THE
COLONIAL HISTORY
SERIES

General Editor
D. H. Simpson

Librarian of the Royal Commonwealth Society

ASHANTEE AND THE GOLD COAST

Ashantee
and the
Gold Coast

Being a sketch of the History, Social State and
Superstitions of the inhabitants of those countries
with a notice of the state and prospects
of Christianity among them

BY JOHN BEECHAM

WITH INTRODUCTION AND NOTES
BY
G. E. METCALFE

1968
DAWSONS OF PALL MALL
London.

First Published in London 1841
Reprinted with introduction 1968

Dawsons of Pall Mall,
16 Pall Mall, London, S.W.1.

SBN 7129 0215 5

Introduction © Wm. Dawson & Sons Ltd. 1968

*Printed in Great Britain
by Photolithography
Unwin Brothers Limited
Woking and London*

INTRODUCTION

JOHN BEECHAM was born at Barnoldy le Bec near Grimsby in 1787. Of his family circumstances and early years nothing has been recorded.[1] The Rector of Irby on Humber helped with his education, intending him for a career in the Established Church.[2] However, when he was some twenty-five years old, Beecham was attracted to Wesleyan Methodism.[3] Becoming in turn an Exhorter and Local Preacher, in 1815 he was accepted for the Intinerant Ministry. He "travelled" in a number of northern circuits of to Wesleyan Connexion until, in 1828, he moved he the Liverpool South Circuit. It was there that he first came into prominence with an uncompromising vindiction of the authority of the Wesleyan Conference against the claims of the local societies as then upheld by the Leaders of Leeds Brunswick Chapel. An expanded version of this speech, published in 1829 as *An Essay on the Constitution of Wesleyan Methodism* was hailed by the historian of the Connexion as one of "the noblest defences

[1] There is an article on Beecham in the D.N.B. The fullest account is the obituary notice by Rev. E. Hoole in the W. M. Magazine, June 1856.

[2] After 1847 Beecham appears in the Minutes of Conference as D.D. but he does not appear to have attended a university and I have not discovered the provenance of this degree.

[3] Hoole connects this change with the circumstances of his father's death in 1812. According to the D.N.B. his father died "when he was a child".

of the bulwarks of our Zion".[1] In 1828 Beecham's "blunt authoritarianism"[2] was not lost on Jabez Bunting, then serving as President of Conference for the second time. It was he who, in 1831, recommended Beecham to one of the vacant secretaryships of the Wesleyan Methodist Missionary Society. This post Beecham retained until his death in 1856 (apart from the year (1850) when he was himself President of Conference). Throughout this period he remained one of Bunting's closest associates in the "ruling clique" which dominated Wesleyanism at that time and whose mouthpiece was the weekly *Watchman*, founded in 1835 when the "Wesleyan virtue" of the directors of the *Christian Advocate*, hitherto the acknowledged if unofficial organ of the Connexion, succumbed to the lures of political radicalism.[3]

Of the four secretaries, who, with two treasurers, formed the Committee directing Wesleyan Missions, Beecham for practical purposes was the senior in residence. Bunting himself was senior in appointment and was a far greater figure in Wesleyan Methodism. By the same token he had less time to spare for his work at the Mission House, especially after 1835 when he became Principal of the new academy in Hoxton (after 1841 in Richmond) for training Wesleyan Ministers. Beecham's junior colleagues were the Rev. Dr. Robert Alder, appointed in 1833 and the Rev. Elijah Hoole, secretary from 1834–72, who before moving to

[1] G. Smith, *A History of Wesleyan Methodism*, 3 vols., 1857–61.

[2] The phrase is Dr. John Kent's, whose *Age of Disunity*, London 1966 includes an admirable study of Methodism in the Bunting era.

[3] Smith, *op. cit.*, ii, 188.

headquarters had served as a missionary in India. Beecham himself, it will be noted, had no first hand experience of missionary work; and never went overseas until in the last year of his life he visited North America to preside over the formation of a separate Conference for the Methodist societies in the Canadas. Although it is accepted usage to speak of the W. M. Missionary Society, it was not, in the strict sense of the word a "society" at all; having no definite membership or regular subscriptions. Its secretaries were, in Methodist terminology, "separated" i.e. relieved of ordinary circuit or pastoral duties, but like any other ministers were appointed by and answerable to Conference. It was their particular task to publicise the work of Methodist missions among the adherents of that church, in order to raise the funds needed to carry it on; in which they had to compete against other local and connexional demands.[1]

In the eighteen thirties Wesleyan missions were expanding rapidly. At home, the mounting volume of business made it necessary to transfer headquarters to more commodious premises in a new Centenary Hall and Mission House in Bishopgate Street, opened in January 1841. Here Beecham for many years entertained returning and outgoing missionaries, received their reports and issued instructions; and it was here that he put the finishing touches to his book on *Ashantee and the Gold Coast* in February 1841. Overseas, expansion was particularly marked by the opening

[1] G. G. Findlay and W. W. Holdsworth, *The History of the Wesleyan Methodist Missionary Society*, 5 vols, London 1921–24 is the standard history.

of new mission fields—in New Zealand, in Fiji and
on the Gold Coast. From the opening of this
mission in 1835 there had been talk of extending
its work northwards into Ashanti. It became
something more than talk when in 1839, T. B.
Freeman paid a flying visit to Kumasi and returned
with the Asantehene's permission to establish a
mission station in his capital. Freeman was not
alone in urging the Committee in London to lose
no time in taking advantage of this offer. President
Maclean of Cape Coast Castle told them that they
and Christian England would incur a serious
responsibility if they had the means to act and yet
allowed the opportunity to go begging.[1]

"If they had the means": it was a searching
question. For if missionary income had more than
doubled in the decade (from roughly £40,000 to
£80,000 a year).[2] it still was not keeping pace with
demand. In 1839 and again in 1840 the Committee
incurred a deficit of £10,000.[3] This was on existing
commitments. However "rich" or "glorious" the
harvest Freeman offered, it could not be garnered
unless the Committee could somehow attract more
revenue both from within the Connexion and from
outside. It was perhaps particularly to this wider
public that *Ashantee and the Gold Coast* was directed.

This helps to explain one curious feature of the
book—the disproportionate emphasis on Ashanti.
Excusable in the historical sections in so far as the

[1] Maclean to Freeman 9/7/1839 M.M.S. An extract
from this letter was printed by T. F. Buxton, *The African
Slave Trade and its Remedy*, London 1840 pp. 246–7.

[2] Findlay and Holdsworth, *op. cit.* vol i print an
interesting graph of missionary income.

[3] *Watchman* 24 xii 1839 and 5/v/1841 where the total
debt is reckoned at over £40,000.

rise of Ashanti forms the dominant theme of the
eighteenth and early nineteenth century, this does
not justify the perfunctory handling of coast
affairs, especially in the period 1820–40. It is
more surprising to find Ashanti enjoying at least
an equal share of the section on mission history,
seeing that here Ashanti represented a purely
prospective and far from certain intention; whereas
by 1840 the future Methodist Church of Ghana was
already established in a score of societies on or
near the coast. Yet Beecham, while discussing the
beneficial effects of this early enterprise, thinks it
important mainly as the possible means by which
the gospel might be introduced into Ashanti. The
fact is that the story of early struggles on the
coast, which, in view of the appalling mortality
among the early missionaries, cannot be said to
want for heroism, emphatically lacked drama. It
carried no special appeal to the British public,
whereas Ashanti might.

For Ashanti could fairly be presented as "one of
the most needed, but most difficult and perilous
missions of modern times" (p. 332 n. below). Most
needed, because, in Freeman's words, *"human
sacrifices* are everyday occurrences, and where
though they do not eat human flesh like the
Fejeeans"—casting a glance at a new competitor
for missionary funds—"the mangled bodies of
human victims are suffered to lay (sic) swelling
and putrefying in the public streets like dead dogs."[1]
On Wesley's maxim about going first to those
who needed you most, unregenerate Ashanti had
prior claims over the peoples near the coast among
whom such practices were rapidly on the wane,

[1] Freeman to W.M.M.C. 9/5/1839, M.M.S.

under pressure from President Maclean. More remote from his influence, if still sufficiently amenable to it to allow Freeman a safe and considerately shortened visit in 1839, Ashanti was the more perilous. Bowdich's pages convey a lively sense of that author's insecurity during his mission to Kumasi. The Ashantis had made themselves known as formidable enemies; and their triumph over Governor MacCarthy in 1824 was still more vividly stamped on the public memory than their subsequent defeats.[1] Beecham does not dwell on African "barbarities" to anything like the extent that Buxton had done in a recent chapter on the "Superstititions and Cruelties of the Africans";[2] and he leaves it to Freeman to indulge in pulpit rhetoric about them (pp. 324–25 below) but he focussed attention on Ashanti from a sound instinct that this was the surest way to persuade the "Christian and benevolent public of this country" to support the W.M.M.S.

For in 1841 there was unprecedented interest in West Africa largely inspired by T. F. Buxton's sensational account of the African Slave Trade, first published early in 1839, and by the subsequent propaganda of his African Civilisation Society, of which Beecham was an active committee member.[3]

[1] Compare Beecham's account of MacCarthy's last campaign (73–76 below) with his notice (81 below) of the battle of Katamansu.   [2] Buxton, *op. cit.*, 226–67.

[3] A number of letters from Beecham to Bunting (also a member of the African Civilisation Society) dealing with arrangements for public meetings in the autumn of 1840 will be found among the Preachers' Letters (Beecham Box) in the Methodist Archives, Epworth House, City Road. I regret that I was unable to see the Bunting letters which are in process of being sorted.

Beecham was anxious to exploit this favourable mood. Sharing Buxton's ideals and proferring his book as a contribution to the work of the Niger Expedition, he was perhaps at the same time concerned lest the Niger engross all the public attention and support. Hence it was important to stress that the Wesleyans were also making an attempt on the African interior and that they too had plans for "experimental farms" which along with the gospel would instill those habits of persevering toil on which all civilisation must be based.

In a letter to Bunting, written just before his book appeared, Beecham hoped that the officers of the Niger Expedition would find time for "pondering well some of the principles to which I have given prominence." If it was necessary, as this enigmatic sentence was perhaps intended to convey, to stress the vital role of Christianity in "civilizing" Africa, it was especially necessary to safeguard the Methodist share in that task. At first Buxton, naively perhaps, had expected that Christian England would agree on some common form of religious instruction for Africa. Disappointed in this he was reduced to hoping that the missionary societies could contrive to partition Africa among themselves so that "each section of the Christian church may have undisturbed possession of its own sphere of labour."[1] There was in 1841 a serious risk that the Methodists might not be undisturbed for long in Ashanti. In the same letter to Bunting, Beecham declared himself thankful to have got his book ready

"at the juncture when it has become so necessary

[1] T. F. Buxton, *op. cit.*, p. 516.

to make some new demonstration as to our *claim* as well as intentions respecting Ashantee".

For in 1841, and for some time afterwards[1] the Wesleyans suspected that the Society for the Propagation of the Gospel had its eyes on Kumasi. It was believed that they meant to avail themselves of the Ashanti princes, surrendered by the Asantehene as hostages for the due observance of the 1831 treaty, and since 1835 educated in England under Anglican auspices. The princes were now about to return to Kumasi and the Wesleyans were anxious that they should there be associated with their own mission and not with a rival enterprise by the S.P.G. This was another reason for stressing Ashanti, where the Wesleyans could claim "the truly apostolic honour" (p. 332 n. below) of being the first in the field, rather than the Gold Coast proper, where the S.P.G. had been the pioneers nearly a century before.[2] At Cape Coast Castle the Wesleyans had entered into other men's labours by drawing for their first leaders, teachers and preachers, on former pupils of the castle school begun by Philip Quaque, himself an S.P.G. product.[3] It was fortunate for them that T. B.

[1] c.f. Freeman to Beecham, 17/4/1842 (M.M.S. Gold Coast 1842–43). Freeman also hoped that the C.M.S. would stick to the Niger and not start work on the Gold Coast.

[2] They were only just the first in Kumasi, as the Basel missionary Andreas Riis visited the Ashanti capital in 1840. Maclean lent his good offices to this visit also, making it a condition that there should be no interference with the projected Methodist work.

[3] F. L. Bartels, "Philip Quaque", *Transactions of the Gold Coast and Togoland Historical Society*, vol. i pt v, pp. 155–77; and *idem*, *The Roots of Ghana Methodism*, Cambridge, 1965.

Freeman had reached a close understanding with
President Maclean so that he and the Committee
of Merchants responsible for the home management
of the forts had ceased to press for a clergyman of
the Established Church to be sent out.[1]   Beecham
clearly believed this Merchant Committee to be
chiefly responsible for the courtesy of an eve-of-
departure call by the princes at the Mission House.
Reporting this development to Bunting he writes:

We are to receive the Ashanti Princes on Wednes-
day to take their farewell of us in Committee. . . . I
have suggested to Hoole that seeing every attempt
is made to impress them with Archiepiscopal and
Propagation Committee shew etc., we should also
do our best, and we intend to fit up temporarily
our saloon and invite all the preachers as well as
the Committee to receive them.

We are indebted, I doubt not, to the Gold Coast
Committee, Messrs. Nicholls and Hutton, for this
visit.   I have had a full explanation with them;
they deeply regret that we should have been so
neglected during the winter; and I expect from
what they told me that they have driven Mr.
P(yne) to write . . . I think it is now pretty plain
that from the beginning he has had something more
in view respecting the Princes than he told us.

You will see that I have mentioned the fact that
the Princes received their first impressions respecting Christianity from Mr. Dunwell's ministry;
but I think I should make it *incidentally* more
apparent that they have not been under our
direction in England, in order to free ourselves, by

[1] On Freeman's relations with Maclean see G. E.
Metcalfe, *Maclean of the Gold Coast*, London, 1962, espe.
pp. 235–45. A Colonial Chaplain of the Established
Church was appointed in 1844 when the Crown resumed
responsibility for Cape Coast Castle.

anticipation, from the *blame* of a failure, should
they become mystified (?) with churchism, or
otherwise conduct themselves improperly. One
cannot help having some uneasy apprehensions
respecting their future course.[1]

To conclude this account of the background of
Beecham's work, we may note briefly what came
of all these hopes and fears. The special Ashanti
Mission appeal preached up and down the country
by T. B. Freeman in the summer and autumn of
1840 got near enough to its target of £5,000 for
the Committee to go ahead with plans for the
Kumasi mission. Freeman was back on the coast
by February 1841 and returned to Ashanti the
following December accompanied by a colleague
who was to be stationed in Kumasi and the two
Princes. Kwantabisa speedily involved himself in
a serious scrape but John Ansa continued to serve
the Wesleyan church for over twenty years, but
on the coast rather than in his homeland. For in
Ashanti the mission languished. The Asantehene
made unexpected difficulties about the school and
when it was finally opened in 1844 no native
Ashanti was allowed to attend it. The preaching
was not notably more successful and in 1850 the
European resident had to be withdrawn and was
not replaced until the twentieth century.

On the other hand nothing came of the supposed
challenge from the S.P.G. which did not resume
activities on the coast until the eighteen-nineties.
There the Wesleyans prospered modestly. Their
work like Maclean's political achievement was put

[1] Methodist Archives, Epworth House. Preachers
Letters (Beecham box). The Rev. Mr. Pyne was the
princes' "moral tutor" during their time in England.

in a favourable light by comparison with the total
failure on the Niger and received honourable
mention in the report of the 1842 Select Committee.
But difficulties increased in the years that followed.
The "experimental farm" at Dominasi was never
much more than a school garden and if a more
ambitious plantation got under way at Beulah
near Cape Coast its very scale was an embarrassment.   Freeman "quite paralysed" by the failure
of the African Civilisation Society to finance the
enterprise soon found his own committee insisting
on retrenchment.   For the forties were a troubled
period for Wesleyans at home and falling membership was reflected in a reduced missionary income.
And when the British Government resumed charge
of the Gold Coast forts in 1844 relations with the
new officials were noticeably less cordial than they
had been with Maclean.   In the eighteen fifties on
the Gold Coast as in England Wesleyan Methodism
did little more than hold its own.

*   *   *

In spite of the circumstances under which it was
written, *Ashantee and the Gold Coast* is much less
a tract than a text-book.   In this it was characteristic of its author, whom a colleague remembered—a shade apologetically—not as a giant of
pulpit oratory (in an age when this was more
common and esteemed than it is now), but as the
efficient committee-man, always careful to prime
himself beforehand with the relevant facts.
Beecham here was above all a methodical and
concise arranger of other men's facts; so much so
that his book has scarcely sufficient autonomy to
rank as a minor classic among the literature on

West Africa—even much of the style is borrowed;
and the task of assessing its quality becomes very
much one of assessing the use made in it of the
sources from which it is composed.

These fall into three main groups. First and of
paramount importance come T. E. Bowdich's
Mission from Cape Coast Castle to Ashantee, which
first appeared in 1819; and Joseph Dupuis' *Journal
of a Residence in Ashantee*, published in 1824. On
these Beecham depends entirely for the history
(mainly Dupuis) and customs (Bowdich rather
more than Dupuis) of Ashanti, and also for much
of what he has to say about the Akan peoples
generally. Secondly come the minor authorities
used in his account of the coastal Akan: mostly
older writers, like Bosman, Isert and Meredith,
but one or two more recent of whom the most
important was H. J. Ricketts' *Narrative of the
Ashantee War*, published in 1831. Finally there
were the primary sources—missionary letters and
journals to which Beecham had access at the
Mission House. These he used to supplement the
printed sources on Akan religion and to provide a
summary account of the progress of the Wesleyan
Mission.

He makes the fullest and also the soundest use
of Bowdich and Dupuis. Both are quoted extensively and almost verbatim. Regrettably he did
not give page references, which have been supplied
in the present edition because *Ashantee and the
Gold Coast* is perhaps most likely to be useful
nowadays as an introduction to these two essential
authorities on old Ashanti. Their own works, vast,
rambling and without benefit of index certainly
need a guide to their contents. Beecham condenses

two bulky tomes into the compass of a pocket
edition by a process of rigorous and on the whole
judicious selection. He reproduces most of their
first-hand descriptions of Ashanti society as they
themselves saw it, which undoubtedly is the most
permanently valuable part of their work. He uses
much less of the narrative passages in which
Bowdich and Dupuis recounted the progress of the
actual missions on which they were engaged. This
is excusable as these were matters of merely
academic interest in 1841. It should however be
noted that the account of Dupuis' mission is much
fuller than that of Bowdich and for both, Beecham,
relies exclusively upon Dupuis, one of the last
authors to be accorded such trust. Finally he
omits almost entirely the copious geographical
speculations which occupy so much space in both
Bowdich and Dupuis. In so far as these were
devoted to discovering the precise course of the
river Niger, about which it is evident that their
Muslim informants themselves had only the haziest
ideas, they too by 1841 had only an academic
interest; for practical purposes they had been made
redundant by the Landers, Laird and Beecroft
who had actually sailed along the Niger from
Rabah to the sea.

It is true, as a reviewer objected at the time, that
Beecham's use of his sources tends to be uncritical.
But this is largely inevitable, having in mind the
dearth of independent witnesses by whom to test
the reliability of his principal authorities. He
does make use of what little came to hand, as in
Abu Bekr's narrative of his captivity (pp. 25–31),
or the testimony of De Graft (p. 6) and Freeman
(p. 12). Where Bowdich and Dupuis disagree

about the Ashanti past their accounts are compared (pp. 4–5, 22) and Beecham in both cases (rightly) accepts Dupuis' version as inherently the more plausible. He therefore tends to follow Dupuis without qualification in his account of Ashanti in the eighteenth century and accepts his dates without comment. It is only very recently that scholars with access to European archives have been able to correct the chronology of the early Ashanti kings.[1]

As far as the events of 1817–24 are concerned however Beecham's reliance on Dupuis becomes downright culpable; both because Dupuis was a highly interested and—as Beecham was aware— very partial actor in the events he describes; and because he makes only perfunctory use for example of Ricketts' *Narrative*, still the principal source for the Ashanti war of 1823–26.

The fact is that the second group of authorities are of very minor importance to Beecham. Even when he is discussing the coastal Akan he prefers to rely on Bowdich, and when he does quote Bosman or Isert, it is almost invariably at second hand, through Bowdich. Meredith seems to have been studied independently for his remarks on Akan religion: and in this connection, as will appear presently, he made some use of original material. But while he brings together into handy compass, widely scattered snippets from the pages of these older writers, to provide a reasonably coherent account of the social history of the Akan, he is much less successful in presenting recent

[1] I. Wilks and M. Priestley "A Revised Chronology of the Early Ashanti Kings" in *Journal of African History*, i (1960), p. 96.

political history, especially in so far as this relates
to Anglo-Ashanti relations.

It may be said that this was not germane to
his purpose, and that it does not much matter as
we can read Ricketts if Beecham did not: but
since he devotes nearly forty pages (48–94) to the
events of 1816–31, and elsewhere seems to have
prided himself on his "historical backgrounds",[1] it
is perhaps worth stressing that his customary
accuracy and sense of proportion fail him here;
and the reader would be well advised to ignore
this section of his work altogether. The root
cause of his failure lies in his persevering reliance
on Dupuis, where Dupuis is least to be trusted;
which produces not only a one-sided account of
the origins of the conflict with Ashanti, but leads
him to accept Dupuis' thesis that Ashanti, or at
least the Asantehene, was anxious for peace
throughout. So while with Dupuis, Beecham
places the blame for the breakdown in Anglo-
Ashanti relations squarely on Hope-Smith and
MacCarthy, in his account of the war that followed
he says little about military affairs—apart from
the stock description of the death of MacCarthy at
Adamanso—but a great deal about the repeated
failure of the British to negotiate. Only this can
excuse the excessive notice taken of Captain Laing
(pp. 68–72 below) whose role in events was rather
smaller than he would have us suppose, but whose
offer to go to Kumasi to negotiate appeared to
Beecham as one of several lost opportunities.
Hence in 1831, peace just happens; there is not a
line about the tortuous efforts that were needed

[1] e.g. in *Watchman* 24 xii 1839 and subsequently in the
1844 edition of Freeman's *Journal of Various Visits . . .*

to open communications with Ashanti. It is true enough that after 1826 the principal opponents of peace were Britain's own allies: but the Asante-hene's renunciation of authority over them, which was explicit in the 1831 settlement, not "virtual" as Beecham has it, would never have been offered before Katamansu. And stable peace in the coastlands was not really to be had on any other terms. Had he chosen to do so, Beecham could have learned much from Ricketts on all these matters.

As Beecham minimises the difficulties of arriving at a lasting peace with Ashanti, so he ignores the problems of keeping it, once it had been signed. He says nothing about the administration of George Maclean. Yet it was precisely in this period that the prospects of "civilisation" as Beecham understood it, notably improved. And it is doubtful indeed if the Wesleyan mission would ever have established itself on the coast, to say nothing of Kumasi, without the countenance and support of the "Governor" of Cape Coast Castle.

In discussing Akan religion, as well as in des-cribing the prospects for Christianity on the Gold Coast Beecham makes some attempt to tap new sources of information. Africans like William De Graft and Joseph Smith, as "men of two worlds", were in his view peculiarly able to interpret African religion to Europeans. There is, in the records of the Methodist Missionary Society, for instance, a questionaire addressed by Beecham to Joseph Smith the schoolmaster at Cape Coast Castle school. It is dated 16 November 1839 apparently for despatch to Smith in Africa, and although from the absence of references to Smith in his book, it seems doubtful whether it was answered, similar questions evidently were put to De Graft in England and form the basis of chapter seven below:

> Have the Africans any idea of a Supreme Being resembling our idea of God? . . . Do they regard him as the Creator of all things, or what power do they ascribe to him and what do they *hope* or *fear* from him? What is the origin of the word fetish? . . . Whether the fetish men offer religious worship to their Deity? If it is not religious worship, what is it, and what is the end to be answered by their ceremonies and practices? What invisible Being or Influence is it which they wish to excite by their practices? . . . Whether the natives have any idea of a future state of being? Do they believe that they have souls which will live somewhere when the body dies? If so what kind of a world are they supposed to live in? Is it a *good* place or a *bad* one? What kind of *employment* will they have? What kind of pleasures or sufferings? And will their condition in that world be influenced by their conduct here? Do they suppose that their Deity lives in that world? Have they any idea of the resurrection of the body? What is the object of burying gold and valuable garments with a deceased person? and also of putting persons to death at the same time? . . . Whether the natives have any idea of a Sunday or Sabbath . . .?

These questions perhaps throw more light on religion in Victorian England than the answers to them did on Akan or Ga beliefs. Beecham is no longer regarded as an important source of evidence on these subjects, and his work is interesting in this connection chiefly as an early attempt to get at the beliefs which inspired West African behaviour

If it sought to understand them within too rigidly conceived terms, it was, for its time, a relatively sophisticated effort, which sprang from the pragmatic conviction that in right belief lay the roots of right conduct; and hence served to demonstrate the practical importance of Christian missions in the great task of "civilisation".

In some ways Beecham's account of the early Wesleyan deployment on the Gold Coast is the most disappointing part of his book; disappointing, that is, in view of the material available. It is an adequate summary of what had appeared in print and it is more accessible in book form than in the pages of the *Watchman* or the *Wesleyan Methodist Magazine*. But seemingly he did not feel free to make use of the letters or journals which he certainly saw but which did not appear in those periodicals, or in *Missionary Notices*. A contemporary critic, making the point that nothing in the book was new, complained of the way in which "the information derived from the missions undergoes an official winnowing at headquarters, when the grain is buried and the chaff given to the public". He went on to accuse Beecham of pandering to "an ignorant and bigoted class of people".[1] While there is substance in the first, the second charge cannot fairly be sustained. *Ashantee and the Gold Coast* is scarcely a work of missionary piety after the style of Miss Tucker's *Abeokuta or Sunrise in the Tropics*. It was addressed to a tolerably lettered public and even

[1] *Watchman* 10 Nov. 1841. The original criticism appeared in the *Athenaeum* and was reprinted by the *Watchman* together with a reply from the *Christian Observer*.

in its peroration the author's caution and matter-
of-factness do not desert him.

It is true that a great deal more might have been
made of the difficulties encountered by the early
societies in dealing with polygamy or slavery, or
in their relations with the leaders of traditional
society on the one hand and the local government
on the other. Something of this has been done
recently by a Ghanaian scholar, F. L. Bartels, in
The Roots of Ghana Methodism, using material all
of which, for the years before 1841, was available
to Beecham. Here no doubt the immediate
occasion for writing, which was after all to enlist
support for the mission and to dispel doubts, not
to sow them, detracted from the permanent
importance of his work. But if Beecham could
not but be aware of these difficulties, and was not
the man to minimise them in private, it is unlikely
that it ever occurred to him to ask whether
Wesleyan systems of discipline or of church
government were the best adapted to this particular
environment, as Brodie Cruickshank was to do
later in *Eighteen Years on the Gold Coast*.[1] To the
end of his life Beecham identified himself too
closely with the dominant principles of Wesleyan
Methodism ever to doubt their efficacy; and, as

[1] It is curious that Cruickshanks's principal doubt, in
1853, was that Wesleyan standards were too strict, he
speaks of "a gloomy and morose austerity"—which
certainly sounds ill-adapted to the Ghanaian temperament;
whereas later critics inclined to think their discipline much
laxer than the Basel Mission and their work altogether
less thorough. Cruickshank hints at the latter when he
says (ii, 113) that he had questioned the wisdom of their
policy of establishing widely scattered stations instead of
concentrating on more intensive development.

we have seen, he was very jealous of their claims on the Gold Coast. If Beecham and Freeman were indeed guilty of believing in the superiority of their faith and western civilisation, it was a sort of virtue that they did not question the African's ability to partake fully and equally of both.

G. E. METCALFE
Hull, 1968.

NOTES

Bowdich, *Mission from Cape Coast Castle to Ashantee:* referred to as B.

Dupuis, J, *Journal of a Residence in Ashantee:* referred to as D.

> In Dupuis pp. i–xxxviii deal with the origin of his mission
>
> > pp. 1–264 embrace the Journal, and sequent events down to 1824 and the history of Ashanti.
> >
> > pp. I–CXXXV (comprising Part II) comprise the geographical sections and appendices.

p. 3 The Mountains of Kong, an invention of the geographer James Rennell, first appeared on his map of Africa of 1798. A corrected (1802) version is most readily accessible in R. Hallett (ed) *Records of the African Association 1788–1831*, London, 1964. The range appears in an attenuated form in Dupuis, who describes it as stretching "nearly as far (east) as Kong (9N 4.40 W). In Rennell's hands the existence of such a range was an argument against the Niger debouching in the Gulf of Guinea; but even after this proved in fact to be the case, the Niger "gorge" south of the confluence with the Binue was identified by the early explorers with the Kong mountains. With Beecham the importance of the range is historic, as affording a rampart against Muslim conquerors from the north. Like his account of early West African history, this represents a great over-simplification of the process of Muslim infiltration, while it is locally true e.g. in Bauchi that pagan pockets held out longest in mountain areas. Curiously his map ignores the Futa Jalon massif, which, as seen by Park, was the only real substance for Rennell's belief in the existence of

the Kong mountains. Futa Jalon was however a
centre of Muslim power.

p. 4   Bowdich mentions a tradition (B 228): B 232 is
the source for the taboo concerning deceased
rulers, and the references to Bosman and Barbot.

p. 3   Dupuis found . . . want of political concert (D.L.)
D XLIX is probably the source of Beecham's
theory about the role of the forest in limiting
Muslim advance.   D L–LI for Ashanti control of
the arms trade to the interior.

p. 5   Migration from their original inheritances . . .
Kong mountains. (D 224–25) "That writer" is
Meredith, *An Account of the Gold Coast of Africa,*
1812.   It is now fashionable (in Ghana) to look
even further north, across the Niger to ancient
Ghana for the original homeland of the Akan, but
this is a twentieth century literary notion, rather
than a traditional belief. The most elaborate,
though not necessarily the most reliable account
of these traditions is E. Meyerowitz, *Akan
Traditions of Origin,* 1952.   Beecham's account is
foreshortened and over-simplified and it is
necessary to distinguish early migration and
settlement extending from c. the 11th to the
16th centuries from the period of state-building
in the 17th and 18th centuries.

p. 6   line 4. "Ashantee" should read "Ahanta"
(B 229–30)

p. 7   there is no Ghulbe or Gulby river. Beecham is
following Dupuis (D XCIII) who describes it as
a river flowing parallel with the Niger and joining
it in Hausa.

p. 8   the founding or enlargement of Kumasi (D 229
c.f. B 231)

p. 9   60,000 warriors (D 225). The conquest of Kwahu
and Gyaman (D 230). The "great mountainous
range" is Beecham's own embellishment. Dupuis,
more accurately speaks of the "desert of Ghofan"
i.e. the sparsely populated plain of the Black
Volta as being the barrier to Ashanti expansion
northwards.

p. 10   The Muslim records referred to by Dupuis.
Dupuis discounted the value of negro information

but relied heavily on the Muslims he met at Kumasi, his command of Arabic being his sole qualification for his post as consul. Dupuis dates the Ashanti rulers of the 18th century by the Muslim era. Beecham follows his dating throughout, although it differs in every particular from that of Bowdich. Wilks I and Priestley M., "A Revised Chronology of the early Ashanti Kings" in *Journal of African History*, i (1960) p. 96 suggest 1712 for the end of Osei Tutu's reign and their successors as ruling: Opoku Ware 1720–50, Kusi Obodum 1750–64, Osei Koje 1764–77, Osei Kwame 1777–1801. It is similarly clear from British records that Kwaku Duah I became ruler of Ashanti in 1834 and not 1838 as usually stated.

Beecham is quoting Dupuis (D 227–8) when he cites Bosman. In fact Bosman dates the Denkyira war in 1701. His work first appeared, in Dutch, in 1704 and the first English version, *A New and Accurate Description of the Coast of Guinea* was published in 1705.

p. 11   one hundred thousand warriors perished (D 228)

p. 13   almost verbatim D 231.

p. 14   Osei Tutu did not lay the foundation of the monarchy. Actually Dupuis (D 229) merely refutes Bowdich's view that he was the founder of Kumasi, conceding that he made it the capital. The point is hardly material as Kumasi was unknown before his reign: c.f., Wilks, I., "A Note on the traditional history of Mampong" in *Transactions of the Historical Society of Ghana*, vol. iv part 2, p. 27.

p. 15   The 'Notes' obtained as a result of the conquest of Akim were those for the Accra forts, the Akims having obtained them after their overthrow of Akwamu c. 1731. The English paid Ashanti 2 ounces (i.e. c. £8) worth of trade goods per month. It was not these notes, but similar demands on Cape Coast Castle that "involved the British and Ashantees in war".

p. 16   Opoku Ware's reforms and the resistance to them (D 235). Bowdich (B 252) and c.f. p. 21 below) rather emphasises the innovations of Osei

Kojo (or Kwadwo) 1764–77, and in this he is followed by a modern scholar who speaks of the "Kwadwoan revolution in Government". I. Wilks, "Ashanti Government" in D. Forde and P. M. Kaberry (eds), *West African Kingdoms in the Nineteenth Century* London 1967.

p. 19   Osei Kojo's war with Gyaman and the Gyamans' use of muskets (D 241).

p. 20   The sultan of Dogho. The provenance of Dogho is uncertain. The name is not used by Dupuis. The reference presumably is to the Alafin of Oyo (arch. Eyeo) the paramount Yoruba chief to whom Dahomey owed a vague and nominal allegiance.

p. 22   The dethronement of Osei Kwamina (D 245). It is Beecham who comments that the captains' fears were probably exagerrated.

p. 23   Osei Apoko II (B 240; D 246) Beecham follows Dupuis.

p. 24   Osei Tutu Kwamina (Osei Bonsu) (B 246; D 247).

p. 36   The river Shama. i.e. the Pra. The "one good fort" of the Brandenburgers — Gross Friedrichsburg at Princes Town two miles from Cape Three Points, sold to the Dutch in 1717.

p. 38   Beecham's account of the invasion of 1807 follows Dupuis (D 250) and Meredith. The other principal source is the despatch of Governor Torrane of 12/vi/1807 in T 30/35, most of which is reproduced in G. E. Metcalfe, *Great Britain and Ghana*, London 1964, pp. 7–12.

p. 39   "a defensive position in the hills of Moisi" (D 252: "between Moisi and Doompassy").

p. 41   Their hearts devoured by the Braffoes (D 255).

p. 44   The king himself acknowledged to Dupuis . . . (D 257).

p. 48   "another invasion in . . . 1817" Actually in 1816. (B 4) reports in T 70/36, part printed in H.C. 4 1 of 1817 and in Metcalfe, *op. cit.* p. 36.

p. 49   The Committee of the African Society at home; i.e. the Committee of the Company of Merchants responsible for the upkeep of the British forts on the Gold Coast. The despatch of 5 March 1817, in T 70/36 and part printed in H.C. 431 of 1817 is not so much evidence of the motive for the Kumasi mission, already decided on in London in November, as of the deep suspicion which prevailed as to Dutch intentions (c.f. B 53, 60). Herman Willem Daendels, Governor of Elmina 1816–18 was the last Dutch Governor to make a serious attempt to recover local initiative for the Dutch.

Hutchinson i.e. William Hutchison a Scot, who finally left the coast in 1832 and died in 1834.

p. 52 "Dupuis . . . states" (D 262–3) Dupuis's authority is Osei Bonsu himself, who is hardly an acceptable witness. It is clear, as Beecham himself recognises, that the Asantehene was not in possession of the Notes before 1817; c.f. Bowdich (B 70) where the Asantehene says that he must have them. This is corroborated by James's report (B 32). They were demanded as a consequence of the invasion of 1816, not that of 1807, and probably—as James conjectured—the inspiration may have come from the mission to Kumasi of the Dutch agent Huydecooper, the previous year. The flattering references to the Dutch and their doubling of their own rent (B 70–71) point the same way. Elsewhere (D 196) defending his recognition of Ashanti sovereignty over the Fantes, Dupuis goes so far as to say that the notes passed into Ashanti hands and that the king had "constantly received his monthly, quarterly or annual pay for the ground rent of the castles themselves as the Fantees . . . originally used to do". This was not the case. In a return of 1814 listing the British payments to local chiefs at their various Gold Coast forts, while in the case of Accra the principal beneficiary was the Asantehene (in receipt of 2 ounces or 160 shillings a month), his name does not appear in the lists at either Cape Coast Castle or Anomabu where the chief payments were of 120 shillings to Adoko of Efutu and 160 shillings to Amonu respectively. (H.C. 506 of 1816; Metcalfe, *op. cit.*, pp. 30–31). Precedent in any case had no bearing whatever on the Asantehene's objections that the Dutch

and the British fort at Accra paid more than
Cape Coast was now offering to do.

p. 53   Copies given by Dupuis (D 120–21; c.f. B 80).

p. 55   Complaints at trade being monopolised by Company servants were as Dupuis (D x) says, fairly
general and contributed to the Government's
decision to wind up the Company, c.f. Metcalfe,
op. cit., 51, 63.

p. 56   Ashantis claim protection under the Treaty.
Strictly (c.f. 57 below) they invoked the Governor's
mediation under article 4.

p. 62   Dupuis' detention on the coast.   W. E. F. Ward
in his edition of Dupuis *Journal of a Residence* . . .
(p. 27) points out that Dupuis' own bad health
made departure before November imposible.
Dupuis (D xxxv) speaks of "upwards of a year's
forcible detention at Cape Coast Castle".

Dupuis' Instructions.   Dupuis regarded himself
as responsible only to the British Government
who appointed him.   But apart from the inherent
imbecility of trying to conduct negotiations with
Ashanti without reference to the only British
authorities who were likely to be affected by
them (i.e. the Government of Cape Coast Castle)
it is very doubtful if the Home Government had
ever intended Dupuis to act in this way.   Instead
they referred him to the London Committee for
advice and instructions (providing none themselves) and the Committee in turn stressed the
importance of working in concert with the
Governor and Council at Cape Coast.   See their
letter to Dupuis 31/x/1818 in C.O. 2/11 printed
in Metcalfe *op. cit.*, pp. 53–4.   Hope Smith's
instructions to Dupuis in January 1820 are in
T 70/1606/1 and Metcalfe, *loc. cit.*, pp. 57–8.

p. 67   Beecham omits to state that Adum had waited
two months longer than the time specified by
Dupuis, i.e. eight months after his departure from
the coast in April 1820 (D 201).

p. 68   "full and unreserved admission of the king's claims
upon Fantee".   The Bowdich Treaty was in fact
far from clear on the question of sovereignty,
inasmuch as Bowdich sought to confine the treaty

to the people immediately adjacent to the forts, while the Asantehene sought to embrace Fante as a whole. A similar ambiguity later attached to the reception of the Dupuis treaty at Cape Coast. It was not the status of Fante but of the Cape Coasters that was in question, and here British and Ashanti views were irreconcileable; the Asantehene regarding them as part of Fante, which they were, and the British insisting on their special relationship to themselves.

Captain Laing; the explorer, later killed in the Sahara after visiting Timbuctu. I have not traced the letters used by Beecham, but Laing was something of a (self) publicist and edited a newspaper while serving on the coast, most of which he apparently wrote himself. MacCarthy's policy in the Gold Coast has never been properly investigated. A number of his despatches have been printed by J. J. Crooks, *Historical Records of the Gold Coast Colony* (Dublin 1924) and by Metcalfe, *op. cit.*, pp. 71–91. From these it appears that MacCarthy's Ashanti policy was a good deal less decided than Laing implied. He was, as Beecham remarks (p. 70 below) working very much in the dark. But there were no general offers of protection or alliance made before the incident at Anomabu (p. 71 below) and small disposition to accept them until after the punitive expedition to Dunkwa to avenge the execution of the sergeant.

p. 71 Laing's offer to go to Dunkwa. It should be pointed out that a request from the acting Governor for the release of the sergeant had already been rejected.

p. 72 "at this critical juncture" Laing's operations occurred in July–August of 1823. MacCarthy did not return to the Gold Coast (from Sierra Leone) until the end of November. Declaring himself anxious for "an honourable peace" which clearly included the independence of his allies (despatch of 12 December) his expectation that the Ashantis were by then disposed to treat, were ended by the news of their advance into Wasaw.

p. 79   Lieutenant-Colonel Sutherland arrived at Cape
        Coast 18 May 1824.

p. 80   The Ashanti repulse before Cape Coast was in
        July 1824.

p. 81   "In the month of September". Actually on 7
        August 1826. The local name for the action is
        Katamansu (or Akatamansu).

p. 84   The terms offered in 1828 are given in Metcalfe,
        op. cit., 114–15. Osei Okoto's reply, *ibid* 116.
        The renunciation of claims to overlordship over
        the allied chiefs in 1831 was explicit. Osu
        Kwantabisa and Osu Ansa were not the hostages
        demanded in 1828.

p. 86   The extent of Ashanti (D 230).

p. 87   Bowdich's opinion of Juaben. "Firm allies in
        war and equal sharers in spoil and conquest"
        (B 232). In form the Bowdich Treaty was with
        both Ashanti and Juaben. It seems that Bowdich
        was in error, although he also noted (B 245) that
        the Asantehene "contemplates the reduction of
        Juaben from an independent ally to a tributary";
        but as this process had overtaken the other
        Ashanti chiefdoms it may be that Juaben was the
        last to be reduced, as it was the first to challenge
        the Asantehene after the debacle of Katamansu.

p. 88   Nta is usually equated with Gonja and sometimes
        with its principal commercial centre Salagha.
        The capital of Gonja is the obscure village of
        Nyanga. c.f. Goody, J., "The Over-Kingdom of
        Gonja" in Forde and Kaberry, *op. cit.*, 179–205.
              Yahndi = Yendi.
              The king told Dupuis (D 171).

p. 89   (D XXXIX)

p. 90   the Ashanti chiefs responsible for the conduct of
        the native ruler = the *adamfo*. c.f. Rattray,
        Ashanti Law and Constitution, 94–8 and Wilks,
        "Ashanti Government" *loc. cit.*, p. 221.

p. 91   (B 128) for the four signatories: Apoku, Odumata,
        Nabbra and Ashantee. Dupuis states . . . (D 166).

p. 94   Apia Nann (B 129).

p. 97   Adjei the second linguist (B 248–49).

p. 98   Hutchison's diary (B 401).

p. 100 Hutchison (B 395).

p. 103   Ashanti cloths manufactured from foreign silks
         (B 331).
         The okras.   (B 291 and c.f., W. E. F. Ward,
         Introduction to Dupuis, p. 48).

p. 105   The court of Juaben (B 125).
         The King of Banna (D 76).

p. 108   Bowdich calculates (B 16–17 c.f. D XXXVIII).

p. 109   Law of succession (B 234, 254).

p. 117   Barka Gana.   Denham D and Clapperton H.,
         *Narrative of Travels and Discoveries in Northern
         and Central Africa*, London, 1826, p. 172.

p. 120   The Gyaman war (D 164).

p. 122   Ashanti proverb (*ibid*). The 3333 wives (B 289–90)

p. 123   Norris, R., *Memoirs of . . . Bossa Ahadee, King of
         Dahomey* . . . London 1789.

p. 123   Clapperton, H., *Journal of a Second Expedition*,
         London 1829, pp. 25, 46.

p. 125   (B 303).

p. 129   "It is supposed . . . by Bowdich (B 129).

p. 131   The population of Kumasi.   12–15,000 (B 24);
         larger than Segu (B 323) Salagha (D XL) Yendi
         (D XC).

p. 132   M'Queen, J., *A Geographical Survey of Africa* . . .
         London 1840, Akrofuom (D 47), Dompoasi (D 57),
         Amoafu (D 61), Asumeja (D 63), Abuontem (D 63).
         Sarasu (D 63) does not appear on the modern
         $\frac{1}{2}$ in. map but was apparently c. 2 miles S.E. of
         Kumasi.

p. 139   Wadstrom, C. B., *Essay on Colonisation . . .
         particularly applied to the Western Coast of Africa*,
         2 vols. 1794–5.

p. 141   The Danish Forts.   Rio Volta presumably refers
         to Ft Kongensten at Ada.   Ft Prinsensten is at
         Keta.   The best account in English of these
         Danish attempts at colonisation is C. D. Adams,
         "Activities of Danish Botanists in Guinea
         1783–1850" in *Trans. Hist. Soc. of Ghana* vol. 3,
         part 1 (1957), pp. 30–46.

p. 148   Dompoasi (B 28) Datiasu (B 29) Assumeja (B 30).
         The King replied . . . (D 167).

p. 149   Simon Lucas's attempt in 1788–9 to penetrate the
         Sahara did not get away from the Mediterranean
         coast.   His report was printed in vol. 1 of the

Proceedings of the African Association (1810).
See R. Hallett (ed) *Records of the African Association*, London 1964, pp. 62–9, and *idem, The
Penetration of Africa to 1815*, London, 1965,
pp. 204–8.

p. 150   James Swanzy, 1767–1823. See H. Swanzy "A
Trading Family in the 19th century Gold Coast",
Trans. G.C. & T. Histy Soc. vol. ii, part 2 (1956).

p. 151   Clapperton, H., *Journal of a Second Expedition
into the Interior of Africa*: 67—the meeting with
the Hausa caravan; 68 the reported death of the
Asantehene; kola the principal cargo; 75 description of the caravan; 109 Comie the king's
ferry; 137 Koolfu and the limit of Bornu
caravans.

p. 156   The recent voyage of Captain Beecroft. His
ascent of the Niger in 1840 of which a notice
appeared in *Proceedings of the R.G.S.*, 1841.

p. 157   100,000 ounces. c.f. Metcalfe *op. cit.*, p. 51 for
the suggestion that £100,000 worth of gold was
nearer the mark.

p. 159   The Lake Buro (D XXXV) probably means the
flood plains of the Volta round Yeji.

p. 166   The dialect of Accra i.e. Ga.

p. 172   The creation story (B 261).

p. 175   The cliff on which Cape Coast Castle stands.
Reef would be more appropriate. Lake Echui
(D XXXI) = Lake Bosumtwi.

p. 176   Some animals (B 265 n. who does not talk about
messengers of the gods).

p. 180   The fear manifested by the Asantehene (D 147).

p. 183   Wholesale murder of his household (B 289, 291
c.f. B 283).

p. 187   Aquambo = Akwamu

p. 190   Sanctuary for fugitives. For an example c.f.
G. E. Metcalfe, *Maclean of the Gold Coast*, London
1962, p. 180.

p. 194   Dupuis on the journey to Kumasi.

p. 195   Hutchison's diary (B 384)

p. 198   Nyankupon c.f. G. Parrinder, *West African
Religion*, p. 9 ff.

p. 201   The oracle at Abura (B 263 n.) i.e. at Nanampong
near Mankessim capital of the Braffo country

(B 218) having superseded Efutu a hundred years
ago (B 250).

p. 205   Bowdich states (B 116).   I have not located the
         origin of the statement about Osei Tutu's illness.

p. 206   The fetishman at Gabon (B 438–39).

p. 207   Sacrifices before Gyaman war (D 114–16).

p. 209   Recourse to Moors (B 93–94).

p. 210   High prices for charms (B 271–2).

p. 211   Eating the hearts of the slain (B 300).

p. 212   During Hutchison's stay (B 391).   On another
         occasion . . . (B 76).

p. 215   The oath draught (D 211 n.).

p. 217   Akromanti (D 231–32) (B 297).

p. 218   Dupuis states . . . (D 232).

p. 219   Taking odum (B 297.   D 211 n. includes the quota-
         tion from Bosman, who makes the O.T. parallel).

p. 220   The slave (B 398).

p. 221   The nephew of the king (B 403).

p. 222   Descriptions of the great festivals (B 285, 287).

p. 224   War for strong man (D 164).

p. 225   Circumcision practised by some: sc the Gas c.f.
         Cruickshank, ii 213.

p. 231   Dupuis states . . . (D LXIV).

p. 232   Bowdich at Kumasi (B 283–88).

p. 237   Funeral custom for Osei Kwamina (B 289).

p. 241   The yam custom seen by Bowdich (B 275–80 with
         illustration).

p. 244   The Adai custom (B 280–82).

p. 245   Hutchison on (B 419).

p. 248   Dupuis description of (D 140–42).

p. 249   Prostitution (B 303).

p. 251   Passages from Dupuis (D 164–65).

p. 254   A negro says Dupuis (D 242).

p. 258   F. L. Bartels, "Philip Quaque" *Trans. Histy.
         Soc. G.C. & T*, vol. 1 part 5 (1955) found no
         evidence that Quaque ever went to Oxford.

p. 259   Andreas Riis did return to the Gold Coast in
         1843 for a few years.

p. 271   A dreadful tyrant.   Kwaku Aka chief of Nzima
         (Apollonia) reg c. 1832–48.

p. 284   Mr. Smith.   John Hope Smith, later (1817–22)
         Governor of Cape Coast Castle c.f. pp. 49, 52–3,
         56–62, 67–8 below.

ASHANTEE

AND

THE GOLD COAST:

BEING

A SKETCH

OF THE

HISTORY, SOCIAL STATE, AND SUPERSTITIONS OF
THE INHABITANTS OF THOSE COUNTRIES:

WITH

A NOTICE OF THE STATE AND PROSPECTS OF CHRISTIANITY
AMONG THEM.

BY JOHN BEECHAM.

LONDON:

SOLD BY JOHN MASON, 14, CITY-ROAD,
AND 66, PATERNOSTER-ROW;
AND BY ALL BOOKSELLERS.

1841.

LONDON:
PRINTED BY JAMES NICHOLS,
HOXTON-SQUARE.

PREFACE.

This volume is intended to meet, in part, the inquiry for information respecting Ashantee, and the countries upon the Gold Coast, which has been excited among the friends of Christian Missions, by the publication of the Journal of the Rev. Thomas B. Freeman's visit to Coomassie in the spring of 1839, and by the measures which have subsequently been adopted with a view to the establishment of a Wesleyan Mission and of Christian Schools in that capital.

The statements illustrative of the general features of Ashantee and Fantee society, contained in the works of Bosman, Isert, Meredith, Bowdich, Dupuis, Hutton, and others, (all now out of print,) the writer has examined, in company with individuals who are themselves personally acquainted with that part of Africa to which those

authors refer; and he has endeavoured to
condense, and to present in a somewhat sys-
tematic form, the information which he has
gathered from the various sources to which
he has had access. Dupuis and Bowdich,
with Hutton, are the only authors who have
written expressly on Ashantee; and while
Dupuis paid particular attention to its history and geography, the sketches which
Bowdich has given of the customs and
manners of the people have the merit of
general correctness.

With the assistance of Mr. Freeman, and
more especially by the aid of Christian
natives of the Gold Coast,—with two of
whom, Mr. Joseph Smith, Head-Master
of the Government-School at Cape-Coast
Castle, and Mr. William De Graft, son of
the linguist, to whom such frequent reference is made by Bowdich and Dupuis, the
writer is personally acquainted,—a full and
connected view is furnished of the dark and
sanguinary idolatry of the people. European travellers may witness and describe
the superstitions of the Heathen, without

understanding the principles on which they rest for support, or being able intelligibly to explain why it is that those principles should operate so powerfully on the hopes and fears of their votaries. But those who have themselves been rescued by the Gospel from the degradation and wretchedness of Heathenism, are enabled, in the light reflected by Christianity, to look back upon the dreary scenes through which they have passed, and can explain, from their own former experience, the reason why superstitions so senseless and extravagant should have exerted such a powerful influence upon their minds and habits.

The notices of the state and prospects of the Wesleyan Mission at the Gold Coast, and the influence which it is beginning to exert upon the interior, are given from the writer's personal knowledge of the circumstances connected with its establishment and progress, and from the communications of the Missionaries themselves, to which, from his official connexion with the Society, under whose direction they have successfully laboured, he has had the privilege of free access.

In common with others who have directed their attention to the subject, the writer has experienced the difficulty presented by the unsatisfactory state of the orthography of African names. Owing to the absence of some uniform rule, the name of a place is sometimes spelt differently by every traveller who has visited it, or had occasion to mention it,—as in the case of Fómunah, a small frontier-town of Ashantee, which is written in no fewer than six different ways by five authors.

In the instances where such confusion prevails, and where he has been able to ascertain the native pronunciation, the writer has spelt the names according to the rule followed in the later works on the languages of Africa, and especially in the Vocabularies which have been prepared for the use of the Niger Expedition. In some other cases, where one mode of spelling has hitherto generally obtained in English publications, the true pronunciation is occasionally indi-

cated by the word being given in paren-
theses, in conformity with the same rule.

The desirableness of a common standard
of orthography being so obvious, the Missionaries of the Society have been instructed, in the formation of Grammars and
Vocabularies, to adopt the Italian sound of
the vowels, and to give to every consonant
one unvarying sound, as in the following
scheme :—*a*, to be sounded as in father ; *e*,
as in there ; *i*, as *ie* in field ; *o*, as in more ;
u, as in flute ; *ai*, as *i* in time ; *au*, like *ow* in
how ; *g*, always hard, as in get ; *j*, always
soft, as in jet ; *ng* initial, as heard in ring ;
ch, as in church ; *hh*, marks a strong
aspirate ; and *ou* is an initial diphthong
which, when combined with *i*, sounds nearly
as the English word we, when articulated
with the lips' drawn together, and projecting, as though the speaker was preparing to whistle.

It is not, however, calculated that this
scale will sufficiently express all the vowel
sounds used by the natives. The orthoëpy
of their languages undoubtedly includes

also the short vowel sounds; as heard in hat, met, pin, pot, and but; and it will therefore be desirable, that Missionaries and others, who attempt to reduce African languages to writing, should specify at least those instances in which the use of the short vowel sounds are indispensably necessary. Such cases will occur as in *ponkor*, the Ashantee and Fantee word for horse. If a Missionary or other visitor were to sound the *o* long in this word, as in more, he would fail to make himself understood by the natives.

J. B.

WESLEYAN MISSION-HOUSE,
Bishopsgate-Street-Within, London,
March 22d, 1841.

CONTENTS.

___

CHAPTER I.

THE EARLY HISTORY OF ASHANTEE.

II.

THE RISE AND DECLINE OF THE ASHANTEE POWER ON THE GOLD COAST.

CHAPTER III.

THE RISE AND DECLINE OF THE ASHANTEE POWER ON THE
GOLD COAST—CONTINUED.

CHAPTER IV.

TERRITORIAL EXTENT, POLITY, AND SOVEREIGN STATE.

V.

DOMESTIC SLAVERY, STATE OF THE FEMALE SEX, POPULATION, AND AGRICULTURE.

CHAPTER VI.

ARTS, TRADE, LANGUAGE, NATIONAL TASTE.

CHAPTER VII.

THE POPULAR SUPERSTITIONS.

CHAPTER VIII.

THE POPULAR SUPERSTITIONS—CONTINUED.

IX.

THE POPULAR SUPERSTITIONS—CONCLUDED.

CHAPTER X.

THE STATE AND PROSPECTS OF CHRISTIANITY ON THE GOLD COAST AND IN ASHANTEE.

CHAPTER XI.

THE STATE AND PROSPECTS OF CHRISTIANITY ON THE GOLD COAST AND IN ASHANTEE—CONCLUDED.

ASHANTEE AND THE GOLD COAST:

&c.

CHAPTER I.

THE EARLY HISTORY OF ASHANTEE.

Spread of the Mahommedan Power in Africa—Retirement
of the Heathen Negro Population Southward—The
Period of the Foundation of the Ashantee Kingdom
uncertain—Tradition that the Ashantees and their
Neighbours sprung from twelve Families—Osai Tutu,
the second Founder of the Empire—Sanguinary War
with Denkera—Osai Apóko—Osai Aquasi—Osai Kujoh—Conquest of Gaman, or Buntuku—Osai Quamina
—Osai Apóko the Second—Osai Tutu Quamina as-
cends the Throne—Great military Achievement—
Story of Abú Bekr, and his Release by Dr. Madden—
The first Buntuku War.

THE spread of the Mohammedan power is one
of the most striking features of African history.
The Great Desert, which had previously presented
an almost insuperable obstacle to the spirit of
inquiry, could not resist the ardour of Arabian
enterprise. In the pursuit of geographical science,
or for the advancement of commerce, the followers
of Mohammed penetrated into the interior of

Africa; and, so early as the tenth and eleventh centuries, various causes, among which war and emigration were the principal, had contributed to the establishment of many Mohammedan kingdoms, or States in which the Mohammedan population was numerous and influential, in the regions through which the Niger rolls its course. Letters and science, which flourished among the Arabians during the dark ages of Europe, attended their footsteps in Africa; and some of the kingdoms which they formed there, appear to have enjoyed a considerable degree of civilization. The glory of those earlier states was, however, eclipsed by the superior splendour and power of Timbuctoo (Tumbuktú). That celebrated place, the very name of which, in later times, has operated with a kind of talismanic effect on the lovers of African enterprise, was founded in the beginning of the thirteenth century; (the year 1215 is specified by the Arabian writers;) and the military prowess of its inhabitants, and its facilities for commerce, ere long elevated it above all its competitors. After various unsuccessful struggles with its rising power, all the surrounding states and kingdoms became tributary to Tumbuktú.

About this period, that portion of the pure Negro race which could not brook the Mohammedan rule, took refuge in the forests of that part of Africa which lies to the south of the vast mountainous range known by the appellation of the Mountains of Kong, and has there maintained its independence to the present day. Dupuis found, on conversing with the followers of the Prophet at Coomassie, (Kumási,) that they ascribe the check which has thus been given to the spread of their religion, to the want of political concert among the Mohammedan states in the interior, and the absence of that energy which distinguished the career of the Arabs. Had it not been for the operation of such causes, they are persuaded that tribes of true believers would not, as is now the case in Ashantee, (As-hánti,) and other states, have been found in subjection to Heathen princes, to whom they are obliged to pay tribute, and whose battles they are compelled to fight; but that every nation, down to the sea-coast itself, long ere this, would have been converted to the service of Allah. These causes are not, however, sufficient to account for the security of the Heathen Negro nations, seeing they successfully fought for and established their independence when the power of the Arabs and their auxiliaries was at its height. Their forest-retreats sheltered them from the cavalry of their enemies, with which, having no similar force of their own, they were unable to cope in the open country; and since, by means of the trade established with Europeans on the coast, they became possessed of

fire-arms, they have, without difficulty, defended
themselves against Mohammedan invasion, and
have kept possession of the territory whose precious mines have ever proved the object of most
eager desire.   Aware of the superiority which
fire-arms confer, they have never allowed the
trade in muskets and powder to extend into the
interior ; which is therefore limited to a very
scanty supply of those articles, brought by the
caravans that cross the Great Desert from the
north.

The precise period of the foundation of the
Ashantee (As-hánti) kingdom cannot be ascertained, partly owing to the circumstance, that the
Ashantees do not possess any written records ;
and partly arising out of the fact, that to speak of
the death of a former king, as well as to inquire
concerning the successor of the reigning sovereign, is regarded by them as a treasonable
offence.   Bowdich mentions a tradition, that the
Ashantees emigrated from a country nearer the
water-side ; and states, that Osai Tutu, who is
said to have conducted the emigration, built Coomassie, and founded the Ashantee monarchy,
about the year 1700, the period when Bosman
and Barbot mention the Ashantees as just heard
of by Europeans.   Dupuis, however, who paid
considerable attention to the subject, traces the
traditional history of Ashantee, as a separate king-

dom, backward for, at least, two hundred years, and states that both the Heathens and Moslems are agreed that the tribes of Ashantee, (As-hánti,) Gaman, Denkera, and Akím, were driven by the believers from their original inheritances, in the immediate vicinity of the Kong Mountains, to the forests of Wangara, the Mohammedan name for that part of Africa which they now possess; and that they spread over the land, down to the margin of the sea, peopling, as may be conjectured, some countries which heretofore lay desolate, like the forests of Fantee, (Fánti,) and Assin, (Asín,) and others, whose primitive inhabitants were not adequate to the defence of their towns. He therefore concludes, that Ashantee is the parent-country, and the stock from which the early generations of Fantees and Denkerans sprung; and the account which Meredith has given of the origin of the Fantee nation is much more favourable to this conclusion, than it is to the opinion of Bowdich. According to that writer, the Fantees were originally an inland people, under the government of the kings of Ashantee; against whom having rebelled, they fled towards the sea, and became an independent state.

Another tradition is mentioned by Bowdich, which deserves especial notice, as furnishing evidence of the relationship which formerly subsisted between the Ashantees and their neighbours.

He represents it to be the popular belief, that the Ashantee, (As-hánti,) Wassaw, Fantee, (Fánti,) Akím, Asín, Aquamboe, (Aquambú,) and part of the Ashantee nations, were originally comprehended in twelve tribes or families,—the Aquonna, Abrutu, Abradi, Esonna, Annona, Yoko, Inchwa, Abadi, Apiadi, Tchweedam, Aguna, and Dumina, in which they still class themselves, without any regard to national distinction; and that men of different nations, belonging to the same primitive family, on meeting, salute each other as brothers. The general correctness of this account is corroborated by Mr. William De Graft, who states, that the chiefs of the several families are distinguished by certain significant emblems, equivalent to the heraldic signs used in European countries. He himself is of the Chudan, (Bowdich's Tchweedam,) or "tiger," family; and he distinctly recollects old Baffu, a chief of the same family at Annamaboe, (Anamabú,) whose ensign of office (his umbrella) was surmounted by a figure of the tiger.   The emblems of the other families are, in like manner, figurative representations of the names which they respectively bear.   In consequence of intermarriages, the distinction between the families must necessarily, to a great extent, be lost; but wherever it is still preserved, or is supposed to exist, the brotherhood is uniformly recognised.   De Graft has known his own father attend the funerals of individuals for the sole reason, that they were members of the same original or patriarchal family with himself; and when he resided, a few years since, at Dix Cove, he was informed, that, some time previous to his going thither, the king of Apollonia sent a present of rice to the inhabitants, when they were suffering from scarcity, as an acknowledgment that he and they were all members of the Inchwa, or " dog," family. This latter fact shows that the tradition extends further than Bowdich was aware, Apollonia not being included in the list of nations which he has given. On another occasion, De Graft, being sent by the governor to publish and explain a proclamation to the natives, was received with the greatest kindness by the chiefs of the Chudan, or " tiger," family, who invariably, wherever he met with them during his journey, which occupied three months, claimed him as one of their own relatives.

After a careful comparison of the various accounts which have been furnished, it may perhaps be concluded, that the Ashantees and their neighbours were originally a part of that great Negro emigration which withdrew, before the Mohammedan arms, from the neighbourhood of the Mountains of Kong; that the Ashantees remained in that part of the country where they are now established; and that other tribes, per-

haps at different times, and impelled by various
causes, retired still further south, and settled in
the country between Ashantee and the sea. With
this general conclusion, it may not prove impossible to reconcile the apparently contradictory tradition mentioned by Bowdich. Under their early
sovereigns, while the Arab influence yet existed
on the Joliba, Kowara or Quorra, and Ghulby
rivers, the Ashantees, although firm and compact
as a nation, were unsettled in their habitation ; and
the seat of government was removed from place to
place, until it was permanently established, by Osai
Tutu, at Coomassie ; which place he enlarged,
(not built, as Bowdich supposes,) and raised, from
an inconsiderable town, to the rank which it now
enjoys as the metropolis of the empire. Now, as
Bequa, last mentioned by Dupuis as one of the
pláces where the government had been occasionally held, is fifty miles to the south of Coomassie,
it is no great stretch of the imagination to suppose, that Bowdich's tradition respecting the emigration of the Ashantees, under the direction of
Osai Tutu, from a place nearer the water-side,
is nothing else but a confused and exaggerated
account of the last emigration of the government
from Bequa to Coomassie. Either in that transaction, or some other movement of the nation
within the territory which lies north of Fantee,
(Fánti,) the tradition most probably originated.

From their earliest history, the Ashantees appear to have been distinguished by their military achievements. In the former part of the seventeenth century, they, with their allies, were able to send into the field sixty thousand warriors, armed with bows and arrows, and a very few muskets; and their courage and ferocity rendered them a terror to surrounding tribes. At that period, Ashantee (As-hánti) occasionally ruled, by its influence, over part of Akím, Asín, Quahu, and Akeyah.

The warlike deeds of Osai Tutu occupy a very prominent place in the annals of Ashantee. On the eastern side he added to it Quahu, which he entirely subdued; and a great extent of country on the west, beyond the Tando river. In the north-west, he reduced Gaman to the condition of a tributary kingdom; northward, he carried his victorious arms beyond Banna, into the neighbourhood of the great mountainous range. Dupuis says, " The auxiliary kingdom of Banna was the right arm of Ashantee in those days, and still is." In the south, he ravaged Asín with fire and sword, for some indignity offered by its monarch towards his person; and conquered both Tofel and Denkera, and established over them his rule.

The overthrow of Denkera was an event which excited a great sensation in the surrounding countries. According to the Moslem records, referred to by Dupuis, the war with Denkera commenced in the year 1719, and was the first great campaign in which the believers were compelled to unite their arms with the Heathen of Ashantee, Banna, Dwabin or Juábin, and other tributary States in the north : and Bosman, who wrote in 1721, represents the Denkeran war as having ended but a few months previous. From this writer it appears that Denkera had assumed so much on account of its power and wealth, that it had become the object of hatred to all its neighbours, who impatiently desired its downfall; although no nation was hardy enough to attack it, until it was invaded by the king of Ashantee.

The occasion of this war illustrates the customs and manners of the people of those countries. Bosiante, the king of Denkera, a young prince who had obtained a high character for valour, sent some of his wives on an embassy to present his respects to the king of Ashantee, (As-hánti,) who honoured them with courteous treatment and many presents; and shortly after returned the compliment, by sending a number of his own wives to assure the king of Denkera of the great esteem which he entertained for his person. One of these was seduced by Bosiante, which so incensed Osai Tutu, that he determined to wash out the scandal with the blood of the offender. Bosiante offered him several hundred marks of gold as a compensation for the injury, which he indignantly refused; and began to make preparations for war, by raising a strong army, and purchasing large quantities of gunpowder on the coast. The Denkerans, either through fear or some other cause, allowed his agents to carry the powder through their own country. While he was thus engaged, Bosiante died; but the preparations for war continued, and the king of Ashantee at length brought a powerful army into the field. Two dreadful battles, in which one hundred thousand warriors perished upon the field, decided the fate of Denkera. It took the Ashantees fifteen days to collect the spoils of the victory which they had won; and Bosman says, "that one of their European officers, who was sent after the battle on an embassy to the king of Ashantee, saw the immense quantity of gold which he had reserved as his own share of the treasures won from the Denkerans." Gold did not, however, satiate the conqueror. The body of Bosiante was disinterred, and the flesh, having been separated from the bones, was given to be devoured by serpents, while the skull and thigh-bones were preserved as trophies. These were to be seen at the Court of Ashantee when Dupuis was there; and, although a century had elapsed since the conquest of Denkera, still the Ashantees, on their solemn days, continued to repeat their insults to the relics of its king and principal men.

The Denkeran war is only briefly adverted to by Bowdich, in his " Historical Notice of Ashantee ;" but he states that the king of Denkera, (Intim Dakari,) the successor of Bosiante it may be presumed, was so considerable a trader in slaves, that the Dutch governor-general paid him a "monthly note" from his own purse, and assisted him against the Ashantees, with two or three small cannons, and a few Europeans. The cannon were taken by the conqueror, and placed as trophies at the top of one of the streets in Coomassie, (Kumási,) where they remained when the capital was visited by Bowdich. The Rev. Mr. Freeman also saw them on his late visit to Coomassie.

The death of Osai Tutu shortly followed the subjugation of Denkera. If the other States, bordering on the coast, wished for the downfall of that haughty power, Akím seems to have had a just apprehension of the rising greatness of Ashantee, and to have been impressed with the importance of keeping back so powerful an invader, and of preserving the equilibrium of the respective nations. It therefore joined Denkera, and lost thirty thousand men in the two fatal battles in which the latter was overthrown. But its misfortunes did not end here. Osai Tutu led his victorious army into the Akím country, defeated the king in a great battle near the frontier, and reduced him to the necessity of suing for peace. This was granted, on the condition that he should become a tributary to the Ashantee crown, and should also defray the expense of the war by a present of two thousand bendas (four thousand ounces) of gold; and two Akím caboceers of high rank were compelled to take Fetish, and were delivered up as hostages for the fulfilment of these conditions.

Owing either to the insincerity of the king himself, or the discontent of his principal men, the contribution was not paid; and Osai Tutu, impatient at the delay, and urged by the reiterated complaints of his rapacious captains, raised another army, which he sent against him, purposing to follow when he had visited the royal sepulchre at Bantama. Accordingly, having presented the usual offerings to his tutelary deities, at that sacred place, he followed the army, accompanied by the flower of his nobility; but before he could join the main body, he was suddenly attacked by a superior detachment of the enemy, as he was crossing the River Prah. On the first discharge, it is said, the king was wounded in the side; but he threw himself out of his hammock, and rallied his men, when a second volley was fired from the forest, and he fell dead upon his face in the river. In the midst of the confusion which ensued, the enemy issued, sword in hand, out of their concealment, and massacred the whole party, amounting to two or three hundred persons, including sixty women and children belonging either to the king or to the nobles by whom he was attended.

Thus ended the life and reign of Osai Tutu, whose qualities in the cabinet and in the field secured for him the epithet of the Great. Although he did not, as Bowdich supposes, lay the foundation of the monarchy, yet he so extended the boundaries and increased the power of Ashantee, (As-hánti,) that he may justly be considered as its second founder. Dupuis evidently regarded him in this light; for he says, " He created an empire, including tributaries and allies, which was strictly of a feudal complexion, by the union of all those kingdoms and principalities between the sixth and ninth degrees of (north) latitude, and between the fourth degree of longitude west from the meridian of London and the River Volta." To the excellences of this monarch the Ashantees still advert with a national satisfaction. They say, he was the Good, as well as the Great ; for, in his reign, justice was ever on the alert, and the claims of his subjects were listened to without distinction of rank or title.

After the death of Osai Tutu, the army, having taken terrible vengeance on Acromanti, (the town which had harboured the enemy the night previous to their attack upon the king, and many of whose inhabitants were in the ambuscade which cut him off,) returned to Coomassie, without even the satisfaction of bearing with them the corpse of their lamented sovereign, for it was never recovered; but they carried up a considerable number of prisoners, who were doomed to be immolated to his shade. Great commotion ensued in the capital: for the principal ministers of state had perished with the king; and before his successor was chosen, and new ministers were appointed, most of the conquered nations had renounced their allegiance to Ashantee.

Osai Apóko, the brother of the preceding monarch, was called to the throne in the year 1731; and his victorious arms obtained for him a renown scarcely inferior to that of his illustrious predecessor. Asín, Akím, Denkera, and Bouromy, all bowed before him, and yielded to his sway. In his conquest of Akím, he first obtained possession of the celebrated "Notes" which afterwards involved the British and Ashantees in war. He also invaded Gaman or Buntuku; chased Abo, its king, as far as the frontiers of Kong; there defeated him in a great battle, and reduced him to unconditional submission.

In the latter part of his reign, Osai Apóko was obliged to fly from his capital before a dangerous conspiracy. He had introduced a new code of laws, and made various important regulations, which the chiefs regarded as an abridgment of their power; and, in defence of their endangered authority, many of them resorted to arms. The king, after endeavouring in vain to hold a kind of convention at Dwabin or Juábin, met, and entirely defeated, the rebels in the province of Akiah. This victory re-established his authority; but he did not long survive. He died suddenly, in the year 1742; and the dissatisfied nobles embraced the opportunity which this event afforded, to secure by policy the object which they had failed to accomplish by arms. The hereditary or elective prince consented to revoke the obnoxious edicts of his predecessor, and restore the old constitution, which guaranteed to all the principal officers of state, and generals, or captains in the army, a proportionate share of influence in the city, a political preponderance in the councils of the nation, and a princely rank in the provinces.

The reign of Osai Aquasi, brother of the two preceding monarchs, was, like theirs, distinguished by war and bloodshed. The caboceers or nobles of Bouromy, Quahu, and Akím entered into a league with the king of Dahomy, who engaged to support them with an army, in order to enable them to regain the independence of their respective countries. Osai Aquasi, however, attacked and defeated them with great slaughter, in the vicinity of the Volta, which they had selected as the most suitable theatre of action, on account of its contiguity to Dahomy. The principal caboceers or vice-kings of Bouromy and Quahu were taken prisoners; and shortly after, the vice-king of Akím, to avoid falling into the hands of the conqueror, blew up himself with gunpowder, together with many of his wives, children, and attendants.

After this, the king of Ashantee, (As-hánti,) contrary to the advice of his most able counsellors, determined to cross the Volta, and take vengeance on Dahomy. Having ravaged the country of one of the tributaries of that crown, he engaged the Dahoman army which had advanced to meet him, and one of the most sanguinary battles mentioned in the records and traditions of the country was fought between the two armies. On the morning of the second day, Osai Aquasi was preparing to renew the contest which the night had interrupted, but was arrested in his plan by some omens pronounced by the priests to be unfavourable; and when the Dahomans, who mistook the inactivity of the Ashantees for want of resolution, came on to the charge, Osai Aquasi precipitately retreated to the Volta, without attempting any defence, and had the mortification to witness the destruction of a great part of his army, in consequence of the want of a sufficient number of canoes to transport them across the river. The Moslems, who were the informants of Dupuis, ascribed this terrible disaster solely to the superstitious fears of the Ashantees; being persuaded that the resources of Ashantee were quite sufficient to have crushed to atoms the whole power of Dahomy. When the news of the defeat became known, the whole kingdom was thrown into mourning; the provinces were ransacked for victims to be sacrificed in the capital, in expiation of offences imagined to have been offered to the national deities, and to appease the shades of the great captains who fell in the war; and the streets of Coomassie, during the whole of the Adai custom,—which custom, with other references to religious observances, will hereafter be explained,—were drenched with blood.

The reign of Osai Aquasi was terminated by a wound which he received in a war with Banna. The crown now descended to another generation. The three preceding kings were brothers; and Osai Kujoh was their nephew. This prince assumed the government in the year 1752, and was speedily involved in a war, acknowledged by the Ashantees to have been the most critical and hazardous in which they were ever engaged. It originated in the refusal of some of the dependent States to pay the arrears of tribute which the new monarch claimed. The king of Gaman having set the example of disobedience, Osai Kujoh twice led his army against him, but was each time defeated with immense slaughter. This is ascribed to two causes; first, that the enemy were armed with muskets as well as the Ashantees themselves; and, secondly, that they were aided by a strong cavalry force from Kong and Ghofan. After each defeat, the Ashantee sovereign returned to Coomassie to offer sacrifices, and consult the national deities; and, encouraged by a favourable response, he advanced a third time upon Gaman, and amply revenged his two former repulses. He led back to his capital a multitude of prisoners, of whom the children were spared alive to recruit the losses which his army had sustained; and the adults of both sexes were either sacrificed, or sent to the great slave-market at Mansu, and sold into West-Indian slavery. Wassaw, another of the rebellious provinces, experienced even a more terrible visitation than Gaman. The incensed king let loose the fury of his soldiers upon its northern confines, and several large districts were entirely depopulated. The principal insurgents were immolated upon the altars of the capital, and two powerful tribes were removed from their native seats, and placed in distant provinces of the empire.

The defeat of Gaman and its allies laid
open the Sarem country to the conqueror, into
which he advanced; and it might have enabled
him, had it been fully improved, to carry his victorious arms as far as Cape Palmas : but he con-
tented himself with receiving the ready submission of the kings and caboceers of those States
which had previously sought the alliance of
Kong.

The fame of Osai Kujoh reached other lands,
and a friendly embassy was sent to his Court from
Dahomy to announce the accession of a new sovereign. Only once before (namely, in the reign of
Osai Tutu) had such a compliment been received
from this formidable neighbour of Ashantee ; and
Dupuis gives it as the opinion of the Moslems,
that this latter embassy originated in the apprehension of the Dahomans, and their ally,—the
sultan of Dogho, the same as Eyeo or Yarriba, to
whom they are in some sense tributary,—that the
king of Ashantee (As-hánti) might be disposed to
carry his victorious arms into Dahomy, in revenge
of the defeat which his predecessor had there
experienced. The Dahoman ambassadors were
received by Osai Kujoh in the most flattering
manner ; public rejoicings took place on the occasion in the capital and throughout the empire ;
and a splendid embassy was sent in return to the
Court of Dahomy to reciprocate the feeling of

kindness and good-will on the part of the king of Ashantee.

According to Bowdich, this Prince was distinguished by other qualities as well as valour, having by his policy succeeded in reducing the number of the aristocracy; but the events of the latter part of his life prove what are the qualifications most esteemed in an African monarch. Being obliged, by the infirmities of age, to confine himself to his palace, his enemies circulated a report that he was dead. This at once threw the distant provinces into commotion. Asín, Akím, and Aquapím, again rushed into rebellion; and when the king sent an embassy, enjoining them to preserve the peace, they killed the messengers, and, in contempt of the aged king, threatened to march to the capital, and place one of their female slaves upon the throne, who would be able to repress disorder and sedition, which his impotence could not accomplish. Vigorous preparations for war were then made; but before the army took the field, the king died.

Osai Quamina, who succeeded his grandfather, Osai Kujoh, in the year 1781, vowed that he would not enter the walls of his palace, or see his wives, until he had obtained possession of the heads of Akombrah and Afosu, the two principal leaders in the rebellion. The vow was strictly performed; and the skulls of the two ill-fated chiefs found a place among the trophies which are preserved in the palace of Coomassie.

This prince, also, was honoured with a congratulatory embassy from Dahomy, and received similar flattering testimonies of friendship from other states; but his reign did not terminate in harmony with the eclat of its commencement. He was deposed by his subjects, in consequence, according to Bowdich, of his absenting himself from his capital, for the purpose of enjoying the company of his favourite mistress, a daughter of the king of Dwabin. Dupuis, however, ascribes his dethronement to his manifest attachment to the Moslems. His innovations, it is said, alarmed the great captains, who feared that the Mohammedan religion would be introduced, and that they should in consequence lose their ascendancy. The Moslems might, however, be mistaken in supposing that the captains were so much afraid of the levelling power of the Mohammedan religion. As the innovations of the king consisted in the suppression of various religious customs and festivals which had the sanction of ages, it is far more probable that his dethronement was suggested by the superstitious fears which those proceedings had awakened.

Osai Apóko, the second of that name, the brother of the fallen monarch, was chosen as his successor. He ascended the throne in the year

1797, and reigned, Bowdich says, a few weeks; Dupuis, two years; which latter term was short enough for the transactions in which he took a prominent part. At the instigation of Kong, the Buntukus or Gamans again took arms, professedly with the design of effecting the restoration of Osai Quamina; and the flames of war raged most fiercely during the period of fifteen months. The entire force of Kong, and of Gaman, crossed the Tando, and gave battle to the king. As his army was not one fourth so large as that of the invaders, he was unable to resist their advance. Their cavalry spread over the open plains of Massy, but could not penetrate that intricate mass of forest in which Coomassie (Kumási) stands. At length the king was joined by the princes and caboceers from the distant provinces; and then, ceasing to act upon the defensive, he gave battle to his enemies in the open plains. After a tremendous conflict of several days, he entirely defeated them, with prodigious slaughter, and returned to his capital, laden with spoils. In this war, the Moslems resident in Ashantee (As-hánti) were compelled to join the army, and fight against their own brethren in the faith in the ranks of Kong and Gaman; many thousands of whom were found in the multitude of captives whom the king led back to Coomassie. It is, however, worthy of remark, that the Moslem prisoners were neither sacrificed nor sold into slavery.

Many of them redeemed themselves, or were ransomed by their friends; others were set at liberty when their sultan sent an embassy to Coomassie; and the remainder were induced, by the kind treatment of the king, to remain in Ashantee, and were incorporated with the Moslem tribes which are settled in the northern provinces of the empire.

In a few months after this victory, Osai Apóko, who was regarded as one of the most promising princes who had ever been raised to the throne, died of a lingering illness, which the Ashantees regarded as the effect of sorcery, practised out of revenge by his dethroned brother.

Osai Tutu Quamina, the prince whose name is so intimately identified with the history of British affairs in Guinea, now ascended the throne. He was the brother of the two preceding monarchs; and commenced his reign about the year 1800, when, according to the Moslems, he was only a beardless boy. Bowdich supposes he was about seventeen years of age. Young, however, as he was in years, his deeds speedily proclaimed the manly qualities which he possessed. Soon after he assumed the government, he was called to take the field against the united forces of Ghofan and Ghobagho; which had defeated the tributary king of Banna, destroyed Banda, his capital, and carried off a great number of captives. The advance of the king of Ashantee (As-hánti) checked their progress southward. After a fierce engagement, which took place between the two armies, near the town of Kaka, the invaders retreated, until they were joined by a large body of reserve; when they again offered battle to the king, who had vigorously pursued them. The entire defeat of the invaders was the result. Beaten at all points, they fled precipitately towards the Volta; with the loss of one hundred thousand warriors, who either perished in the field, or were taken captive by the conqueror. Among the prisoners were two kings; one of whom, the Moslem king of Ghofan, died of his wounds, in the Ashantee camp. This victory gave the conqueror possession of a considerable territory on the north of Banna, to which the crown of Ashantee (As-hánti) had previously only a slender claim.

This account of Osai Tutu Quamina's first campaign, which Dupuis had from the Moslems, receives a striking confirmation, in its main features, from the narrative of the captivity of Abú Bekr, as given by the Rev. G. C. Renouard, in the Journal of the Royal Geographical Society. Abú Bekr was the grandson of an alkáid of Timbuctoo (Tumbuktú); but he removed from that city to Jenneh when he was only two years old. When about nine years of age, he went to Ghónah, to visit the burial-place of his father, who had then been dead about five years; and he remained in that neighbourhood until he was taken prisoner in war, and sold into slavery in the West Indies: from which he was released by the kind intervention of Dr. Madden, in the year 1834. In the following extract, Abú Bekr narrates the circumstances in which his captivity originated. Referring to the period when he was residing with his uncle Mohammed, in the city of Ghónah, he says,—

" At this time we heard the news of the business of Adinkarah, sultán of Buntukú, after the sultán of Bandah, or Inkoransá, who was named Afwá, had been killed. They say, Adinkarah wished to kill Kujóh, governor of Kolongzhwí; a town belonging to the sultán of Ghónah. He wished to kill him, because of what had happened between him and Dikkí, his deputy, [who had been killed by Kujóh]. Adinkarah, therefore, wished to put the latter to death by way of retaliation. Adinkarah, sultán of Buntukú, sent to Kujóh, requiring him to pay a great deal of gold as a ransom for his life, and Kujóh sent what he required; but he refused to accept it, and said to Kujóh's messenger, ' Return to thy master, and say to him, Unless thou increase it by two hundred times as much, I will not accept it ; but my sword shall take his head from off his neck : thou shalt die a swift death.' When this messenger came to his master, and told him these words, Kujóh stretched out his hand, took back the gold, and kept it; and, likewise, sent a messenger to the sultán of Ghónah to tell him what had happened.

"Then was Adinkarah very wroth; and he ordered all his captains to gather all their soldiers together, and follow him, to make war against Kujóh, and to kill him; that they might avenge the death of his servant Dikkí. When the sultán of Ghónah heard that Adinkarah, sultán of Buntukú, and his army, had come against them to kill them, he and all his host, together with Kujóh, rose up to meet them, and marched against them as far as the town of Bolóh, choosing to attack them there : and there they fought from mid-day till evening ; then they separated, and returned to their own places. Seven days afterwards, they again gathered themselves together, and engaged in battle, at the town of Amvighóh. It was a hard-fought battle, and many souls perished on that day. Thus did Adinkarah overcome the king of Ghónah, and take the town of Amvighóh. The people of Ghónah fled ; and some of them passed on [as far as] to the city of Kong.

"On that day was I made a slave. They tore off my clothes, bound me with ropes, laid on me a

heavy burden, and carried me to the town of
Buntukú; and from thence to the town of
Kumási, the king of Ashantí's town: from
thence, through Askumá and Ajimmakúh, in the
land of Fantí, to Daghóh, near the Salt Sea.

"There they sold me to the Christians; and I
was bought by a certain captain of a ship at that
town. He sent me to a boat, and delivered me
to the people of the ship. We continued on
board ship, at sea, for three months; and then
came on shore in the land of Jamaica. This was
the beginning of my slavery until this day."

On comparing this statement with the preceding sketch of Osai Tutu Quamina's first campaign, it will be noticed that both refer in the
first instance to Banda and Coransah, or Inko-
ransa; and speak of an overwhelming calamity
which befell the king of Banda. In the next
place, both agree that something like a drawn
battle was fought between the hostile parties.
And, in the third place, both concur again in
stating, that, after some little time, a second
desperate battle was fought, in which the warriors
of the South gained a most decisive victory over
their enemies.

Various considerations show that these two
narratives describe one and the same campaign.
Abú Bekr was right in stating, that Adinkarah
(or Dinkara) was then ruler of Buntuku or

Gaman; but that prince was not an independent
sovereign. Both Buntuku and Banna were, at
that period, dependencies of Ashantee (As-hánti);
and Dinkara could not have sustained any other
character in this war than that of viceroy or
general of the king of Ashantee. That he
would take a prominent part in the war, on
account of his contiguity to the theatre of the
campaign, is very probable. When Odumata,
the Ashantee general, conquered Banna, and
reduced it to the condition of a tributary State,
his army, for the same reason, was composed
almost exclusively of Buntukus. Abú Bekr
must, therefore, have been mistaken, in supposing
that Dinkara was a principal in the war. And it
is not surprising that circumstances should have
combined to impress the mind of a boy, that the
affair between Dinkara and the governor Kujóh
was the cause of the war; when, in fact, its
origin ought to be traced to the overthrow of the
king of Banna by his enemies, whose ultimate
object was to subvert the throne of his superior,
the new king of Ashantee.

The conclusion, that Abú Bekr was one of the
prisoners whom Osai Tutu Quamina carried back
with him through Buntuku to Coomassie, (Kumási,)
is strengthened by the further agreement of the
two narratives with respect to time. The Rev.
Mr. Renouard calculates, that Abú Bekr left

Africa about the year 1807 or 1808; but Dr.
Madden, whose humane exertions procured Abú
Bekr his liberty, supposes, that he embarked for
Jamaica about 1804; which latter period agrees
within two or three years with Dupuis's date of
the first campaign of Osai Tutu Quamina. The
war in which Abú Bekr lost his freedom cannot
be fixed at a later period than that which Dupuis
specifies: for it was in 1807 that Osai Tutu
Quamina invaded Fantee; and, previous to that
invasion, the Ashantee empire had enjoyed profound peace during a period of five years. But
when it is considered that some considerable time
must necessarily have elapsed between the cap-
ture of Abú Bekr, and his embarkation for the
West Indies, the discrepancy between Dr.
Madden and Dupuis almost entirely disappears.

As Abú Bekr may probably be cited as a
witness in a subsequent part of this work, it will
be interesting to glance at the proof of his
veracity, deducible from the brief account which
he gives of his journey from Coomassie to the sea-
side. He states, that he went through Askuma
and Ajimmakuh, in the Fantee (Fánti) country,
to Daghóh, where he embarked; and the fact is,
that all these three places were noted depôts for
slaves before the legal abolition of the slave-trade
by Great Britain. The slaves from the interior
were brought down to the great slave-mart at

Mansu, and were marched from thence, in different directions, for the sea; and those who were to be embarked at Daghóh (the native name of the place, called Lago by Europeans) went from Mansu by Askuma (Asikúma) and Ajimmakuh. William De Graft has visited the three places; and has often heard his father, and other elderly persons, speak of them as having been formerly depôts for slaves. Now, on no other principle can it be accounted for, that an old Negro, who had been upwards of thirty years a slave in the West Indies, should describe those places so correctly, but that their names were indelibly imprinted upon his memory, as he was dragged through them from the land of his fathers to a distant captivity. That was a period in his life which could never be forgotten; and its attendant circumstances would naturally form the subject of his constant meditation, and become inter-woven with all his liveliest recollections.*

The martial prowess of Osai Tutu Quamina was next displayed in that war with Gaman which has been termed the first Buntúku war of his reign. This was occasioned by the revolt of part of the Gaman people from the govern-ment of the vice-king,—the representative of the Ashantee sovereign,—who aimed at regaining

* See Note A.

their national independence, under the nephew of their late monarch. This young prince had enjoyed the protection of the sultán of Ghofan, who, as has been stated, lost both his army and his life, in the attempt to overthrow the government of the new monarch of Ashantee. The rising of these brave people (for so the conqueror himself characterized them to Dupuis) was speedily suppressed; and a profound peace of five years' continuance followed. During this period of tranquillity, Ashantee (As-hánti) enjoyed a higher reputation than she had ever perhaps attained at any former period; and alliance with her illustrious sovereign was generally courted. Before the events are narrated which disturbed this general repose, and finally involved the character and interests of Great Britain, it will be proper to notice the state of those countries which more immediately border upon the sea.

CHAPTER II.

THAT part of the coast of Guinea which is distinguished by the appellation of the Gold Coast commences with Apollonia, where the Ivory Coast ends, and reaches to the River Volta, where the Slave Coast begins. It first became known to Europeans in the sixteenth century. At that period the spirit of discovery which, during the middle ages, had been confined to the Arabs, manifested itself in Europe in a most remarkable manner. The Portuguese, who led the way, prosecuted their researches with enthusiastic ardour along the western coast of Africa; and from various points penetrated into the interior, in the hope of finding the far-famed Prester John,* whose empire, first supposed to be in Asia, and afterwards transferred in imagination to Africa, excited the most intense curiosity, and became the ultimate object and aim of the enterprises of the Portuguese. The great end to which all their researches in Africa were rendered subordinate was the discovery of this mysterious kingdom.

The English first commenced trading with Guinea in the latter end of the reign of Edward VI.; but the merchants who engaged in such commerce were exposed to considerable risk, in consequence of the pretensions of the Portuguese, who, having built the fort of St. George del Mina, endeavoured to enforce their claim of an exclusive right to

* The origin of the name is doubtful; but Rubruquis and other early travellers having reported that there was a Christian sovereign of that name in Asia, an ineffectual search was made for his kingdom; when another rumour arose, that a Christian monarch did actually reign somewhere on the eastern coast of Africa, from whence his dominions stretched far into the interior, and the research was in consequence renewed in that quarter of the globe.

trade with the Gold Coast as well as the other parts of Western Africa.

In the reign of James I. the trade began to be encouraged by the Government; and under Charles II., in the year 1662, a chartered Company was formed, entitled, "The Company of Royal Adventurers of England, trading to Africa." This step was taken with a view to the protection of the trade from the aggressions of the Dutch, who, having deprived the Portuguese of all their forts and settlements on the Gold Coast, attempted in their turn to monopolize the entire commerce of Western Africa; although the English had long had a fort at Cormantine, and had also established factories at other places on the Gold Coast, and thus enjoyed as good a right to participate in the trade as themselves. A war between the English and Dutch followed; at the end of which, in 1667, the English Company were left in possession of only one fort, that of Cabo Corso, or, as it is now called, Cape-Coast Castle, which had been taken from the Dutch.

As the war had exhausted the resources of the Company, they surrendered their charter to the crown, and a new Company was incorporated, in the year 1672, under the name of "The Royal African Company of England," with ample powers and privileges for the purpose of prosecuting and protecting the trade between Africa and England. The

following enumeration has been given of the establishments on the Gold Coast, at the time of the
incorporation of this second Company. The Dutch
were in possession of the strong fortress of St.
George del Mina, (Elmina,) and of the fort at
Cormantine, called Fort Amsterdam, which they
had taken from the English during the war. And
they had likewise another, named Fort Anthony, at
Axim; a fourth, called Fort Sebastian, on the river
Chamah; a fifth, called Fort Nassau, at Mouree;
a sixth, called Crevecœur, at Accra (Akráh); and
a seventh, named Fort Conraadsburg, at St. Jago,
within gun-shot of Elmina. The Danes were in
possession of one small but impregnable fort,
(afterwards called Fort Royal,) on the top of a hill,
within gun-shot of Cape-Coast Castle, and of
another at Accra, to the eastward of the Dutch
fort at the same place. And the elector of Bran-
denburgh had one good fort at Cape Three
Points.

The second English Company, finding themselves in possession of only one fort, proceeded
to strengthen their position; and, for this purpose,
they enlarged Cape-Coast Castle, and built one
fort at Accra, another at Dixcove, a third at
Winnebah, a fourth at Succondee, and a fifth at
Commenda, and rebuilt a sixth at Annamaboe.
Three of these forts were only about musket-shot
distance from Dutch forts. The Company like-

wise purchased Fredericksberg, or Fort Royal, from the Danes. By these exertions the English interest was put on an equal footing with that of the Dutch, to the great mortification of the Dutch Company, who had endeavoured, by force of arms and other means, to prevent the erection of the new forts.

In the year 1752 this second Company was divested of its charter by Act of Parliament; and their forts, castles, and all their other possessions, were transferred to a third new Company which was then formed.

The Gold Coast, which from the time of its discovery had been the cause of so much contention among the maritime powers of Europe, was divided into several independent States. Of these Fantee (Fánti) was the most considerable. The capital of the British settlements, Cape-Coast Castle, is situated in the Fetu country, formerly governed by a dey; but that State fell under the influence of Fantee, to the laws, regulations, and customs of which the people were obliged to submit. The unfortunate governor, Meredith, who himself at length became a victim to the violent conduct of the natives, in a letter to the Directors of the African Institution, written about the period when the Ashantees were beginning to make their power felt upon the Gold Coast, thus expresses himself as to the turbulent character, as well as influence, of the Fantee people :—

" The Asiantees are threatening to pay us another visit; and it is the current opinion, that the Fantees must be either subdued by the Asiantees, or means devised to restrain their ungovernable conduct, before the country is tranquillized, or before much improvement is effected. The Fantees are now to be considered a large body : they have brought under their subjection, either by threats or favourable promises, a number of small estates ; so that from Cape Coast to the extremity of the Agoona country may be put down as governed by the Fantees. To say that such and such places bear distinct names, is now merely to signify that they were formerly inhabited by a distinct people."

The irruption of the Ashantees into the Fantee country first brought them into collision with the British, in the year 1807.

This invasion originated in a dispute between two of the principal chiefs of Asín, a dependency of Ashantee, (As-hánti,) immediately contiguous to Fantee (Fánti) on the north. The grave of a distinguished caboceer, a subject of Amu, who ruled over the eastern half of Asín, was plundered of a quantity of gold by a near relation of Apoutai, joint ruler with Chibbu of the other half of that country ; and the offender having made his escape, Amu applied

to Chibbu for redress. This was refused; and he
then appealed to the court of Coomassie (Kumási).
The king delayed for a considerable time to give
judgment, in the hope of effecting a reconciliation
between the parties; but being disappointed in this
expectation, he at last decreed that the offender,
Apoutai, should make compensation to the relatives of the deceased, to the amount of the property
which had been stolen. Apoutai refused to submit
to the decree, and a war followed between him and
Amu, in which the latter at length prevailed, and
ravaged the territories of his opponent. The king
now interfered, and endeavoured to reconcile the
contending chiefs, by sending to each of them a
present of gold; and Amu had the prudence to
submit to the authority of the king, by taking up
a merely defensive position in the hills of Moisi.
A second embassy was then sent from Coomassie,
with other presents, to both chiefs; and Amu
was required to break up his camp, and leave the
palaver as it stood until the next Adai custom,
while Chibbu was commanded to keep the peace,
and not molest Amu on his homeward march.
Apoutai appeared to acquiesce, and drew off his
troops; but afterwards came upon Amu by surprise, when he had quitted his defensive position,
and completely routed him: and, in further
contempt of the king's authority, he barbarously
murdered the royal messengers, and a number of

other Ashantees who were in the camp, and
tauntingly suspended their mutilated bodies upon
trees on the border of the province.

Forbearance on the part of the king was now at
an end. He immediately placed himself at the
head of a powerful army, and advanced into the
Asín territory. Chibbu and Apoutai having in
vain attempted to impede his progress, retreated
towards the Prah; but, before they could cross
that river, were entirely defeated, and, according
to the popular Ashantee songs, thirty thousand of
their troops perished in the field. The two Asín
leaders, however, effected their escape, and were
cordially welcomed by the Fantees, who pledged
themselves to protect them to the uttermost of
their power. Apparently anxious to obtain possession of his enemies by friendly negotiation, the
king despatched an embassy to Akum, the caboceer of Asikuma, which, although a Fantee province, was in some sense dependent upon Ashantee,
(As-hánti,) requiring the surrender of Chibbu and
Apoutai. The liberal present which the king sent
was accepted; but the Council of Abrah, the capital
of Fantee, (Fánti,) refused either to deliver up the
fugitive chiefs, or to appoint deputies to go to the
royal camp to assist in settling the differences by a
legal investigation. The king then sent to demand that he might march through Fantee in
pursuit of the remnant of the Asín army; but

this application was also rejected, and his messengers were put to death, and their bodies treated with savage indignity.

The king, having waited in vain for the return of his messengers, and probably suspecting their fate, ordered his army to advance under the conduct of two of his generals, who defeated the united forces of Asín and Fantee (Fánti) upon the frontiers; but Chibbu and Apoutai again saved themselves by flight. Another battle afterwards took place, between the retreating army which had rallied and the van of the Ashantee army, when, the king coming up with the remainder of his forces, the Ashantees gained a complete victory; and part of the survivors fled to Abrah, and others, among whom was Chibbu, towards the sea-side. Apoutai then made offers of peace, which the king accepted, acceding to all his proposals; and, as an evidence of a perfect reconciliation, he sent large presents to both Chibbu and Apoutai. The proposals of peace had, however, been made in duplicity, either to gain time, or accomplish some other object; which end having been obtained, the mask was thrown off, and the messengers whom the king had despatched with the presents were, like the former, inhumanly butchered. Their hearts were reported to have been devoured by the Braffoes while yet palpitating; and the carcasses of the unfortunate victims were suspended upon the boughs of the trees, while their heads, after experiencing disgusting treatment, were placed in a row along the path on which the king would have to advance. The Asíns and Fantees then retreated towards the south, persuading themselves that the king would not dare to prosecute the campaign among the large towns, and especially those placed under the guns of the British and Dutch forts; but the sequel showed how miserably they were deceived in their calculations. The king was now excited to the highest pitch of indignant feeling, and he took the "great oath" that he would never sheath his sword, or return to his capital, until he had obtained the heads of Chibbu and Apoutai.

From this moment the war assumed the most determined character; and nothing less than the utter extermination of the Fantees appeared likely to satisfy the infuriated monarch. Orders were given to spare neither age nor sex; and, for a time, those orders were executed to the letter. Desolation and ruin followed in the track of the Ashantee army, and the silence and solitude of death reigned over the country through which they had passed. The king, after a sanguinary battle, having taken and destroyed Abrah, the capital, appeared to be somewhat appeased; and sent to several other Fantee towns, promising that, on their submission, the lives and property

of the people should be protected. Among the
rest, he despatched two of his sword-bearers to
Emperou, with pacific proposals; but Quasi Beni,
a caboceer of Abrah, having escaped with a few
troops from the destruction of the capital, persuaded the inhabitants, who had already engaged
another body of auxiliaries, to unite with him in
resisting the Ashantees; and the royal messengers were treated with indignity, and then massacred. This outrageous proceeding again roused
the king to action; and a division of the army
was immediately sent against Emperou. The
enemy greatly outnumbered the Ashantees, who,
in the onset, were repulsed, and driven back upon
the main army; but a charge made, by the king
in person, upon the flank and rear of the Fantee
army, decided the contest. It is stated that, with
the exception of about one hundred persons, who
fled before the town was assaulted by the victorious Ashantees, not one of its inhabitants, of
either sex, nor a single individual of the army
which had bravely attempted its defence, was left
alive. Several of the caboceers of the place, after
killing their own wives and children, destroyed
themselves; and all the rest fell beneath the sword
of the conqueror, or perished in the flames which
reduced the town to a mass of ruins. When
Dupuis passed this place, twelve years afterwards,
portions of the walls, which exhibited the action

of fire, were still standing, and the surface of the earth, in various places, was whitened with ashes and bleached human bones and skulls.

The king now directed his course towards Anna-maboe, (Anamabú,) then the largest town upon the coast, whither Chibbu and Apoutai had fled, after the destruction of Abrah.   But as it is the policy of the Ashantees, on invading a country, to leave no enemies in the rear while they press forward to the seat of the government, or other principal town of the enemy, he left one half of his army to destroy the remainder of the Fantee towns, and to exterminate the entire population. The king himself acknowledged to Dupuis that, at that period, none were taken prisoners, except a few principal caboceers, who were reserved for punishment at the rejoicings to be celebrated in the capital on his return.   Among the towns which were then destroyed was Mankasím; which, from the extent of the ruins still visible, Mr. Freeman is of opinion must, at least, have been half the size of Coomassie (Kumási) itself.

The advanced guard of the Ashantee (As-hánti) army, under the command of the viceroy of Den-kera, first reached the sea-coast at Cormantine, three miles eastward of Annamaboe.   This town they destroyed, and took possession of the Dutch fort, known by the name of Fort Amsterdam.   The near approach of the Ashantees now began to

excite uneasy apprehensions at Annamaboe; and
Mr. White, the governor of the castle, sent a
messenger with a flag of truce, to inquire respecting the king's intentions. An unsatisfactory
answer was returned; at which Mr. White expressed his regret, offering to use his influence
to obtain from the Annamaboes redress for any
just grievances which the king might be able to
substantiate; but stating, that unless the king
could produce sufficient cause of complaint, he
should afford the inhabitants protection against
any hostile attack on his part.

A week elapsed before anything further
occurred, when a reconnoitering party of Ashantees were discovered in possession of a point of
land about a mile distant from Annamaboe
(Anamabú). Almost all the inhabitants capable
of bearing arms sallied forth to attack them,
and succeeded in driving them from this position; but while they were engaged with this
small party, the king was employed in securing
all the passes leading to the town; and on the
following morning advanced to attack it. The
armed inhabitants were again drawn forth to
meet him, but were soon put to flight, and driven
towards the town in great confusion. The alarm
now became general, and the aged men, women,
and children crowded into the area of the castle
for protection; while one or two great guns were

fired, with a view to deter the Ashantees from advancing. The supposition that this would inspire the Ashantees with fear, argued a great ignorance of their character. Undismayed, they pursued the flying inhabitants through the town, down to the beach, mercilessly destroying all who came in their way; and then, in despite of the guns of the fort, the discharges from which made great havoc in their ranks, they advanced under its very walls, and carried off the women for whom room could not be found within. The fort itself was soon reduced to the utmost extremity; for the Ashantees, advancing almost to the very muzzles of the cannon, shortly rendered them useless, by the severity of their well-directed fire; and, at the same time, assailed the gate with such vigour, that had not night come to their aid, the little garrison would not have been able to repel the assailants.

After a lapse of two or three days, the king prepared to renew his attack upon the fort. Six thousand choice men were selected, half of whom were to attempt to blow up or scale the walls, under cover of the continual fire of the other half; but the very morning of the day on which the king had vowed, by the help of his gods, to seat himself in the governor's chair, a flag of truce was lowered from the walls. A negotiation ensued, and the king declining to go to Cape-Coast

Castle, the governor-in-chief, Colonel Torrane, went to the royal camp, and concluded a treaty of peace. Chibbu and Apoutai, the originators of the war, had quitted Annamaboe (Anamabú) previous to the approach of the Ashantees, and taken refuge at Cape-Coast town; from which place, Apoutai again made his escape, but Chibbu was delivered up to the king, and, after suffering the most exquisite tortures in the rejoicing which took place at Coomassie on the return of the army, his head became one of the principal decorations of the death-drum of the king. Of the inhabitants of Annamaboe, at least eight thousand perished in the contest; and many of the survivors were carried off by the king as prisoners, either to suffer death in other forms, or to be consigned to slavery. The elder De Graft, the linguist, was one of the brave defenders of the fort on that memorable occasion, and received a musket-shot, which he carries in his arm to the present day.

A second invasion of Fantee (Fanti) by the Ashantees took place in the year 1811. This was occasioned by the Fantees having determined to wreak their vengeance on the people of Elmina and Accra, (Akráh,) because they had not taken part against the Ashantees in 1807. The king having been informed, by the Dutch governor of Elmina, of the warlike proceedings of the Fantees, sent four thousand troops to protect Elmina, and another

army of twenty-five thousand more to defend
Accra (in the trade of which he was interested)
against that body of the Fantees who had proceeded to attack it. The force which was sent to
aid Elmina defeated the Fantees in several engagements; but the army intended for Accra
became involved in war with the chiefs of Aquapím and Akím, who had thrown off their allegiance to Ashantee : and the Fantees in that quarter
thus escaped the chastisement which the king had
designed to inflict.

Another invasion, in the year 1817, reduced the
Fantees to the greatest distress. Incalculable
misery resulted from the devastation committed
by the Ashantees. They swept the country before
them, destroying the whole of the plantations;
and famine and wretchedness attended all their
movements. William De Graft has a vivid
recollection of that awful period. He was then
only a boy, and well recollects that, on one
occasion when it was expected that the Ashantees would force their way into Cape-Coast
town, a friend of his family caught him under
his arm, and ran with him into the castle for
protection. The British, having interfered to
protect the natives, rendered themselves obnoxious to the invaders, who sat down before
Cape-Coast Castle, and continued to blockade it
with such determined perseverance, that the

government found it necessary, in order to avert the imminent danger with which the place was threatened, to advance a large sum of money, which the king demanded from the Fantees. With this the invader was willing to content himself, and he again returned to his own capital.

These repeated irruptions produced such a feeling of alarm and insecurity, that the local government was led to prefer an earnest request to the Committee of the African Society at home, to authorize and provide for an embassy to be sent to the court of Ashantee; with a view to conciliate its powerful monarch, and negotiate an extension of commerce. This request was acceded to; and on the 22d of April, 1817, Mr. James, governor of the fort at British Accra, Mr. Bowdich, nephew of Mr. Smith, the governor-in-chief at Cape-Coast Castle, Mr. Hutchinson, and surgeon Tedlie, set out on a Mission to Coomassie. How great was the importance which the local government attached to the establishment of friendly relations with Ashantee, (As-hánti,) will appear from an extract of a Despatch from Cape-Coast Castle, which was laid before a Parliamentary Committee in 1817. It is dated March 5th of that year, a few weeks only before the embassy was undertaken.

"From circumstances which have lately transpired, we have reason to think that General Daendels is intriguing with the king of Ashantee,

and using every means to bring the English into
disrepute; but he carries on his designs so
secretly, that we cannot produce any proofs. We
shall, however, use every exertion to counteract
his plans; and have full reliance in being able to
succeed. To our assistance, in accomplishing this
desirable object, the presents for the king of
Ashantee, by the store-ship, have arrived most
opportunely; and they are such as we consider
will be highly gratifying to him. An Ashantee
messenger, deputed by the king to the Fantees,
is now at Abrah: to him we have sent an invitation to visit Cape Coast; and he promises to be
down in the course of ten days. On his return,
we purpose selecting an intelligent native to
accompany him; to whom we shall give the requisite instructions to the king, regarding the
embassy which we are desirous of despatching
previous to the setting in of the rains. We shall
observe your instructions relative to the arrangement of the Mission; and we are very sanguine in
our expectations, that the consequences attending
the result of it will prove highly beneficial, not
only in the extension of British commerce and
influence with the nations of the interior, but
from such information being collected as may
considerably contribute to science, and be an
accession to the stock of geographical knowledge.
The commercial intercourse with the Ashantees

has been for the last ten months extremely flourishing, and is now evidently daily improving.
The necessity of a close alliance with the king of
Ashantee becomes, therefore, more obvious than
ever; and it is only by cultivating and promoting
this connexion that an inland trade can be
thoroughly opened, and through his means
inquiries may be directed to the interior, which
may gradually open an extensive intercourse with
the natives."

The British embassy were favourably received
by Osai Tutu Quamina; but no sooner had they
proceeded to business, than a misunderstanding
arose respecting the Fantee "Notes." When the
African Company established itself upon the Gold
Coast, it did not obtain any territory either by
conquest or purchase; but merely hired sufficient
land for the erection of forts, and gave pro-
missory notes to the native chiefs for the regular
payment of the stipulated rent. The other
European Companies, also, were placed under
similar obligations for the land on which their
forts were built. On the subjugation of the
countries upon the coast, by the king of Ashantee,
(As-hánti,) these notes fell into his hands; and
at the time of the embassy's visit, he had received
the rents for the Dutch fort at Elmina, and the
English, Dutch, and Danish forts at Accra (Akráh).
On the same ground, the right of conquest, he

claimed the Fantee notes; and Dupuis expressly
states, that the treaty of peace which Colonel
Torrane negotiated with the king at Annamaboe,
in the year 1807, was a formal and solemn acknowledgment that the whole of Fantee (Fánti)
belonged to the king, to whom he paid the arrears
of rent then due for the ground on which the
Annamaboe (Anamabú) Fort and Cape-Coast
Castle stood.

The king did not, however, as it would appear,
obtain at that time actual possession of the notes
for these two places; for, at a later period,
Amoney, king of Annamaboe, and Adoko, chief
of the Braffoes, prevailed upon Governor Smith to
write other notes, engaging to pay the king of
Ashantee four ackies of gold per month for the
two forts; reserving for themselves the remainder
of the rent specified in the original notes, which
they retained in their own hands. These were
the notes concerning which the king demanded
an explanation from the embassy; and the answer
which Mr. James gave appears to have confirmed
the suspicions of the king, that the governor-in-
chief had combined with the Fantees to defraud
him of his due. The conduct of the king and
his captains, in consequence, became so violent,
that Mr. Bowdich, in a state of alarm, interposed,
and assured the king that the governor would do
right; and proposed that messengers should be

sent down to Cape-Coast Castle, to receive his explanation of the whole affair.

The result of this appeal to the governor was, that Mr. James was recalled, Mr. Bowdich was placed in his stead at the head of the embassy, and the demands of the king respecting the notes were acceded to. The governor explained the circumstances in which he had been deceived into a compliance with the wishes of the Fantee chiefs, Amoney and Adoko, by writing the notes of which the king complained; and sent the king two other notes for four ounces of gold per month, (copies of which are given by Dupuis,) in which the governor stated, that, in consequence of the conquest of the Fantee country by the king of Ashantee, the notes for Annamaboe Fort and Cape-Coast Castle were, by consent of the former owners, transferred to the conqueror ; and, at the same time assured the king, in his accompanying letter, that the amount of these notes should thenceforth be regularly paid to his receiver, on behalf of the Company, at Cape-Coast Castle.

The affair of the Fantee notes having thus been settled to the satisfaction of the king, the negotiation proceeded, and a friendly treaty was finally concluded. By virtue of this treaty, Mr. Hutchinson was left as British resident at the court of Ashantee ; and Mr. Bowdich returned to Cape-Coast Castle.

CHAPTER III.

WHEN the news of this treaty reached England, His Majesty's government resolved upon sending a consul to Coomassie, (Kumási,) for the purpose of cultivating the friendly relations which had been entered into with Ashantee (As-hánti); and with a view to foster the trade between that country and the British settlements on the Gold Coast, and to induce the king eventually to suffer the traders from the more inland districts to visit the British markets in common with the Ashantees themselves. Mr. Dupuis, whose long residence in Barbary had contributed to qualify him for such an office, was accordingly appointed consul; and, after being detained in England about nine months from the date of his commission, he set sail for the coast of Africa in the month of November, 1818.

On his arrival, Mr. Dupuis found that the king of Ashantee was engaged in hostilities with his vassal Dinkara, king of Gaman, who had thrown off his allegiance; and that Mr. Hutchinson had left Coomassie on the eve of this, the second Buntuku, war, and was then at Cape-Coast Castle. He learned, moreover, that a considerable trade with Ashantee had resulted from Mr. Bowdich's successful negotiations; but that it was a matter of general complaint without the walls of the castle, that the trade had been to a great extent monopolized by a few leading servants of the Company. He also discovered that his own appointment as consul at the Ashantee capital was viewed with much jealousy; and he persuaded

himself that the local government was willing
to risk a rupture with the king, for the purpose
of defeating the objects for which that appointment was made by the British government.
Be this as it may, a misunderstanding soon took
place. Reports of doubtful origin arose, to the
effect, that the king had been defeated by the
Buntukus; and these reports were joyfully
received by the Cape-Coast people, who expressed
their hopes that the power of Ashantee would
be overthrown, and proceeded to treat with disrespect the Ashantee captain who was placed as
resident among them. He reported those proceedings to his master; and the visits of the
Ashantee traders were, in consequence, to a great
extent discontinued.

While things were in this critical state, two of
the king's messengers visited Cape-Coast Castle, in
order to complain of the conduct of the people of
Commenda. They had been sent thither by their
sovereign to convey some jaw-bones, as trophies
of his victory over the Buntukus; but, instead of
meeting with a courteous reception, they had been
treated with violence, and contemptuously turned
out of the town. The messengers then repaired
to Cape-Coast Castle, and claimed the protection
of the British by virtue of the treaty; but the
government refused to interfere in the affair, and
the messengers were obliged to depart without

obtaining redress.   Shortly after this, another
untoward event took place in the death of the
Ashantee resident at Cape-Coast town; the sud-
denness of which excited a suspicion that he was
cut off by poison secretly administered.   And
further provocation was given to the king, by the
rejoicings of the Cape-Coast people, at the report
of his defeat and death; which report, although
encouraged at the castle, was treated as a mere
idle rumour at all the neighbouring settlements.

The arrival of a messenger, bearing a gold-
hilted sword, put an end to the delusion.   He
stated, that he had been despatched from the
camp to complain of the treatment which his two
messengers had received at Commenda; to claim
the interference of the governor on the ground of
the treaty; and to say, that, if the governor still
refused his friendly interposition, he should send
down some troops to Commenda, and avenge his
insulted dignity in another way.   The messenger
was moreover instructed to express the anger and
regret which the conduct of the Cape-Coast
people had produced in the mind of the king;
and to request the governor to exert his influence to prevent a recurrence of those matters of
complaint.

To this message the governor returned an
answer which was regarded by the king as uncour-
teous and unfriendly; and the elders and chiefs of

the town were encouraged to arm the people, and build a mud wall for their protection against the Ashantees. The king, however, would not believe that the governor had really sent the reply which was delivered to him. Having subjected his messenger to the torture, he threw him into prison, intending to put him to a cruel death, if he discovered that he had made a false report; and he then despatched another messenger to Cape-Coast Castle, to ascertain the exact truth of the whole affair. In the mean time, the news that the Cape-Coast people were fortifying their town, reached the royal camp in Gaman; on which the captains instantly unsheathed their sabres, and requested permission to go down and punish them without delay. To this the king objected, on the ground that he held a " book," or treaty, with the white men; but engaged that he would apply for redress, for he was persuaded that an imposition had been practised upon the governor.

In fulfilment of this promise, a third messenger, of high rank, accompanied by a large retinue, was sent down; who, at a public audience in Cape-Coast Castle, recapitulated all the grievances of which his master had cause to complain; and, producing the treaty from a box, presented it to the governor, desiring him to read it, and say whether its provisions did not authorize the king to demand satisfaction; and telling him, in conclusion, that should he still refuse to fulfil the obligations of the treaty, he might retain it; for the king could not reconcile it to his views of honour and good faith to go to war so long as he kept the treaty in his own hands. The formal reading of the treaty was commenced, and was proceeded with to the fourth article; * when the Ashantee messenger again arose, and, in the name of his sovereign, demanded satisfaction upon the faith of that article; declaring that if it were not complied with, the natives of the town would suffer the vengeance of Ashantee; for, although with respect to the castle, the king did not wish to make war with white men, his own people must obey him, or pay the forfeit of their disobedience. This demand was enforced by the loud clamours of the messenger's attendants; when some of the town-chiefs, fully awakened to a sense of the impending danger, endeavoured to clear themselves from blame, by throwing the responsibility upon the government, alleging, that they had only acted at the instigation of the whites. When order was restored, the messenger desired that the remain-

---

* "In order to avert the horrors of war, it is agreed, that, in any case of aggression on the part of the natives under British protection, the king shall complain thereof to the governor-in-chief, to obtain redress; and that he will in no case resort to hostility, without endeavouring, as much as possible, to effect an amicable arrangement."

ing clauses of the treaty might be read; and, at
the seventh article,* he again arose, and required
satisfaction upon the faith of that article also.

From the demands which the messenger made
in this interview, no explanations or arguments
could induce him to recede. He declared that his
orders were peremptory; and that, unless the
local authorities promised to do the king justice,
he had no alternative but to leave the treaty
at the castle. At this juncture, Mr. Dupuis
requested the governor to make known to the
messenger his consular appointment to Coomassie;
on the announcement of which, the messenger
bowed to Mr. Dupuis, and took him by the hand
in token of respect and good-will. This circumstance gave another turn to the whole affair.
The messenger appeared for a time at a loss to
decide whether he should give up the treaty, or
take it back, and leave it to Mr. Dupuis to talk
the palaver with the king; but at length he
resolved to keep possession of the treaty, and
remain at Cape Coast until he could obtain fresh
instructions from Coomassie, as to the course he
ought to pursue.

After a considerable lapse of time, the alarming

* " The governors of the respective forts shall, at all
times, afford every protection in their power to the persons
and property of the people of Ashantee, who may resort to
the water-side."

news was brought, that a large body of Ashantee troops was at hand; which proved, however, to be another embassy. The king had sent one of his own nephews, with a train of twelve hundred attendants, who entered the town with a display of splendour which had not been witnessed on the coast from the time that the king himself was there. This new ambassador formally reiterated all the grievances of which his relative had to complain; denounced the Cape-Coast people as rebels; signified the royal displeasure at the conduct of the local authorities; and concluded by demanding sixteen hundred ounces of gold as a fine from the natives, and sixteen hundred additional from the castle.

A fruitless negotiation ensued, when the ambassador again demanded an audience in the hall; in which he repeated the claims of the king upon the castle and the town; declaring that it was the fixed determination of the king, not to allow the aggression of the natives to pass unpunished; and that, although he wished to live in friendship with the whites, unless the most ample satisfaction were promptly made, it would be sought by an appeal to arms. Conciliatory measures were now seen to be indispensably necessary; and the governor in council at length resolved to facilitate the departure of Mr. Dupuis to Coomassie; and, in consideration of the critical state of affairs, greatly to increase the number and value of the presents which Mr. Dupuis had brought with him from England, for the king of Ashantee. Thus, after having been detained upon the coast, by various causes, upwards of twelve months from the time of his landing, Mr. Dupuis set off for Coomassie, in the beginning of the month of February, 1820. At his leaving, however, another circumstance occurred, which not only furnished additional proof of the absence of cordial co-operation between himself and the Cape-Coast government, but was in itself sufficient to warrant the apprehension, that his mission would not be productive of the results which its projectors so ardently desired. On opening the papers which were given to him, on the eve of his departure, he found that the governor and council had prepared copious instructions for his guidance; and he was informed, that unless he accepted those instructions as his rule of conduct, the governor would withhold the presents, and send another person to convey them to the king. With such conditions, however, Mr. Dupuis judged that he could not comply, without proving faithless to the trust reposed in him by His Majesty's government, from whom he had directly received his commission; and he therefore left the instructions with a friend to be returned to the Castle, accompanied by a written protest, when he should have got so far on his journey as to be beyond the governor's reach.

On his arrival at Coomassie, (Kumási,) Mr. Dupuis was favourably received by the king, who appeared disposed to settle the existing differences without having recourse to arms. A lengthened negotiation accordingly ensued; during which, the feelings of the king were frequently excited to fury, when adverting to the conduct of the Cape-Coast people, and the treatment which he alleged to have received from the local government. At length, when convinced, by a reference to Mr. Bowdich's treaty, that its provisions did not authorize him to demand a fine from the governor, he gave up that claim; but no argument or persuasion could induce him to relinquish his demands upon the town. A second treaty was finally concluded, in which the king bound himself to receive and acknowledge Mr. Dupuis, as his Britannic Majesty's consul at Coomassie; promised fidelity to the crown of Great Britain; acknowledged that all differences between himself and the English were adjusted; and bound himself to support and encourage commerce between Ashantee (As-hánti) and Cape Coast and its dependencies, by all the means in his power. On the part of the British government, Mr. Dupuis again acknowledged the sovereignty asserted by the king of Ashantee over the Fantee territory, on the express condition, that the king agreed to allow the natives, residing under British protection, to enjoy the benefit of British laws; and to be amenable to them only in case of any act of aggression on their part.

To this treaty, supplementary articles were annexed; by one of which the king, to eradicate, as he said, from his dominions, the seeds of disobedience and insubordination, excluded the natives of Cape-Coast town from participating in the benefits of the treaty; but, at the same time, bound himself that, whatever plans he might see fit to adopt to bring them under subjection, he would not destroy the town, nor allow a gun to be fired into it, or suffer his troops to commit any act of hostility or depredation therein on the inhabitants or on their property. In another of those articles, the king further pledged himself to afford protection, in person and property, to Missionaries or others, being subjects of His Britannic Majesty, who might wish to establish themselves in any part of his territory, for the purpose of propagating the Christian religion; and at the same time formally and cordially invited to his country such well-disposed men. This treaty, with the supplementary articles, was executed on the 23d day of March, 1820.

Mr. Dupuis then returned to Cape-Coast Castle, accompanied by some Ashantees of rank, whom the king sent as ambassadors to the British court, to maintain a good understanding between the two countries, and deliver numerous presents to His Royal Highness the Prince Regent. The reception which Mr. Dupuis met with on his return was not flattering. Sir George Collier, the commander of the British squadron upon the coast, had been applied to by the local authorities to support them in their opposition to the Ashantees; and, encouraged by his promise of assistance, they refused to accede to the treaty which Mr. Dupuis had negotiated, on the plea that it transferred the sovereignty of the Fantee country to the king of Ashantee. The palaver respecting the fine which the king had imposed upon the Cape-Coast people was reserved, when the treaty was executed, for final adjustment on the spot; but the local authorities withdrew the proposal which they had previously made, to give the king one hundred and fifty ounces of gold, as a peace-offering on behalf of the town; and further decided that the payment of the tribute or rent, which the king had been accustomed to receive, should be discontinued.

Mr. Dupuis made a formal protest against the proceedings of the local authorities, and applied to Sir George Collier, when he returned from his cruise, to interpose so far as to support his protest against the adoption of any rash and hostile proceedings, until the sentiments of His Majesty's ministers, in relation to the treaty, should be known. Sir George, however, declined all interference, and also offered reasons for refusing to convey the Ashantee ambassadors to England; on which Mr. Dupuis made the ambassadors acquainted with the actual state of affairs; and, having sent a message to the king of Ashantee, entreating him to remember his oath, and maintain peace, he proceeded to England with Sir George Collier, for the purpose of laying the whole case before the government at home.

At this period an important change took place in the administration of affairs on the Gold Coast. The British connexion with that part of Africa had for some time occupied the serious attention of ministers, and the whole subject had been fully investigated by Committees of the House of Commons, in the years 1816 and 1817. As the result of those inquiries, a Bill was brought into Parliament, in 1821, for abolishing the African Company, and transferring to the Crown all the Company's forts and possessions. This Bill passed into law, and the forts on the Gold Coast were placed under the authority of Sir Charles M'Carthy, who had for some years ably conducted the government of Sierra-Leone.

When Sir Charles arrived at Cape-Coast Castle, in the month of March, 1822, things were found in an unsatisfactory state. Prince Adum, the Ashantee ambassador to the local government, after waiting patiently for communications from England, two months longer than the time specified by Mr. Dupuis, had withdrawn with his retinue to a short distance from Cape-Coast town, and placed it in a state of blockade; and the whole of the trade with Ashantee had been transferred from that place to the Dutch settlements.

Whether the policy which the new governor was led to adopt was, in all respects, the best, may, perhaps, be doubted. Let it be admitted, for the sake of argument, that Mr. Dupuis betrayed great want of moderation and temper in his disputes with the local authorities, and that his evident partiality for the Ashantees, in many cases, blinded his judgment; still there are certain well-established conclusions, the consideration of which serves to show that a warlike policy on the part of the British was not that which best harmonized with a due regard to the honour of their country. That the king of Ashantee (As-hánti) had established the right of a conqueror over the countries on the Gold Coast, and that the British had acknowledged that right from the days of Governor Torrane to the time of Governor Smith, are facts, the stubbornness of which will not yield to any sophistical arguments, or special pleading whatever. The assertion of Major Ricketts, that

the "natives of Cape Coast were never conquered
by the Ashantees," and the objection made by the
local authorities to Dupuis's treaty, on the alleged
ground, that it transferred the sovereignty of the
Fantee country to the king of Ashantee,—cannot
annihilate the published despatch of Governor
Smith, in which he had previously acknowledged
the sovereign rights of the king over Fantee,
(Fánti,) and, with the consent of the Fantee chiefs
themselves, had transferred to him the notes for
Annamaboe and Cape-Coast Castle, and bound
himself to pay regularly to the king the ground-
rents for those places. This full and unreserved
admission of the king's claims upon Fantee constituted, in fact, the very basis upon which Mr.
Bowdich's treaty was concluded.

A paragraph from the letters of Captain Laing
sufficiently explains the course which Sir Charles
M'Carthy was induced to pursue.

"The natives of the Gold Coast," he remarks,
" soon comprehended the nature of our policy,
as explained by Sir Charles M'Carthy, who was
looked upon by them, in a very short time, as
their deliverer, both from internal and foreign
oppression; they beheld with satisfaction the privileges that were conferred upon them by the
change; and they had full confidence in the promises he made to them of British protection.
The name of M'Carthy rung along the coast

from Cape-Apollonia to the mouth of the Volta; and the great influence which he gained over these people—the hitherto-acknowledged subjects of the king of Ashantee—was viewed with silent and gloomy indignation by that monarch, whose pride was not only stung at the sudden revolt of his subjects, acknowledged as such by British treaty, but at the neglect of his authority and dignity on the part of the British, in not sending to him a complimentary embassy."

In thus proceeding to widen the breach and precipitate a crisis, by setting the king of Ashantee at defiance, and exciting revolt among those who had hitherto been acknowledged as his subjects, by British treaty, the new governor was doubtless induced to believe that the claims of the king in vindication of his honour, and in maintenance of his authority, could not have been consistently conceded; but a feeling of regret, that Sir Charles did not first try the effect of peaceful measures, is perfectly consistent with a due appreciation of the excellences which he combined in his character. The king of Ashantee had been placed in perplexing circumstances by the unhappy disputes between the Company's government and Mr. Dupuis; and it was a matter of moment, that the national character of Britain should be placed before the barbarian sovereign in its true light. Considering the desire manifested by the court of Ashantee to maintain friendly intercourse with the British, it is not altogether improbable that the adoption of a peaceful policy would have been attended with success; but if this had failed, the *ultima ratio regum* would then have been resorted to under circumstances more honourable to the British name.   Had Sir Charles understood the true position of affairs, he would probably have pursued such a course; but he was placed in a trying situation.   The servants of the Company which had just been abolished by Act of Parliament, it would appear, had entered into a compact, not to accept office under, or hold any communication with, him; and Mr. Dupuis had failed to meet his earnest wishes for full information on all the points in dispute.   In these circumstances, he was left to explore his way as well as he could, and to adopt such measures as an imperfect acquaintance with the various matters in dispute might suggest.

A considerable period elapsed before hostilities actually commenced. The king having, as it would appear, indulged the hope, that the new governor would pursue a different line of policy from that of his predecessor, remained in inactivity until his plans should become sufficiently manifest. Preparations were then made for war by the Ashantee monarch, with the accustomed sacrifices, and consultation of the national deities; and while these things were going on, the oath-draught, it was understood, was administered to the traders coming down from other parts of the coast, enjoining them to entire secrecy as to what was taking place in Ashantee. A dead silence in consequence ensued, which the governor construed as a sign that the king was over-awed, and dared not attempt to carry his warlike threats into execution.

The first act of hostility on the part of the Ashantees took place at Annamaboe, (Anamabú,) from the great square of which a Negro serjeant in the British service was carried off, on the pretence that he had spoken disrespectfully of the king. The governor, who, imagining that tranquillity was established, had gone to Sierra-Leone, returned to Cape-Coast Castle; when Captain Laing nobly offered to proceed on an embassy either to Donqua, where the serjeant was confined, or to Coomassie itself, if that should be deemed necessary. Had this offer been accepted, it is not unlikely that important results would have followed, as it was afterwards understood that the king had resorted to this step only to try the temper of the British, and perhaps with the hope that it would bring about a negotiation. The governor, however, apprehensive for the captain's safety, declined the offer, and neglected to take any other decisive step; when the serjeant was executed; and the

king sent a message to the governor, that he
would shortly convert his head into one of the
ornaments of the royal death-drum of Ashantee.
But even then he appeared unwilling to proceed
to extremities until he had made another pacific
overture.   The Dutch governor at Elmina was
the medium of this communication; and a statement of grievances was delivered by the Ashantee
deputies, which statement, according to Captain
Laing's own admission, contained much truth:
but this attempt at negotiation proved abortive,
and the war then commenced in reality.

At first, separate detachments only of the
Ashantees made their appearance, over which
Captain Laing gained some decided advantages;
but those reverses had no other effect upon the
king than to induce him to make a more extensive preparation for the struggle.   He called upon
his chiefs and vassals for a further augmentation
of his troops, and sacrificed several human victims
daily to ensure success.   At this critical juncture,
Sir Charles appeared disposed to pause; and Captain Laing was of opinion, that had not some
fatal counsels interposed, he would have endeavoured to arrest the further progress of the war
by friendly negotiation.   The golden opportunity
was, however, unhappily neglected, and intelligence was ere long received, that the Ashantees
were rapidly advancing through Wassaw, and that

the allied native forces were precipitately retreating before them towards the coast.

The governor was at the camp at Djuquah when these tidings were announced, and he immediately determined to cross the Prah, and meet the enemy. Without waiting for the arrival of the troops, who were with Major Chisholm, at the camp at Ampensasu, he accordingly pushed forward with the whole of the force which he had with him at Djuquah, and a body of armed natives under their own captains. Having crossed the Prah, he waited a few days at Assamacow, and sent his secretary, Mr. Williams, to inform the retreating Wassaws and Denkerans of his advance, and to persuade them to halt, and await his arrival. With much difficulty, the secretary prevailed upon them to remain at a spot which he had chosen for a camp, on the bank of a small river, towards which place the governor shortly proceeded; but before his arrival an alarm was given that the Ashantees were approaching. A messenger was immediately despatched to him; but he had unfortunately formed too low an estimate of the military skill and courage of the Ashantees, and treated the intelligence as an idle report. He, however, reached the camp on the morning of the following day, January 21, 1824, and the horns and drums of the advancing enemy were shortly heard. Having been induced, by

some information which he had received, to believe that many of the Ashantees were disposed to
join him at the first opportunity, Sir Charles
ordered the bugles to sound, and the band of the
Royal African corps to play " God save the
King ;" to which the Ashantee chiefs responded
only in warlike strains, as they marched their
divisions down to the opposite bank of the river.
The Ashantee chiefs are distinguished in battle
by their own peculiar military airs; and, on
this occasion, a native from Coomassie, who was
in the British camp, was able, on hearing the
music, to tell the name of every chief as he
advanced.

The battle commenced with great spirit on both
sides, and a heavy firing was kept up across the
river, until the troops under the governor's immediate command had nearly exhausted their ammunition. The enemy then attempted to cross the
river, but were received with the bayonet, and
repulsed with great slaughter. A large body, however, having, at an earlier part of the day, crossed
the river higher up, for the purpose of cutting off
the retreat of the governor, now attacked his
forces on the flank and in the rear, and literally
cut them to pieces. Sir Charles, who had himself
received several wounds, seeing all was lost on his
side, retired to that part of the field where the
king of Denkera and his people were still bravely

resisting the enemy. An attempt was then made to check the Ashantees by discharging a field-piece among them; but nothing could resist their progress; and the Denkerans were compelled to give way, while Sir Charles and some of his officers vainly endeavoured to effect their retreat through the woods. They had proceeded only a short distance, when they were assailed by a party of the enemy, by whose fire Sir Charles had an arm broken, and was wounded in the chest. Mr. Williams also, his secretary, shortly fell, stunned by a ball; but was recovered to his senses by the application of the Ashantee knife. At this critical moment, when a slight gash had actually been made in the back of his neck, a captain came up who recognised Mr. Williams as a friend from whom he had formerly experienced kindness, and gave command that his life should be spared.

On looking round, Mr. Williams witnessed the appalling sight of the headless trunks of Governor M'Carthy, Mr. Buckle, and Mr. Wetherell. He remained for some time a prisoner in the Ashantee camp; during the whole of which period, he was regularly locked up at night in the same place with the heads of his unfortunate companions, which, by some peculiar process, were kept in a state of perfect preservation. Sir Charles's head presented nearly the same appearance as when alive.   As to his body, it is stated, that his heart was eaten by the principal Ashantee chiefs, in order that they might, as they imagined, imbibe his bravery; and his flesh, having been dried, was divided, together with his bones, among the men of consequence in the army, who kept their respective shares about their persons, as charms to inspire them with courage. Whenever they executed any of their prisoners, Mr. Williams was placed on one side of the great death-drum, while they decapitated the unfortunate victim on the other.   One of the prisoners, Captain Raydon of the Cape-Coast militia, met with a peculiar fate.   He had received five wounds in the action; and five being, in such cases, the sacred number, he was sacrificed to the fetish.   Captain Ricketts, and Mr. De Graft, the linguist, then acting as lieutenant of militia, succeeded in making their escape from the field of battle; and, aided by a native guide, they at length reached a village, where they met Major Chisholm, who had set out from the camp at Ampensasu, with a view to reinforce the army of the governor : but having heard of his defeat, the major resolved to retire to Cape-Coast Castle, to which place he expected the victorious Ashantees would immediately urge their way.   Captain Laing, who had been out in another direction, on receiving tidings of the governor's defeat, also hastened to Cape Coast, and great exertions were made to place it in a state of defence, and collect a sufficient force to meet the enemy. But, although thirty thousand natives had taken arms in support of the common cause, the victory of the Ashantees produced such a general feeling of dismay, that only few appeared willing to enter the field against them.

Instead of improving their decisive victory by an attack upon Cape Coast, the Ashantees manifested a desire to renew friendly relations with the British. Although they were still fifteen thousand strong, and were well prepared for the prosecution of the war, they halted a few miles from the field of action; and, after a little delay, they engaged the Dutch governor Last, at Elmina, to write to Cape-Coast Castle, inviting a conference for the purpose of negotiating a peace. Captain Ricketts, accordingly, proceeded to Elmina, and met the Ashantee deputies, who stated that their sovereign had not sent his army to fight with the Whites, but to bring him Kujoh Chibbu,—the vice-king of Denkera,—and the chiefs of Tueful, and Wassaw, who had revolted from him; that if these were delivered up, the army would immediately return; but that if this condition should be rejected, they had orders to take Kujoh Chibbu, in particular, by force of arms, although he might be locked up in Cape-

Coast Castle. They also positively denied that
the king had given orders to execute the
British serjeant at Donqua; and declared that
the act was perpetrated by those Fantees who
were at that time acting in unison with the
Ashantee troops. Captain Ricketts having
replied, it was agreed that hostilities should not
be re-commenced while the negotiation was pend-
ing, and the deputies returned to the camp.
Before the conference broke up, Governor Last,
having learned that Mr. Williams was still alive,
requested the deputies to inform their general
that he would best evince his sincerity, in offering
to make peace with the British, by sending the
prisoner back to his friends. And in about a
week, Mr. Williams was brought to Elmina in a
state of nudity, with his hands tied behind his
back, and delivered up to the Dutch governor.

This negotiation was attended with no other
practical result. Kujoh Chibbu, afraid that he
should experience the fate of Asín Chibbu, and,
like that unfortunate chief, be delivered up as a
peace-offering to the Ashantees, although repeat-
edly assured that his fears were groundless,
resolved upon crossing the Prah, and attacking
the enemy. Arrangements were made, by the
British officer in command, to support this movement; but it had no other effect than to arouse
the Ashantees again to action, who shortly fought

their way down into the neighbourhood of Cape-Coast Castle.

At this juncture, Lieutenant-Colonel Sutherland arrived with a body of troops; and preparations were immediately made for attacking the Ashantee army before the arrival of the king, who was understood to be on his way down from Coomassie, with a strong reinforcement. The marines were accordingly landed from the squadron, by whom the castle and towers were garrisoned, and the whole of the military, with the native allies, proceeded to attack the enemy. A hard-fought battle took place, which was not attended by any decisive advantage on either side; and on the following day, the native forces having generally dispersed, Colonel Sutherland recalled the troops within the walls of the castle. At the same time, the king of Ashantee joined his army; and it was then ascertained, that Osai Tutu Quamina was no more, having died a natural death, at Coomassie, shortly after the commencement of hostilities against the British.

The new king, Osai Ockoto, the brother of the deceased monarch, shortly after his arrival at the camp, having sent a message of defiance to the governor, advanced with his whole army so near to Cape-Coast Castle as to be distinctly seen on the heights. The most vigorous exertions were made to put the place in a state of defence. All the male inhabitants of the town were ordered to offer the most determined resistance; and the seamen and marines from His Majesty's ship "Victor," and the seamen from merchant-vessels in the roads, were landed to man the guns, and aid in opposing the enemy. And, in a few days, this force was strengthened, by the arrival of another ship of war, with men and officers of the Royal African corps. About five thousand armed natives from Accra, (Akráh,) besides others of the natives allies from different places, also arrived about the same time. Another general engagement took place, which was only terminated by the darkness of night. It was expected that the action would be renewed the following day; but the dreadful ravages of the small-pox and dysentery, and the want of provisions, had produced such a feeling of dissatisfaction in the Ashantee army, that the king deemed it prudent to withdraw. The same causes were, at the same time, producing the most fearful effects in Cape-Coast town, and in the castle, within the walls of which many thousands of native women and children were cooped up, to preserve them from the fury of the enemy. The scene was too painful to be described; and, had it not been for the timely arrival of a partial supply of provisions from Sierra Leone, and that some vessels had been despatched from England with rice, famine must have swept off those whom disease had spared : for the Ashantees had reduced the surrounding country to a perfect wilderness.

About two years after this period, in the month of September, 1826, another, and, as it proved, decisive, battle was fought near the village of Dodowah, twenty-four miles north-east of British Accra, between ten thousand Ashantees and eleven thousand British and allied native troops. The Ashantees were the assailants, and fought with desperate bravery. About the middle of the day, they were driving back the centre of the allied army; when Colonel Purdon brought up the reserve, and met them with discharges of rockets and grape-shot. The rockets, in a great measure, decided the contest. The Ashantees, having never before witnessed the effect of those formidable engines of destruction, were thrown into confusion; and, although they continued the battle through the day, they were not able to rally again. Many of their principal chiefs were killed; and the whole of their camp and baggage fell into the hands of the allies. Among the trophies was a human head, enveloped in a silk handkerchief, and a paper covered with Arabic characters; and over the whole was thrown a tiger skin, the emblem of royalty. On the supposition that this was the head of the unfortunate Sir Charles M'Carthy, it was afterwards sent to

England by Colonel Purdon; but it was really the head of Osai Tutu Quamina, which the new king carried about with him as a charm. It is said, that, on the morning of the battle, he offered to it a libation of rum, and invoked it to cause all the heads of the Whites to come and lie near it; and it is further stated, that, during the day, when intelligence was brought to him of the death of any of his principal officers, he immediately, in the heat of the battle, offered human sacrifices to their shades.

After this action, the allied troops lay on their arms all night; the king having been seen at the close of the day walking in front, as though he was meditating some desperate enterprise; but, instead of renewing the attack, he withdrew the remainder of his army, and returned to Coomassie. The native allies of the British manifested no disposition to pursue him, but retired to Accra (Akráh) with the booty which they had obtained.

In a few days, the new governor, Sir Neil Campbell, who had succeeded General Turner, landed at Cape-Coast Castle; and one of his first acts was to send for Kujoh Chibbu, who had greatly distinguished himself in the battle, and the other principal native chiefs, to thank them for their brave and successful exertions, and to propose to them that peace should be made with the Ashantees. Independently of higher considerations, this was the truest policy which he could possibly adopt; for it was obvious, that the native allies could not be depended upon for the continuance of the war. Major Ricketts confidently asserts, that had the Ashantees delayed for a few weeks their attack upon the allied forces, their overthrow could not have taken place; for the native union would have melted away, and the Ashantees would have been left in undisputed possession of the country.

The chiefs objected to proposals of peace being made to the king of Ashantee, (As-hánti,) although the governor assured them that no treaty would be concluded, except on the condition that their safety and interests were secured. At length, he told them that the orders which he had received from the king of England to put an end to the war, were peremptory; and, dismissing them, made arrangements to send messengers direct to Coomassie, (Kumási,) with a view to improve the recent victory by negotiating an honourable and lasting peace: but this conciliatory plan was defeated by the continued opposition of the chiefs. At length, however, by a combination of favourable circumstances, Major Ricketts succeeded in opening a negotiation; when the terms proposed to the king, with the approbation of Kujoh Chibbu and the other native leaders, were, that he should lodge four thousand ounces of gold in the Castle at Cape-Coast, to be appropriated in purchasing ammunition and arms for the use of the British allies, in case the Ashantees should again commence hostilities; and that two of the royal family of Ashantee, whose names were mentioned, should be sent to Cape-Coast as hostages.

To these terms the king of Ashantee, although manifesting a great desire to be at peace with the British, was evidently unwilling to accede, and the negotiation languished for years; until, at length, in the month of April, 1831, the king sent down to Cape-Coast Castle one of his own sons, named Quantamissah, and Ansah, son of the late king, as hostages, with six hundred ounces of gold to be lodged there as a security for his future good conduct; and thus virtually abandoned the claim which, on the ground of previous conquest, he had previously urged against the natives upon the coast.

CHAPTER IV.

ASHANTEE is included in that extensive general division of Western Africa which Europeans, for reasons not now well understood, have denominated Guinea; a name with which the natives themselves are unacquainted. Ashantee, however, is a native term, although incorrectly pronounced by the English; who accentuate the last syllable instead of the second, and unite the *s* and *h* in one syllable; when there is good reason to

believe, that the Ashantees are wholly unacquainted
with the combined sound of *s* and *h*, as heard in
ash. Meredith, in the quotation previously given,
follows Bosman and Barbot in substituting the *i*
for the *h*, and writes the name " Asiante ; "
which is a nearer approach to the true orthography than Ashantee. At all events, if the aspirate
be retained, it should commence the second syllable, and the word should be expressed as though
it were written, As-hánti, the first syllable being
articulated as rapidly as possible, and the last like
ty in duty. The accent is on the penultimate.
With respect to the first syllable, it may be
added, that Bowdich, Hutton, and Dupuis,
when quoting the exact language used by the
king on certain occasions, altogether drop the
a ; and certain it is, that in the pronunciation
of the word by the two Ashantee princes, Quantamissah and Ansah, little else is heard in the
first syllable, but the hissing sound of the *s*.

The empire of Ashantee is not so much one
State placed immediately under one government,
as an assemblage of States owing a kind of feudal
obedience to the sovereign of Ashantee. According to Dupuis, the empire extends westward from
the River Volta about four geographical degrees,
and, reckoning from the neighbourhood of the
coast, four degrees of latitude ; comprising an area
of about sixty thousand square miles. Over the

whole of the countries within these limits, the king of Ashantee, he says, exercises supreme sway; all kings, viceroys, or caboceers, being his absolute and unconditional vassals, as tributaries or not; and most of them holding their governments by virtue of an appointment from the court. The opinion entertained by Bowdich, that Dwabin, or Juábin, only about a day's journey from Coomassie, (Kumási,) is an independent kingdom, is repudiated by Dupuis, who states, that the king of Ashantee was greatly irritated when he (Dupuis) expressed a wish to see him, indignantly demanding whether there was any other king than himself; and declaring, that if Bowdich's treaty represented the chief of Dwabin as king, it was a gross imposition. Dupuis adds, that he is not even entitled by courtesy to the title of *Ohen,* (the Ashantee word for king,) although the tributary rulers of Banna and Gaman both use it. Whether this be correct or not, it will be seen, on reference to the signature of Bowdich's treaty, that his name is appended without the royal appellation of *Osai,* which is invariably used by all the kings of Ashantee. The fact, that the chief of Dwabin is united by the ties of consanguinity to the royal family of Ashantee, is sufficient to account for those attentions shown him by the king, which Bowdich mistook as a recognition of his independence.

In marking out the boundaries of the empire,

Dupuis does not, however, make the Volta the limit of the king of Ashantee's influence in that direction; for Inta, or Ghunja, the capital of which is Salgha, and Dagumba, whose metropolis is Yahndi, are allied with Ashantee. Bowdich says, the kings of Inta and Dagumba are excused from attending in person at the annual yam-custom celebrated in Coomassie; but they send some of their principal caboceers to represent them on that great national occasion. He states, moreover, that the capitals, and other large towns of these two countries, pay, as an annual tribute to the king of Ashantee, five hundred slaves, two hundred cows, four hundred sheep, four hundred cotton cloths, and two hundred silk and cotton cloths; and that the smaller towns are proportionately taxed. In the enumeration which Dupuis gives of the tributary princes and allies to whom, on one occasion, the king was despatching presents, both Inta and Dagumba are mentioned; and some of the subjects of the latter State are represented as being actually in attendance at Coomassie, who formally presented thanks to the king for a former present which he had sent to their sovereign. On the same occasion, the king told Dupuis, that he had sent to the king of Dagumba for fifty girls, and fifty boys, (some of whom had already reached Coomassie,) whom he should dress in rich clothes and gold, and send as a present to the king of England. And, in his chapter on the geography of Western Africa, while he says that Yahndi is not a part of the empire of Ashantee, he admits that Ashantee influence carries great weight in the councils of the sovereign of Dagumba, and expressly mentions Inta, or Ghunja, as a province, and again as a tributary, of Ashantee ; and, after giving the names of Salgha, the chief city, and several frontier towns on the Dahoman side, he explicitly maintains, that although the people of all these places are left to the government of their caboceers, and the jurisdiction of their own laws, yet are they compelled, whether Moslems or Heathens, to serve in the wars of Ashantee. Inta, or Ghunja, therefore, if not Dagumba, ought to be included within the Ashantee empire, as well as the other dependencies, and its limits must be regarded as proportionately extended to the eastward of the Volta river.

Adverting again to the political constitution of the Ashantee empire, it may be remarked, that others of the dependent States, as well as Inta, or Ghunja, are left under their former laws, as administered by a native ruler. But the people have the privilege of appealing from their own tribunals, and claiming a judgment upon their respective cases, according to the laws of Ashantee ; and over every one of these States an Ashantee chief is placed, who is held responsible by the king for the conduct of the native ruler. This superior chief generally resides at Coomassie, and seldom visits his province except to receive the tribute. To the oppressive conduct of the superior chiefs may be principally ascribed that spirit of dissatisfaction and revolt which so frequently manifests itself in the dependencies of the empire.

The king of Ashantee, (As-hánti,) although represented as a despotic monarch, having the lives and property of his subjects at his absolute disposal, is not, in all respects, beyond control. He is placed in a situation somewhat similar to the kings of the ancient Medes and Persians; among whom it was a principle, that what had once passed into law, the power of the sovereign himself could not change. The imperative mandate of Darius was quite sufficient instantaneously to consign to the jaws of the lions all the individuals, and their wives and children, who had been the occasion of procuring the decree for the ruin of the prophet Daniel; but the utmost power of the king could not save the prophet himself from its operation.* Now, the king of Ashantee is under a somewhat similar obligation

* Daniel vi. 14—24.

to observe the national customs which have been handed down to the people from remote antiquity; and a practical disregard of this obligation, in the attempt to change some of the customs of their forefathers, cost Osai Quamina his throne.

The caboceers and captains, moreover, claim to be heard on all questions relating to war and foreign politics. Such matters are considered in a general assembly; and the king sometimes finds it prudent to yield to the views and urgent representations of the majority. Four individuals, representing the general assembly of caboceers and captains, signed Bowdich's treaty at the same time with the king himself, after it had been agreed upon at a full meeting of the caboceers, tributary princes, and captains. And Dupuis states, that the treaty which he afterwards negotiated at Coomassie (Kumási) was criticised and scrutinized by a full court of the principal nobles and captains, and was the subject of a most laborious discussion, before it obtained the royal signature. The Ashantees advocate the participation of the caboceers and captains in the consideration and management of war and foreign policy, on the principle, that it makes the nation more formidable to its enemies, who feel that they cannot offer provocation with impunity, where there are so many guardians of the military glory.

But while the caboceers and captains, in their

collective capacity, possess considerable influence
in the management of questions relating to foreign
policy, as individuals they are subject to the
most despotic authority, and frequently become
the victims of the jealousy or displeasure of
the king.   A few cases of recent occurrence
will sufficiently illustrate the temper of the
chiefs, and the character of the Ashantee government.   When the king of Ashantee conquered Wassaw, he placed the king, or principal chief of that country, under the care of
Aprakú, the captain of Bantama ; and the captive
chief so ingratiated himself with his guardian, or
keeper, that he obtained permission from him to
return to his own country.   It was presumed
that, in the lapse of years, the captive was almost
forgotten, and that his withdrawal would not even
come under the notice of the king ; or that,
should he become acquainted with the transaction,
it would not call forth any serious expression of
dissatisfaction.   The event proved the fallacy of
the hopes which were thus entertained.   The
king was immediately informed of what had happened, and required from Aprakú an immediate
explanation.   But the answer of the guardian
chief, so far from being deemed satisfactory, was
regarded as wanting in due respect for the king's
authority ; and his life became the forfeiture of
his two-fold offence.

Shortly after this affair, another of the most distinguished caboceers or nobles likewise perished. Dampti, general of the household troops, surnamed Boadaban, or "bark-breaker," an appellation figuratively descriptive of his military prowess, had become an object of the king's jealousy, partly, if not exclusively, on account of his wealth. Aware of the danger to be apprehended from falling under the suspicion or displeasure of his sovereign, he determined to strike the first blow, and formed a conspiracy to attack and burn the capital. But before this plan could be carried into effect, the whole plot was discovered to the king, and Dampti's neck was submitted to the stroke of the executioner. The chief or bashaw of the Moors was implicated in this conspiracy, and was, in consequence, a prisoner in his own house, chained to a log of wood, at the time when the Rev. Mr. Freeman visited Coomassie.

The king of Ashantee maintains such an efficient system of espionage, that it is difficult for his subjects to speak or act in any manner derogatory to his authority without his being made acquainted with the offence. He employs a number of clever boys, trained for the purpose, who are placed as spies upon the conduct of the great men, and convey to the king a report of all they see and hear. While Mr. Freeman was at the frontier-town of Fómunah, waiting for permission to go

up to the capital, some of those boys were in
attendance upon him. When he was at meals,
one would enter, and, placing himself at a distance, would silently mark all that passed; and
wherever Mr. Freeman went, he had reason to
believe that his proceedings were subject to their
scrutiny.

Offending or suspected chiefs are most frequently called to account when the yam-custom
takes place. At that great annual festival all the
caboceers and captains, and the greater number
of the tributary kings or chiefs, are expected to
appear in the capital; and the nobles or captains
against whom the king has cause of complaint
are then placed upon their trial. Often, on those
and similar occasions, a chief goes up without any
suspicion that he has excited the jealousy or
displeasure of the king, when he is met with
charges founded on the reports which have been
conveyed to the palace, and degradation or death
is the usual result. This was the case of a distinguished caboceer, whose trial Bowdich witnessed.
Apia Nanu, the general of an army which had
been employed on distant service, returned to the
capital; and a fit opportunity presenting itself,
he was publicly accused of having spoken disrespectfully of the king. He denied the charge;
when he was confronted by witnesses, who had
heard him, while absent with the army, complain

of the conduct of the king, and who had been kept in a secluded part of the forest in order that they might surprise and confound him by their sudden and unlooked-for appearance when he should be placed upon his trial.

To speak disrespectfully of the king is a treasonable offence, which, from the facilities possessed for obtaining information, seldom escapes detection; and, when discovered, is ever visited with severe punishment. A reference to the state of feeling among the Ashantees on the subject of unbecoming language used towards the sovereign, and the difficulty of committing this offence without detection, may enable the biblical reader to enter more fully into the meaning of the inspired preacher : " Curse not the king; no, not in thy thought; and curse not the rich in thy bed-chamber ; for a bird of the air shall carry the voice, and that which hath wings shall tell the matter." *

Apia Nanu, not being able to rebut the evidence of his accusers, was deprived of his stool, —the emblem of his dignity,—and of the whole of his property ; but he was allowed to retire with three wives and ten slaves. The sequel strikingly illustrates the notions of honour which are prevalent among the Ashantees. On the following

* Ecclesiastes x. 20.

day, the king, who considered that none but the meanest spirits could endure to live after severe disgrace, on hearing that the degraded caboceer still lingered in the capital, exclaimed that no man who was actuated by a proper feeling would bear so much shame before all the people, rather than abandon his home; and ordered that, as an additional punishment for this baseness, only one wife should be left to him. This was more than the high spirit of Apia Nanu was able to brook, and he immediately became his own executioner.

Sometimes a chief who suspects that he has become obnoxious to the king, will not trust himself in the capital without the means of defence or intimidation. A powerful caboceer might be named, who, on a recent visit to Coomassie, (Kumási,) impressed with the critical circumstances in which he was placed, as an object of the king's jealousy, deemed it prudent to take with him three thousand armed attendants.

The king has the property, as well as the lives, of his people within his power. He is the legal heir of all his subjects, whose gold he can claim at their death. Bowdich's story of Aga recognises this peculiarity in Ashantee law, and shows too that the king is not always patient enough to wait for the natural death of his rich subjects. On one occasion, it appears, Osai Tutu Quamina acknowledged that he entertained a prejudice against a wealthy captain; when his principal linguists, always inclined to support him, said, "If you wish to take his stool from him, we will make the *palaver*." But Aga, who had singularly gained the king's confidence, immediately sprung up and exclaimed, "No, king, that is not good. That man never did you any wrong. You know, all the gold of your subjects is yours at their death; but if you get all now, strangers will go away and say, 'Only the king has gold;' and that will not be good. But let them say, 'The king has gold, all his captains have gold, and all his people have gold;' then your country will look handsome, and the bush people will fear you."

It is recorded to the honour of Osai Tutu Quamina, who, whatever might be his faults, possessed some noble qualities, that this individual, Aga, had secured his confidence by his fearless honesty. He was a poor boy who carried salt from Aquomo to Coomassie for sale; and, being taken into the service of the caboceer of that place, he was present when his master was brought before the king on a charge wrongfully preferred against him at the instance of the government. The caboceer being confused by the misrepresentations of the king's officers, the boy Aga suddenly started up and said, "King, you have people to wash you, to feed you, to serve you; but you have no people to speak the truth to you, and tell you when God does not like your *palaver.*" Immediately an unanimous cry arose in the assembly, that he ought to be carried out, and have his head struck off; but the king commanded him to proceed; and Aga, in a speech of three hours, convinced the king of the innocence of his master, and obtained his acquittal. The king then took Aga into his own service; and, having had further proof of his ability and integrity, appointed him to the office of linguist, and presented him with wives and slaves, a house, and gold to support his establishment. And as an additional reward for his honesty in the case first mentioned, the king raised him to the rank of second linguist, and greatly increased his property. Mr. Hutchinson had an opportunity of witnessing the boldness of this individual. The king having detected the misconduct of one of his captains, wrought himself up to such a height of passion, that none of the chiefs dared to arise in his presence, till Aga stood up, and, in his usual energetic manner, requested His Majesty to remember that an Englishman was the witness of his conduct.

To return from this digression: It is stated that the king usually takes a considerable portion of the gold which a deceased caboceer has

left behind him in dust; leaving to his successor only a small amount. Sometimes a
chief will attempt to defraud the king of his
claim, by presenting to his children large sums of
gold, when he imagines himself to be near death;
and Bowdich mentions the son of one who displayed, with impunity, the property which he had
thus acquired; but this, it may be presumed, was
a somewhat hazardous experiment.

The rich nobles, however, convert a considerable portion of their gold into ornaments, which
usually descend to their successors;—although
not invariably, for even these, whether manufactured or otherwise, are occasionally taken away.
The principal matter of which Apia Nanu had
complained against the king, was, that on the
death of his brother, to whose stool he had succeeded, the king had claimed some rock-gold,
which belonged to the inheritance, and had
doubtless been worn among the ornaments of
the family; for on state occasions, many of the
nobles appear with rude lumps of rock-gold
suspended from their left wrists. But, it is to
be remarked, that if the ornaments of the
chiefs are generally allowed to descend to their
heirs, the king has a check upon his subjects to
prevent them from multiplying such articles so
as wholly to defraud him of his claims at their
decease. On every occasion, when a chief adds to

his stock of ornaments, he has to pay a tax to the
king, amounting, as appears from an instance
quoted by Bowdich, to one-fifth of the value of
the gold thus appropriated.

Once in their life-time those caboceers and
principal men who are favourites of the king,
and believe themselves to be free from palavers,
make a public exhibition of their riches, in a noisy
procession through the public places of the capital.
Mr. Hutchinson had the opportunity of witnessing the display which Apóko made on such an
occasion.   Among the articles which he noticed
were gold chains for the neck, arms, and legs ;
ornaments of all descriptions for the ankles, consisting of manacles with keys, bells, chains, and
padlocks ; armlets and various ornaments for his
numerous family of wives, children, and captains ;
a superb war-cap of eagles' feathers, fetishes,
(which will be hereafter explained,) Moorish
charms, caps, and silk dresses ; purses, bags,
and other articles made of monkey-skin ; fans,
with ivory handles, made of tiger-skin, and
decorated with silk ; gold swords, and figures of
birds, beasts, and fishes, of the same metal ;
ivory arrows and bows, covered with silk and
skin ; drums, and various instruments of music,
covered with tiger-skin, and having red belts ;
and many other weapons of war, and articles
suited to the taste of the owner.   The orna-

ments made of gold weighed upwards of sixteen hundred ounces.

The income of the king must be very large, for the produce of the gold mines is not private property, but belongs to the Crown; although this would be much greater were the mines better worked. The customs paid by those who engage in trade, the taxes from the provinces, and tribute received from conquered nations, are a further augmentation of the royal revenue. The gold contained in the soil of the market-place of Coomassie is also the property of the king. On two occasions, in the reign of Osai Tutu Quamina, the washing of the soil yielded about sixteen hundred ounces of gold. Frequently after a heavy rain, lumps of gold are laid bare, but they are carefully covered up again, as the person who should take any would expose himself to the penalty of death. While Bowdich was at the capital, an individual was actually beheaded for picking up a piece of gold in the market-place.

The court of Ashantee (As-hánti) affords a more striking display of barbarous splendour than any of the principal courts in the interior. Those of Eyeo, or Yarriba, Sackatoo, (Sakátu,) and Bornou, as they are described by travellers, are far less imposing in appearance. The court of Ashantee is seen to advantage on the public reception of

visitors at the capital. The king is magnificently
attired in silk, with necklaces, bracelets, knee-
bands and ankle-strings of gold and beads, and
many other ornaments, some of which are in massive gold, and others are ingenious devices and
representations delicately wrought in the same
metal. With these a variety of charms are intermingled. His fingers are covered with gold
rings, and he has been seen to wear on his finger
and thumb a pair of gold castanets, by the clap-
ping of which he enforced silence. The manners
of all the Ashantee kings known to Europeans
have been uniformly represented as dignified yet
courteous.

The royal throne, or " stool," is literally covered
with plates of gold. Behind the king are his
guards, with belts encased in gold, having ornaments of the same metal representing jaw-bones ;
and the muskets of the guards are also covered
with gold. There too are placed the royal messengers, with breast-plates of gold, holding in a
reversed position their large crooked sabres, so as
to render conspicuous the golden hilts. The principal officers of the king's household display a
splendour in accordance with their rank. The
keeper of the treasury is known by the blow-pan,
boxes, scales, and weights, all of solid gold, which
are exhibited in his retinue. Gold canes, tied in
bundles like *fasces*, and elevated in all directions

by their numerous attendants, distinguish the four linguists. The chamberlain, the gold-horn blower, the captain of the messengers, the captain for royal executions, the captain of the market, the keeper of the royal burial-ground, all sit surrounded by the emblems of their respective offices, and attended by a large retinue. The royal cook also displays a number of table-services, punchbowls, tankards, waiters, and other utensils of massive silver plate. The okras, slaves peculiarly devoted to the king, and various other officers, are adorned with large stars, crescents, and gossamer wings of solid gold. And, to complete the list of persons in immediate attendance upon the sovereign, as well as to exhibit the union of barbarism and magnificence, must be mentioned the royal chief-executioner, a man of gigantic size, bearing a massive golden hatchet, and having exhibited before him the execution-stool, clotted with human blood, and partly covered with a cawl of fat.

The appearance of the caboceers and their principal captains and attendants is imposing. Many of them wear Ashantee cloths of great value, manufactured from costly foreign silks, which have been unravelled, in order to weave them anew with every variety of colour and figure. These robes are of great size and weight, and are thrown over the shoulder like the Roman toga.

A profusion of gold necklaces, and other ornaments, mixed with charms, are also worn by the
nobles ; and to their left wrists are attached rude
lumps of rock-gold which, on account of their
weight, are supported on the heads of their hand-
somest boys, who are selected for this office.
Like the sovereign, they wear sandals of leather,
of various colours. They are also surrounded by
a great number of attendants, some bearing gold-
headed canes, and others swords with gold handles, from which are suspended representations of
the heads of wolves and rams, as large as life, cast
in gold. And their stools, the emblems of their
dignity, which descend to their successors, made of
wood, elaborately carved, from each of which two
bells are suspended, are on these occasions con-
spicuously exhibited on the heads of confidential
officers, around whom are seated crowds of boys
flourishing elephants' tails curiously mounted.
The tails of elephants are ensigns of distinction,
which are sometimes borne by sons of the
king before the principal caboceers. Osai Tutu
Quamina had, when a boy, carried an elephant's
tail before Apóko. The elephants' tails waved
before the sovereign are spangled with golden
ornaments. The captains attend in their war-
dresses, each of which consists of a cap with gilded
horns projecting in front, and adorned with immense plumes of ostrich feathers ; a vest of red

cloth covered with fetishes, charms, and various
ornaments; and loose cotton trousers, with immense boots of dull red leather, reaching half-way
up the thigh, and fastened by small chains to their
cartouch or belt.   The caboceers, as well as the
king, are shaded by immense umbrellas, many of
which are large enough to cover twenty or thirty
persons.   These are made of the most showy
cloths and silks, and are crowned at the top with
emblematical representations of birds and beasts,
either gilt or of solid gold.

The interest on public occasions is not unfrequently heightened by the presence of some of
the tributary kings and princes.   Bowdich saw
the court of the king of Dwabin, or Juábin, when
on a visit at Coomassie, and represents it as almost
equally crowded with that of the king of Ashantee.   And when Dupuis made his public entrance
into the capital, he witnessed the king of Banna,
surrounded by a numerous and splendid retinue,
seated near to his liege lord.   The stool of this
monarch was covered with silver plates, none being
permitted to sit enthroned in gold but the sovereign prince of the whole empire.

Every caboceer or noble has his band of music,
and, as the visitant approaches, it plays his own
peculiar air or tune, by which he is distinguished
from his compeers; and in these bands are drums
adorned with thigh-bones, teeth, and other human

relics. Each of these drums is carried on the
head of one man, and beaten by two others. The
simultaneous playing of such a number of bands,
accompanied with discharges of musketry and
other sounds, produces an almost deafening
noise.

After the visitant has performed the laborious
task of saluting in succession all the distinguished
personages present, and last of all the king, he is
then conducted to a distance, and placed in a
convenient situation to receive their salutations in
return. Another scene then takes place, baffling
all adequate description. The caboceers pass,
according to their respective ranks, followed by
their captains and retinue. Each noble is attended by his flatterers, who proclaim, in boister-
ous songs, the "strong names" of their master,
while his band plays in warlike strains, and various
dances are performed. The chiefs courteously
salute the stranger as they pass. On the occasion
alluded to, when the king of Banna was present,
as that monarch approached Dupuis, having commanded silence by an authoritative wave of the
hand, he snatched a scimitar from one of his
attendants, and, commencing a violent dance, in
which he wrought himself up to a height of fury,
he loudly dwelt upon the warlike achievements of
his sovereign lord. Women sang of the thousands
and tens of thousands slain in battle by Saul and

David;* but the military glory of Ashantee's king was thus proclaimed by a monarch only inferior to himself.

The king and his attendants close the procession. All his officers of state display their respective insignia as they pass along; among which are prominent the executioners, with their blood-stained stools, and the great death-drum, decorated with jaw-bones and skulls of vanquished foes. This drum is beaten at the moment when a human victim is beheaded. The people well understand its sound. On one occasion, when Mr. Freeman was in a distant part of the capital, the drum was heard; on which his interpreter said, "Hark! do you hear the drum? A sacrifice has just been made, and the drum says, 'King, I have killed him.'" A circumstance occurred on Mr. Freeman's public reception, which forcibly illustrates Ashantee manners. The king had saluted Mr. Freeman with great courteousness as he passed; but he had not proceeded many paces, when he suddenly snatched a sabre from one of his attendants, and aimed a violent blow at an individual who was beating a drum. The drummer, terrified, ran and placed himself under the protection of a powerful caboceer, who, as Mr. Freeman afterwards learned, pleaded for him; when the

* 1 Samuel xviii. 7.

king consented to spare his life, but sentenced
him to lose an ear, saying, "The drum ought to
have been played properly, in honour of the
Englishman who had paid him a visit!"

At those state-exhibitions, the market-place,
which is about a mile in circumference, is generally crowded. Mr. Freeman calculated that forty
thousand persons, half of whom were soldiers,
were present at his public reception. Such a
length of time is occupied with the formalities
which etiquette prescribes on those occasions, that
the day sometimes closes before they are concluded; and the glare of torches, which are fed by
oil contained in vessels of gold, and the brilliant
glow of the stars in an African sky, throw a new
interest over the extraordinary scene.

That the king should be able to parade so large
a body of troops on public occasions, will not
cause surprise, when it is remembered that the
Ashantees are a nation of warriors; all the males
being trained to arms from their youth. Bowdich
calculates that Ashantee Proper can alone send
two hundred and four thousand soldiers into the
field; and its disposable force, since the Ashantee
invasions, has been estimated by old residents at
upwards of one hundred and fifty thousand. The
discipline of the Ashantee army has ever been
spoken of with commendation by the English, as

often as they have had opportunity to witness it.
When the Ashantees first came down to the sea,
in the year 1807, the governor and his officers, on
entering into negotiation with the king at Annamaboe, (Anamabú,) were surprised to find, not
only that the king himself was polite and well-
behaved, but that he and his troops understood
and observed the rules of war as they are maintained among civilized people.   And Mr. Williams, the secretary of the unfortunate Sir Charles
M‘Carthy, who was for some time a prisoner in
the enemy's camp, stated, on his return, that he
was astonished at the discipline of the Ashantee
army, and at the regularity with which the officers
and soldiers performed their respective duties.

The Ashantee monarchy is hereditary; but the
order of succession is peculiar.   The crown does
not descend from father to son, but passes from
brother to brother.   This arrangement most probably originated in the necessities of a military
government, which would not allow the sceptre to
be placed in the hands of infancy; an event that
doubtless would have been of frequent occurrence, had the lineal order been preserved
amongst a people whose principal occupation is
war.   A female cannot ascend the throne; but if,
when the last of the line of brothers dies, his
sister has a son, the crown descends to him.   The

heir-apparent, it would appear, is generally
marked out during the life-time of the reigning
sovereign. When Bowdich was at Coomassie,
Ockoto, the brother of the king, who actually
succeeded him at his death, was then acknowledged as his heir; and Quako Kujoh, son of the
sister of the present king, is at this time recognised as the future sovereign of Ashantee. The
native term used as the title of the heir-apparent,
and indeed of all the princes of the blood, is
Ossu.

The government of Fantee (Fánti) appears to
have been formed, at the commencement of its
independence, on a different model from that of
Ashantee. According to Meredith, when the
Fantees resisted the authority, and fled out of the
dominions, of Ashantee, they proceeded to elect an
individual to act as governor among them. But
as they were afraid, that, for a reward, or on a
promise of favour, he might be induced to betray
them to their old masters, they resolved to prove
his devotedness to their interests by a severe test,
and required from the successful candidate for the
government, that he should lose his left hand.
While he hesitated to give this proof of his attachment to their cause, a general murmur arose
among the people; and his cane-bearer, stepping
forward, declared that *he* was willing to sacri-

fice a hand for their good, although his master was not. His offer was immediately accepted, and, his left hand having been taken off, he was constituted the Braffo, that is, captain or leader of the people; and his family was provided for by the State. At length his descendants and family-connexions formed themselves into a separate State or community; and the district in which they resided acquired, in consequence, the name of the Braffo country, of which Abrah was the capital, and became the source of all the laws and customs of the Fantee country.

The power of the Braffo does not appear to have been absolute in the first instance. Bosman, who wrote at the beginning of the last century, represents the Braffo, although the chief governor, and having greater power than any other person in the whole land, as somewhat closely restrained by the old men, who were a sort of national counsellors, " not unlike," he remarks, " some European Parliaments; acting perfectly according to their own inclinations, without consulting the Braffo." He further states, that " every part of Fantee had also its own particular chief, who would sometimes scarcely acknowledge himself subject to the Braffo, who had only the ineffectual name of the supreme power."

In process of time the Braffoes extended their power and authority, until they became so ob-

noxious to the people, that when Adú, who had
reigned very tyrannically, died, his family was
rejected, and Adokú was called to the stool, which
he occupied, with more limited authority, during
the Ashantee invasions. He was assisted in the
administration of public affairs by twelve officers,
whose dignity was hereditary in as many families.
These state-officers, when they went abroad, lived
at the public expense, and took for themselves
whatever they pleased of the property of others.

With regard to the Fantees it may, however, be
generally remarked, that, although they have long
been the most powerful people upon the coast,
they were never so united as to form one compact
political body. They have been classed in distinct
communities, with their respective chiefs, and held
together only by general ties, under a nominal
head. At present there are two principal Fantee
chiefs, dignified with the name of king; Agri,
who resides at Cape-Coast town, and Otú, whose
authority is exercised in the Braffo country.
There are several inferior chiefs, each of whom
exerts a ruling influence in his own limited district. In all the towns there are native magis-
trates, called pynims, to whom, under the chiefs,
is committed the administration of justice. The
principal chiefs, on public occasions, make a somewhat imposing appearance. Otú, for instance, at
such times, is dressed in silk, with gold orna-

ments, and seated on a stool with cushion and bells. Behind him an attendant stands, with a large umbrella; and on each hand are placed officers with swords under their arms, the gold handles of which project in front; and others, with gold and silver-headed canes.

In the other countries on the coast, the forms of government vary. Westward of Fantee, in Apollonia, the government is an absolute monarchy; and in the Ahanta country, it is a kind of aristocracy. At Accra, (Akráh,) eastward, the aristocracy is checked by a democratic influence.

CHAPTER V.

DOMESTIC SLAVERY, STATE OF THE FEMALE SEX, POPULATION, AND AGRICULTURE.

Slavery characteristic of African Society—In Mahomme-
dan States, Number of Freemen to Slaves but few ; in
Pagan States, still greater Disparity—Rev. Mr. Freeman at Fómunah—Slaves sometimes rise to Power—
Barka Gana—Slave-Trade cherished in some Instances
as Means of reducing an abundant Slave-Population—
The popular Superstition promotes native Wars—
Number and Condition of the Wives of Kings of
Ashantee, Dahomy, and Yarriba—In Courtship, the
Female herself but little consulted—The Husband
lives alone—The Children neglected—Degrading Em-
ployments of Females—Evils of Polygamy—Popula-
tion of Ashantee, of Fantee, and neighbouring Coun-
tries—Splendid Forest Scenery—Miraculous Berry—
Mode of Agriculture—Cultivation of the Palm-Tree—
Danish Settlement in Aquapím under Dr. Isert—
The Plough introduced—Miss Roer instructs the
Negro Women in household Occupations—Mr.
Schionning's prosperous Plantation.

THE absence of enlightened freedom is one
of the most striking characteristics of African
society. In the nations of Western and Central
Africa, the few are despots, and the great mass of
the people slaves. Although the followers of " the
Prophet" are forbidden by their religion to enthral
those who are their brethren in the same faith, yet,
in the principal Mahommedan States, the num-

ber of Pagan Negroes held in a state of slavery is far greater than that of the free population. Clapperton found that in Kano, one of the principal towns in Hausa, under the dominion of the sultan of the Felatahs, the proportion of slaves to freemen was as thirty to one; and he also incidentally mentions a village in the immediate vicinity of Sackatoo (Sakatú) where only one in seventy was free.

In the Pagan States, however, slavery prevails still more extensively. Every caboceer or noble of Ashantee (As-hánti) is the possessor of thousands of slaves, and the inferior chieftains and captains own a lesser number. The lives and services of the slaves are at the disposal of their masters. A person may take away the life of his own slave with impunity; and if he kill the slave of another, he can only be required to pay the market-value of his victim. The slaves are employed in cultivating the plantations of their masters, or in trading for them; and have such an allowance for their support, as their owners may deem sufficient.

A caboceer, or principal chief, derives an indirect benefit from the slaves of his captains. Every captain or subordinate chief gives up, in the form of a tax, a certain portion of his income to his superior; and he, again, pays a tax to the king. While Mr. Freeman was detained at Fómunah, he frequently saw the captains of Korinchi bring their respective quotas, amounting from one toku, value five-pence, to four tokus; but by what rule those payments were regulated, he did not ascertain. The superior chief, however, on some occasions, at least, acts as though all the property of his captains was his. When Mr. Freeman first arrived at Fómunah, Korinchi sent him and his attendants to the house of one of his captains, who hospitably entertained them during the whole of their stay in that place; but when Mr. Freeman was about to make a suitable acknowledgment to his attentive host, he was given to understand that Korinchi was the person to whom he ought to express his gratitude, as the captain was only Korinchi's slave. A similar fact is mentioned by Clapperton. On one occasion he asked the king of Yarriba to furnish him with some food in return for certain presents; when the king told him to go to the caboceers, and they would provide him with supplies. To this, however, Clapperton objected, saying, he had not visited Katunga in the character of a beggar; but he was corrected by the king, who informed him that the caboceers were all his own slaves, and that whatever they possessed was his property.

Humiliating as is that state of dependence in which the life and services of an individual are at the absolute disposal of another, the treatment of slaves in Africa is not uniformly harsh and severe. In Ashantee, (As-hánti,) a slave sometimes succeeds to the stool and property of his deceased master; which custom may serve to illustrate the circumstances of Abraham previous to the birth of his son Isaac. " Behold," says the patriarch, " to me thou hast given no seed; and lo, one born in my house is mine heir." * Was not this presumptive heir of Abraham the son of one of his own domestics, and may it not be concluded that the As-hantee custom has thus descended from remote antiquity?

In many instances, slaves rise to power and office. The case of Barka Gana, mentioned by Denham, affords an apt illustration. This individual was. the general of the sheikh of Bornou, and governor of six large districts. He had a considerable number of slaves of his own, and enjoyed, in a high degree, the favour of his master. This, however, he forfeited, by an act of disrespect. The sheikh, having inadvertently presented him with a horse which he had promised to some one else, sent for the animal back, which so offended Barka Gana, that he returned all the horses previously given to him by the sheikh; declaring, that in future, he would either walk, or ride his own horses. On receiving

* Genesis xv. 3.

this message, the sheikh immediately summoned him to appear, and, reminding him that he was only a slave, caused him to be stripped in his presence, and ordered that he should be immediately sold to the Tibbu merchants. That this order was not ultimately carried into effect, was solely owing to the returning kindness of the sheikh.

Sometimes slaves acquire such power as to become the objects of the sovereign's jealousy. The king of Ashantee, (As-hánti,) in conversing with Mr. Hutchinson, advocated the slave-trade, for the reason, that the slave-population in the country was too numerous for the public safety; and to show that his apprehensions were not groundless, he instanced the conduct of a number of slaves who rose against him in the Buntuku war, and joined the standard of his enemies. He said, he had at that time one slave who had a thousand followers at arms, and expressed his fears that he might disturb the public peace like Kujoh Kuma, who was a slave of his when he revolted, and who, independent of run-aways, had at his command a force of ten thousand men. When Clapperton was passing through Yarriba, he found that there had been a servile war in that country. The Hausa slaves, encouraged by the Felatah invaders, had risen against and murdered their masters; and, after a severe struggle, had secured their independence.

A careful investigation of the state of African society will serve to show, that the foreign slave-trade is valued by the native princes, not only on account of its pecuniary advantages, but also as an outlet for what they deem a redundant slave-population. In many cases the slave-trade is the immediate cause of the internal wars by which Africa is ravaged; and the horrors of such wars as are promoted by the slave-dealer for the purpose of supplying the foreign market with human flesh and sinews, are affectingly illustrated in the autobiography of a captured Negro from the neighbouring Slave-Coast, which will be inserted in the Appendix.* But were the slave-trade to be immediately extinguished, peace would not, as a necessary consequence, be restored to Africa. There are other causes of war besides that inhuman traffic. On examining the historic sketch which has been given of the wars of Ashantee, (As-hánti,) it will be seen that the obtaining of slaves was not their primary object: they were undertaken in resistance to aggression, to revenge some insult, or in maintenance of alleged rights. The suppression of the foreign slave-trade, however desirable, would not, therefore, of itself, remove such causes of internal commotions. Unless remedial measures be intro-

* See Appendix I.

duced into Africa herself, the endless disputes which take place among her savage or semi-barbarous tribes will still prove the occasion of frequent wars; and those wars will probably become more sanguinary in their results, should not the slave-trade enable the conquerors to avoid the apprehended danger of placing their prisoners among their own people. Ten thousand of the prisoners taken in the Gaman or Buntuku war were put to death by the Ashantees in cold blood, in a way most revolting to humanity; and the motives which dictated this horrible massacre were thus explained to Dupuis by the king himself:—
"When I fought Gaman, I did not make war for slaves, but because Dinkara (the king) sent me an arrogant message, and killed my people, and refused to pay me gold, as his father did. Then my fetish made me strong, like my ancestors; and I killed Dinkara, and took his gold, and brought more than twenty thousand slaves to Coomassie. Some of these people being bad men, I washed my stool in their blood for the fetish. But then some were good people, and these I sold or gave to my captains: many, more-over, died, because this country does not grow too much corn, like Sarem; and what can I do? Unless I kill or sell them, they will grow strong, and kill my people."

Under the influence of similar views, when Mr.

Norris refused to purchase from the king of Dahomy, the prisoners whom he had taken in a recent war, and recommended that he should make them boilers of salt, as they came from a country which supplied them with that article, or that he should employ them in some other occupation which he might deem preferable; the king utterly refused to listen to any such proposal. He said it would not be safe to keep people in his country who might utter seditious language, and set a bad example; for that his was a peculiar government, and those strangers might prejudice his own people against it, and infect them with sentiments incompatible with its principles and requirements. For these reasons, the king declared he should put the prisoners to death. Such was the conclusion of another despot, who dreaded an increase of the slave-population of his own country, and had not an opportunity to relieve himself, in another way, of the captives whom he had taken in war. And unless, during the process by which the foreign slave-trade shall be extinguished, suitable means be simultaneously used to enlighten the public mind of Africa, and to construct society there upon a new principle, not only will wars continue to prevail, but those wars will either prove more bloody in the field, or will serve to add new horrors to the national superstitions, by furnishing a greater number of human sacri-

fices for the annual customs and other festival
occasions; for it is a settled principle of the
popular superstition, as explained by the king
of Ashantee, in vindication of his inhuman
butcheries, that " the fetish makes war for strong
men every where, because then they can pay
plenty of gold, and proper sacrifice."

Polygamy is another of the distinguishing
features of society in Africa. The kings and principal persons have usually a great number of wives.
It is stated that the law allows the king of Ashantee (As-hánti) to possess three thousand three
hundred and thirty-three; but in what consists the
charm of this mystic number, which is carefully
kept up, does not appear. The king has seldom a
greater number than six with him in the palace
at the same time; the rest live at the country
residence of the king, and in the capital, where
two streets are devoted to their use. No persons
are permitted to approach them but their own
female relatives, or the king's messengers; and
these only communicate with them at the en-
trances, which are closed at each end with bamboo
doors, where a guard is placed. When they go
abroad, which is not often the case, they are
attended by a great number of little boys with
whips of elephants' hide, with which they lash
severely all who do not immediately turn aside

into another path, or throw themselves into the bush with their hands before their eyes. Sometimes the offenders are also visited with a fine. It is stated, that their appearance in the more public parts of the city occasions great confusion. Caboceers and captains, as well as slaves and children, are seen tumbling one over another, to avoid their approach.

When the king of Ashantee signed Bowdich's treaty, three hundred of his wives, however, were present as witnesses of the transaction; and at a public entertainment given by the king of Dahomy, Mr. Norris saw seven hundred and thirty of the wives of that monarch, who marched in file, bearing liquors and provisions upon their heads; and these were followed by many hundreds more, classed in troops of seventy each, who walked in greater state. In Yarriba, even a caboceer has been known to possess two thousand wives; while the king of that country told Clapperton that he did not know how many wives and children he had; but he was sure that his wives alone, hand to hand, would reach from Katunga, the capital, to Jannah,—a distance, as appears from the maps, of considerably more than one hundred miles! On one occasion, he actually visited the traveller in company with five hundred wives.

This latter sovereign makes the services of his

wives subservient to his pecuniary interests; for Clapperton remarks that, in their journey from Badagry to Katunga, they found in every place some of his wives trading for him, and, like other women of the common class, carrying large loads upon their heads from town to town. The wives of the king of Ashantee, it appears, are not thus degraded; but live in a state more in accordance with their dignity. Bowdich says that the three hundred whom he saw at the signing of the treaty, were arrayed in all the magnificence which a profusion of gold and silk could furnish. According to Dupuis, however, their influence is not great. Their mediation is considered unavailing in state affairs, and they are not permitted, nor do they expect, to receive presents from foreign ambassadors. Whereas in Barbary, as in the East, it is of the first importance to secure female mediation; for the determination of the sultan is generally formed under the influence of the harem or seraglio.

The number of wives which caboceers and other persons possess depends partly on their rank, and partly on their ability to purchase them; for the practice which prevailed in the remote ages of patriarchal antiquity, is perpetuated among the descendants of Ham. With them also, it is the rule that the parent receives a sum for his daughter, instead of giving a fortune with her, as is the practice in European countries; and it consequently follows, that a large family of daughters is a source of wealth to an African father. Nor has the husband cause to complain, that he is required to pay for every wife; for in Fantee, (Fánti,) and the countries near the coast, if a man can only obtain six or ten wives, the fruits of their labour are sufficient to enable him to lead a life of indolence.

In the affair of courtship the wishes of the female are but little consulted; the business being chiefly settled between the suitor and her parents. No Ashantee, however, compels his daughter to become the wife of one whom she dislikes: but if she refuse to receive as her husband one of whom her father approves, he instantly withdraws from her his support and protection, and prohibits her mother also from affording her any aid or countenance whatever. It is not unfrequently the case that infants are married to each other, to promote the connexion of families; and infants are also frequently wedded to adults, and even to elderly men. In such cases, the husband sends a present to the mother, who brings up the child for him, until she is old enough to be removed to his own house. The Ashantee caboceers speak of this as a good plan for a man who wishes to get gold; for the most innocent freedom, when the girl becomes ten or eleven years old, proves the occasion of a serious palaver with the husband; and as these marriages are not generally known, it happens that such palavers frequently occur, and a person has to make compensation for taking liberty with a wife when he supposed that he was only playing with a child. It is, moreover, a custom in Ashantee, (As-hánti,) to contract for a child before it is born. When a man takes a fancy to the wife of a caboceer in a state of pregnancy, he *consaws* the infant in the womb, by the payment of a sum, varying from two to ten ounces of gold; and should the child prove to be a girl, she is brought up for him as his wife.

The domestic arrangements, in places where polygamy prevails, are formed on a different principle from that which regulates an English domicile. In Ashantee, (As-hánti,) Fantee, (Fánti,) and the neighbouring countries, the husband lives separate from his wives, who dwell in houses or sheds built contiguous to each other, in the form of a square; and in some cases they continue with their mothers. They cook and carry food to their husband, but are not allowed to partake of a meal in his presence. Sometimes his children eat with him, but more frequently he eats alone. On one occasion, when Mr. Hutchinson paid a visit to the croom of Apóko, one of the greatest men in Ashantee, he had the opportunity of witnessing a domestic scene. About the middle of the day, a large pot of yams, and another of boiled fish, were placed in a side room, whither Apóko repaired and dined; after which he divided the remaining yams and fish into a given number of portions, when the door opened, and about twenty of his sons and daughters received their respective shares in calabashes with which they came furnished. In the after-part of the day, four of his wives arrived from Coomassie, a distance of about three miles, with some prepared food; but as he was disposed to sleep, he sent them word that they were not to enter the room, but leave the meat, and go back again to town.

The children are left chiefly to the care of their mothers, and grow up without correction, until at length, when the perverseness of a boy can no longer be endured, the Ashantee father punishes him by cutting off an ear. Some of the Ashantees, however, appeared to admit the force of Mr. Freeman's arguments in favour of early and moderate correction.

Unfaithfulness on the part of the wife is treated with severity. Death is sometimes the penalty which both the guilty parties have to pay; but more frequently the injured husband is satisfied with a fine from the parents of his offending wife, and another from her paramour. Sometimes he cuts off her nose, if her family are too powerful

to be provoked with safety by putting her to death.
It is not uncommon, however, that the wives and
daughters of even men in power are employed
by their husbands and fathers to allure the other
sex into crime, in order to involve their victims
in a palaver, which has ended in their being
sold into slavery, when they have not been rich
enough to pay the required fine.

In Ashantee, (As-hánti,) a peculiar provision is
made with reference to the female sex.   One of
the king's sisters is constituted the governess of
the empire, or queen over the females.   When
this personage, on a certain occasion, honoured
Dupuis with a call, she was accompanied by about
one hundred and fifty women and girls, many of
whom were described as the wives and daughters
of men of high rank.   All the females in the empire are said to be placed under her direction and
control ; but whatever may be the nature and
object of the training to which she subjects them,
it is certain that it is not intended to make the
wife the rational companion and confidential
friend of her husband ; for if an Ashantee wife
is detected in listening to a private conversation of her husband, her curiosity is sure to
cost her an ear ; and if she betrays a secret with
which she has by any means become acquainted,
her incensed husband punishes her by cutting
off her upper lip.   The sight of women who

have suffered such inflictions is as common at this day in Coomassie as it was in the time of Bowdich.

With regard to the employment of the female sex, it may be remarked, that the weightiest duties generally devolve upon the wife, who is to be found "grinding at the mill," * transacting business in the market, or cultivating the plantation. The females of the higher classes in Ashantee (As-hánti) may be exempt from such drudgery; but the condition of Fantee (Fánti) wives, in general, is similar to that in which Clapperton found the wives of the king of Yarriba.

In countries where polygamy prevails, it might be presumed, that either there is a great disparity between the sexes, or that all do not marry. According to Bosman, the number of women among the natives on the coast, in his day, was much greater than that of the men; but it is supposed that the proportion of women to men in Ashantee, is not two to one; and it is the fact, that the majority of the males live without wives. Sometimes a caboceer will give his daughter to a confidential slave; but celibacy is the condition of far the greater proportion of the slave population, which principally constitutes the military force of Ashantee. From this unequal state of things, the

* Matthew xxiv. 41.

grossest irregularities naturally follow. In despite of the penalties with which incontinence is visited, the violation of the marriage-contract is notoriously common; and prostitution is openly countenanced. In some instances, females are provided by the State, and are set apart to their office by public formalities and religious ceremonies. As many as two hundred and fifty females of this description have been seen together on state-occasions at the court of Dahomy. But scarcely any single circumstance tends to show so clearly the demoralization of Negro society, as the fact that wealthy females on their death-bed regard it as one of the most meritorious acts which they can perform, to bequeath to the public a few female slaves. What must be the moral condition of a people, where the State lends its authority to legalize crime, and the sanctions of religion are employed to invest vice with the attributes of virtue!

The large towns of Ashantee (As-hánti) contain a considerable population. The inhabitants of the capital have been variously estimated.* This has partly resulted from the circumstance, that the towns of this part of Africa are surrounded by a number of plantations belonging to the inhabitants; and the natives always include the slaves on those plantations in their estimates of the population of the towns to which they are attached. Bowdich fixed the resident population of Coomassie (Kumási) at fifteen thousand; but says, the Ashantees persisted in asserting that, when it was collected, it was upwards of one hundred thousand; and he himself admits, that, including the slaves in the suburban plantations, the population is probably much greater than that of Sego, which was estimated by Park at thirty thousand. Dupuis does not expressly specify the population of the capital ; but he compares it with other towns in reference to their size ; as, for instance, he states that Juábin " is to be reckoned about one-third the size of Coomassie, (Kumási,) and its population is estimated at seventy thousand souls;" and that Salgha, the great emporium of Inta or Ghunja, " is reported to be twice the size of Coomassie, and its population (of whom one-sixth part are Moslems) to be about four hundred thousand." If the writer is to be understood as intimating that the population of these towns is proportionate to the number of houses which they contain, and the ground they respectively cover, it follows, that Coomassie, according to his calculation, contains two hundred thousand, or two hundred and ten thousand inhabitants. This estimate is, doubtless, too high ; but Mr. Freeman is of opinion that Bowdich's is too low ;

and Mr. M'Queen, in his recent work, has judiciously avoided both extremes, and, following the Ashantee census, has fixed the population of Coomassie at one hundred thousand souls.

The total number of considerable towns in Ashantee (As-hánti) is unknown to Europeans. The capital is "environed by numerous large and small towns;" and it has been ascertained that many others are situated within the track of the great roads or pathways, eight of which, named after the kings in whose reigns they were formed, are cut through the immense forest in which Coomassie is embosomed, and extend from the capital to the most distant parts of the empire; these again being intersected by numerous cross-paths in various parts of the provinces. Dupuis gives the population of several towns which he saw on the pathway leading from Coomassie (Kumási) to Cape-Coast Castle; among which may be instanced Akrofrúm, with eighteen thousand inhabitants; Dumpási, with fifteen thousand; Majúri, with ten thousand; Amoafo, with seven thousand; Asiminia, with seven or eight thousand; Abointem, with three thousand; and Sarasú, with eight thousand. Dwabin, or Juábin, already referred to as being one-third the size of Coomassie, (Kumási,) is situated about sixteen miles from the capital, on another pathway, in a south-easterly direction. The same writer also gives the names of sixteen principal towns, accessible by the pathway leading from the capital to the northern boundaries of the empire; of fourteen others, on the pathway to Salgha; and of several others, in various directions. Yahndi, the capital of Dagumba, is represented as much larger than Salgha; which town is said to be twice the size of Coomassie. The two pathways leading to Dagumba and to Salgha are called the "old roads," from their antiquity and pre-eminence.

Taking Bowdich's estimate of one million as the amount of the population of Ashantee Proper, Murray calculates that the empire of Ashantee, (As-hánti,) including all its subjects and vassals, must contain more than four millions of people.* To those who look fully and fairly at the subject, this calculation probably will not appear extravagant. A person, travelling direct from the coast to Coomassie, without diverging on either hand into the forest, through which the main track lies, is in danger of underrating the population. Mr. Freeman remarks, that, when he first went to Fómunah, he had not the slightest idea of the extent to which the neighbourhood was inhabited; and was afterwards surprised, in his perambulations around the town, to find many

* Encyc. of Geography.

crooms or villages, containing a considerable population, situated in places where he had supposed there was nothing but a dense forest. The most populous provinces, however, if the testimony of the natives is to be depended upon, lie northward of Coomassie, where the country is much more open than in the vicinity of the capital and towards the south; and the district around the large trading town of Salgha is reported to be thickly inhabited.

The general conclusion adopted by Mr. M'Queen is, that, with the exception of a small portion of the sea-coast, this part of Africa is exceedingly populous; that it "swarms with population;" which conclusion is supported by a consideration of the scale on which the wars of the Ashantees and their neighbours have been conducted. In the war between Ashantee (As-hánti) and Denkera, one hundred thousand men perished in a single engagement; and in the battle in which Abú Bekr was made captive, the king of Ashantee destroyed upon the field, or made prisoners, one hundred thousand of his enemies. Admitting that all the males are trained to arms, yet it is impossible to conclude otherwise than that nations which can conduct war on so large a scale, and sacrifice such multitudes in a single conflict, must undoubtedly have great resources.

The countries of Asín and Fantee, (Fánti,)

supposed to have contained at one period between three and four millions of inhabitants, had suffered so greatly from the wars which have been partly described, that their population, inclusive of the large towns of Fantee, did not, at the time when Bowdich and Dupuis went to Coomassie, amount to more than three or four hundred thousand. Since the peace, however, the population of Fantee has rapidly increased; in evidence of which Mr. Freeman states, that, during the three years immediately preceding his visit to England last year, not more than ten of the native converts attached to the Wesleyan Mission had died, but that two hundred and fifty of their children had been admitted into the Christian church by baptism. It is not perhaps too much to assume, that Mr. Freeman, owing to the system of regular itinerancy on which he acts in prosecuting his Missionary labours, is more intimately acquainted with Fantee than any other European; and it is his opinion, that the tract of country included within the curvature of the river Prah, the borders of Akím and Aquapím, and the sea, has, at the present time, a population of eight hundred thousand or a million of souls.

Immense forests (which, from the gigantic size of many of the trees, the flowering shrubs and climbers with which they are intermingled, and the exquisite parasitical plants with which they are covered, exhibit a combination of magnificence and beauty equally novel and surprising to an European eye) luxuriate in Ashantee (As-hánti) from about the seventh degree of north latitude down to the neighbourhood of the coast. The rich and fertile soil produces cotton, indigo, coffee, rice, sugar-cane, maize or Indian corn, yams, plantains, bananas, and most kinds of tropical fruit. Pine-apples are so plentiful, that they may be bought on the coast for a penny each. A remarkable fruit grows spontaneously inland, which has obtained the appellation of " the miraculous berry." It leaves such an effect upon the palate, for an hour or two after it is eaten, that the most acid lime tastes like a luscious orange, and vinegar may be mistaken for sweet wine. Cabbages, peas, turnips, carrots, cucumbers, melons, various salads, and other esculents, can be produced in any quantity, at a moderate distance from the coast.

The native mode of agriculture is very imperfect. When a suitable spot has been selected for cultivation, the slaves are employed to clear away the thicket, and to lop or cut down the large trees, excepting those which are regarded with superstitious veneration, and others of a useful kind, as the high and low palm, bamboo, tamarind, papa, cocoa, and some which bear valuable nuts. The trees, branches, and brushwood, which have thus undergone the operation of the bill-hook, are spread upon the surface until dried by the heat of the sun, when the whole is burned, and the ashes are scattered over the field as manure. Holes are then made in the ground, with a small hoe, at regular distances; in which the grain is deposited, and left to germinate without much further care or attention.

As the traveller from the coast advances into Ashantee, (As-hánti,) the plantations become more flourishing and extensive; and on approaching the capital, they are seen placed with much regularity in triangular beds, each surrounded by a small drain, and carefully cleared from weeds. Leaving Coomassie (Kumási) again for Salgha, the road lies through a beautiful country, and the crooms through which it passes are all environed by extensive plantations. Some of the districts of Ashantee are more open and cultivated than others. Yomoho in Akím, for instance, has a large agricultural population, and supplies the markets of Dwabin, or Juábin, Bequa, Sarasú, Dumpási, and other towns, with corn and yams. Quahu is also represented as a very fruitful province; in many parts of which the land is clear and open, even down to the Volta, where there is a valuable fishery, that gives employment to many thousands of the natives. The northern provinces, generally, are much more open than those in the south.

The palm-tree is in some places cultivated by the natives, for the sake of the wine which it yields, and also for its nuts, from which the oil is expressed. When a tree is seven years old, it is then mature enough to produce wine. There are two methods for obtaining it. Sometimes the tree is left standing, and the branches are cut off nearly to the bole. An orifice is then made in the bole, near the top, from which the liquor begins to ooze out. But it is preferred to cut the tree down; and, after lopping off the branches, to burn a few dry leaves under it before it is tapped. The juice continues to flow for a fortnight, at the rate of a gallon in twenty-four hours. The wine drawn in the morning is fresh for about four hours. By the middle of the day it begins to ferment, and is then intoxicating. After the fermentation is over, (say, on the following morning,) it is good vinegar. The wine of some of the trees is too sweet for the taste of the men, and is chiefly drunk by females.

Some attempts to introduce an improved method of cultivation into this part of Africa, deserve especial notice. In the year 1792 the Danish government, having arranged for the final relinquishment of its share in the slave-trade in ten years from that time, resolved, as a preparatory

measure, to form an agricultural settlement in the
vicinity of their forts, near the river Volta.   Dr.
Isert, having travelled in that part of Africa, and
collected much valuable information, was appointed by the government to proceed thither
again, and select a suitable locality.   In the first
instance, he fixed upon a large and beautiful
island in the Volta; but the natives, under the
influence of the white slave-dealers, opposing his
design, he finally established a settlement among
the mountains of Aquapím, fifty miles from Accra,
(Akráh,) the same distance from the Volta, and
about thirty miles from the Poní, a small stream,
navigable by boats.   The native caboceer, or chief,
granted as much land as was necessary for the
purpose, at a monthly rate of eight rix-dollars,
about sixteen shillings sterling.   At this spot a
number of the Negroes, who were first enfran-
chised by the Danish government, were collected ;
and some European agriculturists were sent, who
introduced the use of the plough.   The early
efforts of the settlers were attended by an encouraging measure of success ; especially in the cultivation of Guinea corn, millet, and cotton ; and
the Danish government expressed its sense of the
services of Dr. Isert, by raising him to the rank of
captain.

The philanthropic exertions of that gentleman,
however, shortly terminated by his death ; and

Lieutenant-Colonel Roer, who had paid much attention to botany, and had, moreover, great experience in West-Indian cultivation, was appointed to take the management of the new settlement. He was accompanied by his sister, who laudably exerted herself in instructing the Negro women in spinning cotton, and other domestic occupations. The state of the settlement in the year 1795, about three years after its formation, is thus described in a letter from Mr. Moe, published by Wadstrom, in the appendix to his work :—

" I have the satisfaction of acquainting you, that I have been in Aquapím, and have seen the late Captain Isert's colonial establishment at that place. It is situated on a high and mountainous tract of land ; but so distant from navigation, that it appears to me very inconvenient for commerce. But, for the rest, I have good reason to think that the soil, air, and water are all very good. There are but few Europeans ; but they were in the best state of health during my stay among them. Mr. Flint, who, till the arrival of Lieutenant-Colonel Roer, takes care of this infant colony, has established another similar one at the foot of the mountains, nearer to Accra ; and I saw growing, at both places, a considerable quantity of cotton-trees and maize, all of which flourished and throve very well. The dry and wet seasons are not so distinct at Aquapím as near the coast; for rains fall there in all the other months of the year, as well as in the rainy season.

" I observed that, near the Danish forts at Rio Volta, Printzenstein, and Quitta, the commanders of those places and a certain merchant have begun to plant cotton, sugar-canes, and different kinds of garden-stuffs, such as greens and sweet-peas.

" In the neighbourhood of Christiansburg, at Accra, an old respectable Negro, a native of Dunko, at a considerable distance up in the interior part, has established himself on a solitary spot, and has planted large fields with cotton, maize, and various kinds of provisions and garden-stuffs. By his intelligent and laborious cultivation he has distinguished himself so much, that he is now come into great repute. He raises such quantities of provisions, that he supplies not only Christiansburg, but also most of the neighbouring Negro villages."

The Danish government, in further prosecution of its design, in the year 1798, sent out Mr. P. Thonning, to investigate the capabilities of the country, and make botanical researches; and shortly after Mr. H. Schmidt was sent on the same service. The latter gentleman did not long survive; but Mr. Thonning made a survey of the country from Accra to the Volta, and returned to

Europe with forty-two new *genera,* and two hundred and four *species,* of plants.

All who have visited Aquapím represent it as well adapted for agriculture. Mr. Schionning, the governor of Christiansburg Castle, at Danish Accra, says, " As to beauty of prospect, pleasing variety, and local advantages, I never saw any thing equal; nor can I compare any part of the world where I have been to it; in short, you may compare it to what poets describe when they depict nature in all her elegance." He further expresses the opinion, that wheat would grow well in Aquapím; and remarks, that all European garden-productions thrive as well there as in Europe. The sugar-cane grows to an immense size inland, out of the reach of the ants.

Mr. Schionning himself had an extensive plantation, about fifteen miles from Accra, (Akráh,) which promised an abundant increase previous to the Ashantee war. His proceedings and prospects are thus described by himself :—

" In October, 1808, I put some coffee-berries in the ground; and in the following June I transplanted about sixteen thousand young trees. I have every year added to this stock; and in November last (1810) I had growing thirty-six thousand five hundred healthy coffee-trees, of different ages. Last year I had a nice crop; and I am sure that I should have had from sixteen to twenty thousand pounds' weight of coffee this year, had not the Ashantee war put a stop to my exertions. I calculate upon a pound and a half annually, (from each tree,) when the trees are four years old. To keep my plantation in good order, one person is necessary to one thousand trees. On high land the coffee-tree thrives much better than on level or marshy ground. High-land coffee is far superior in flavour, but not so advantageous as the low-land coffee, which, being much larger, is, of course, much heavier."

The writer is not possessed of information as to the present state and prospects of these establishments; but the success attending the earlier efforts of the Danish government is sufficient to show what might be accomplished by the application of suitable means.

CHAPTER VI.

ARTS, TRADE, LANGUAGE, NATIONAL TASTE.

Mode of building—Ingenious Workmanship in Gold—Iron
manufactured into Swords of very fine Temper—Carpenters' Work — Tanning of Leather — Pipe-Heads
bought in the Market of Coomassie—Weaving—Manu-
facturing Towns of Ashantee—Trade not so extensive
in Ashantee as in some other Countries—Illustration
of the scriptural Parable of the Talents—Policy of the
Kings of Ashantee not to allow Intercourse between
the Coast and the Interior—Intercourse with the Interior Eastward—Caravans from Bornou and Hausa to
the Borders of Ashantee, crossing the Niger at Komi—
Gora or Kolla Nuts—Not improbable that Tidings
from the Niger Expedition may be received by Way
of Ashantee—Washing for Gold-Dust—Precious Gold-
Mines—Exports of Gold—Other Exports—Ivory—
Exports from the Gold Coast—Importance of Lan-
guage in tracing the Origin of Nations—Probable that
the Languages of Africa are of common Origin—Dr.
Prichard notices an Analogy between the Kaffer and
Coptic—His Classification of Dialects of Western
Africa—Grammatical Outline of the Fantee Language
—Native Oratory—Prevalent Taste for Music—Musical
Instruments—Native Band at Cape-Coast Castle.

THE natives of the countries contiguous to the
coast, as well as the Ashantees, build their houses
of mud and sticks, which composition is called
"swish." The fronts of the houses in Coomassie
(Kumási) are nearly uniform. A kind of plat-

form, about two or three feet from the ground, projects some distance from the wall; from the front of which, pillars rise, to support the overhanging roof. On this platform the master of the house, who is at least a captain in rank, sits, to hold palavers and drink palm-wine. The wall and the front of the platform are ornamented with various devices, which were executed when the plaster was soft; and, the platform being polished with red ochre, while the wall above is finished with white clay, the whole has a somewhat pleasing appearance. No windows are to be seen; and a door, at one end of the platform, is the only means of ingress and egress in front. On entering this door, the visitor finds himself in a square yard, or court, surrounded by a number of sheds, or small buildings, in which dwell the chief, his wives, and the domestic slaves. This yard, in some instances, leads into another, and that into a third, according to the number of persons in the establishment. The houses in Coomassie are all of one story, and built of the same materials; with the exception of the stone-house, called the Castle, which was erected by Osai Tutu Quamina, in honour of the king of England. The plan of enclosing a square with small sheds, or huts, for the separate residence of the master and the other members of the family, generally prevails in this part of Africa.

The Ashantees and Fantees are ingenious artists in the precious metal which their country produces. Among the specimens of native manufacture which the writer has had the opportunity of examining, were chains and rings, executed in a very creditable manner. The writer has been told, by an artist in London, that a valuable gold-chain of English manufacture, which had been repaired by a native of the Gold Coast, was put into his hands by the owner, and that he was not able, after a careful examination, to point out the new links which had been added. Some of the rings are of solid gold, ornamented with various devices; others are formed of a hoop, entwined with net-work; and others, again, are composed entirely of gold net-work, which enlarge or contract, according to the size of the finger. The Ashantee artists are expert in moulding gold into the form of birds, fishes, and various animals.

Iron is also manufactured to a considerable extent; and some of the swords made by the Ashantees are said to show very fine workmanship.

The native carpenters' work is not despicable. The writer has before him a stool, made of a white, soft wood, neatly carved; and a low chair, brought by Mr. Freeman from the interior, which displays considerable taste: it is also made of

white wood, and carved, and is studded all over
with brass nails : the bottom is of strong leather.
The chair shuts up like a camp-stool, and has, on
the whole, a somewhat elegant appearance.

The tanning of leather is also understood.   The
writer has in his possession a large, round cushion,
made of red-coloured leather, ingeniously ornamented with various devices cut in the substance
with a knife.   The cushion is stuffed with the
cotton produced by the silk-cotton tree.

Various specimens of pipe-heads, bought by
Mr. Freeman in the market of Coomassie,
(Kumási,) similar to those sent by Bowdich, with
one of the above-mentioned cushions, to the
British Museum, support the favourable opinion
which that traveller has given of Ashantee
pottery.

The art of weaving has made considerable progress among the Ashantees.   The principle of
their looms is the same as that of the hand-loom
of the English ; but the web which they manufacture never exceeds four inches in breadth.
They purchase the richest silks, in order to un-
ravel and interweave them with their own thread ;
and their best cloths are extolled for their fine-
ness, variety, brilliance, and size.   The colours
used by them in dyeing are, red, blue, and
yellow, and a green produced by a union of the
two last-mentioned colours.

In Ashantee, (As-hánti,) the several arts and
manufactures are, in some cases, carried on in
the same town.   Dumpási, for instance, is mentioned by Bowdich as a very industrious town,
where cloth, beads, and pottery were manufactured in all directions ; and the blacksmiths'
bellows were always at work.   At other places,
only one kind of manufacture is found, as at
Datiasú, the inhabitants of which are exclusively
employed in potteries, and at Asiminia, where
almost the entire population is engaged in
weaving.

The spirit of commercial enterprise does not
prevail to so great an extent among the Ashantees
as in some of the adjoining countries.   When
Dupuis endeavoured to impress the king with
the importance of making his capital a depôt
of British manufactured goods, and of African
produce, and explained to him that, were he to
adopt the principle on which commerce is conducted in Europe, where every article pays a
relative custom to the officers of the state, in
support of the government, he would derive a
great revenue from the encouragement of trade ;
the king replied, that the people who lived
nigher to the great water—the Niger—understood
these things better than the Ashantees ; that *they*
were a nation of warriors ; and that, according

to *their* fashion, only the king and great men engaged in trade. The king, the caboceers, and captains, are, in fact, the only merchants; and it is principally by trading that the great men of Ashantee acquire their wealth. It may be remarked, in passing, that Ashantee trading furnishes a striking illustration of the well-known scriptural parable of the talents.* The king will frequently lend, for a period of two or three years, a few ounces of gold to a subordinate captain, for the purpose of testing his qualifications; and if, on rendering his account, it is found that he has made considerable gain by the use of the gold, he is raised by the king to a station of superior dignity and more extensive authority. Dupuis was present on one occasion when the unfaithfulness of a captain, who was thus on probation, was brought to light; on which the king indignantly ordered the loan of gold to be returned.

But although the commerce of Ashantee (Ashánti) is confined to the king and great men, an extensive trading intercourse is kept up with the countries in the interior, as well as with the towns upon the coast. Upwards of half a century ago, Mr. Lucas learned from the sheríf at Tripoli, that there was a commercial commu-

* Luke xix. 13.

nication between that place and Ashantee; and the sheríf, with the utmost cheerfulness and confidence of safety, offered to conduct him by the way of Fezzan and Kashna, across the Niger, to the latter country. He appeared quite familiar with the neighbourhood of that river, and mentioned a fact which he could scarcely have known but from personal observation; namely, that fire-arms are not found in any of the countries south of the Niger, (which he professed to have visited,) because the kings nearer to the coast would not allow the populous inland States to obtain possession of those powerful instruments of war. It has undoubtedly ever been the policy of the kings of Ashantee to prevent communication between the Gold Coast and the interior. Mr. Swanzy, in his examination before a Parliamentary Committee in 1816, stated, that he had never known any people come down to Cape Coast from Hausa, or any other country beyond Ashantee; although traders, natives of Ashantee, (As-hánti,) very frequently came down to the forts upon the coast. Many Fantee traders, in return, go to Coomassie, (Kumási,) but they are not allowed to advance beyond it.

Dupuis found that many Moors from the interior frequently visited Coomassie; and that, occasionally, Tunisian and Tripolitan merchants, and natives of Cairo, of the Great Desert, and of Medina and Mecca, travelled as far as that capital. Three of the imperial sherfa,* who are regarded as descendants of the Prophet's family, were at Coomassie during the reign of Osai Tutu Quamina ; and one of these, the sheríf Ibrahim, who was there at the same time with Bowdich, returned to Cairo, with a large caravan of pilgrims under his care.

That the intercourse between Ashantee (Ashánti) and the countries in the interior, lying in an easterly or north-easterly direction, has been long established, may be presumed from the fact previously noticed, that the two pathways from Coomassie (Kumási) which, on account of antiquity and pre-eminence, are called the old roads, are those leading to the Volta, opposite to Salgha, the great emporium of Ghunja, and Yahndi, the capital of Dagumba. The extent of the traffic carried on between Ashantee, and the countries in this direction, appears from the notices given by Clapperton. He states that caravans travel regularly between Bornou, Hausa, Ghunja, and Ashantee. The Bornou caravans come no further than Kulfu ; but several of the Bornou traders proceed from that place, with the Hausa caravans, to the borders of

* The plural of the Arabic word sheríf.

Ashantee. On his journey from Badagry to
Boussa, (Búsah,) he met with one of those
caravans at Kiama, a town through which they
regularly pass, and found, accompanying it, a
trader from Bornou, with whom he was acquainted on his former visit to that country.
The caravan was on its way from Ghunja and
Ashantee; and the taya, or head man, told
Clapperton that they had been detained in
Ghunja twelve months on account of the wars,
and also, that the king of Ashantee (As-hánti)
was dead. The substantial correctness of this
statement—for the war between the Ashantees
and English was then raging, and Osai Tutu
Quamina had not long been dead—is evidence
of their acquaintance with Ashantee.

This caravan consisted of one thousand men
and women, and beasts of burden. Clapperton
thus graphically describes its appearance as he
overtook it again on the road, after leaving
Kiama. "At ten o'clock," he says, "we fell in
with the Hausa caravans. They occupied a long
line of march: bullocks, asses, horses, women,
and men, to the amount of a thousand, all in a
line, after one another, forming a very curious
sight; a motley group, from the nearly naked
girls and men carrying loads, to the ridiculously
and gaudily dressed Ghunja traders riding on
horseback; some of these animals being lame,

and going with a halt, and all in very bad condition. The poor girls, their slaves, are compelled
to travel with a heavy load on their heads; yet
are as cheerful and good-natured as if they
were at home, grinding corn in their own native
country."

In this description it will be noticed, that
traders from Ghunja were accompanying this
caravan into the interior. Clapperton elsewhere
remarks, that Ashantee merchants visit Kano,
the great emporium of Hausa. On reaching
Komi, or the king's ferry, represented by our
traveller as the great ferry to and from Hausa,
and the countries already mentioned, they met
another caravan going to Ghunja; and a scene
of great animation presented itself. "The village," Clapperton remarks, "is built on the
high ground, the bank shelving gradually down
to the river side, where there is a second temporary town composed of the huts of the merchants; here and in the village all was bustle
and confusion. A caravan going to Ghunja was
halted on the eastern bank; on the western the
kafilah from Ghunja, with kolla nuts, &c. The
village was filled with horses and men dressed
out in their gayest trappings: here merchants
were offering horses for sale; there their slaves,
with gay glass beads, cords of silk, unwrought
silk, and tobes, and turkadoes for sale; some

dancing and drumming; while others, more wicked, were drinking and rioting."

At this ferry the Quorra, or Niger, is about a quarter of a mile in width, and runs at the rate of two miles an hour. On the 10th of April, the day when Clapperton went over, the water was ten or twelve feet deep in the middle. The ferry is crossed by canoes of about twenty feet long and two broad. Cattle are occasionally made to swim over.

By crossing this ferry, it may be remarked, the caravans from Hausa to Ghunja and Ashantee avoid the town of Búsah, and proceed to Kulfu, the great trading town of Nufi, where they meet caravans from Bornou, and halt a considerable time.

It would appear that gold is not exported in any considerable quantity from Ashantee into the interior eastward, unless, however, it be carried by way of Hausa, through Fezzan, to Tripoli. Clapperton expressly says, gold is neither found in Bornou, nor is brought into it; and adds, that a small brass basin tinned to drink out of, is there esteemed as a present for a sultan. Four or five dollars, or a Soudan tobe, will scarcely purchase such an article. In the Kano market, he remarks, a few silver trinkets are to be found, but none of gold; and in the enumeration which he gives of the mer-

chandise carried by the Hausa merchants from
Ghunja and the neighbouring countries to Kulfu,
the first great mart after crossing the Niger,
he specifies only "a *little* gold."

The gora or kolla nut is the principal export
from Ashantee (As-hánti) in this direction. This
was one of the articles in great request in the
time of Mr. Lucas. The sheríf described the
taste of this nut as that of a pleasant bitter, and
spoke of it as so "grateful to those who are accustomed to its use, and so important a corrective to
the unpalatable or unwholesome waters of Fezzan,
and of the other kingdoms that border on the
vast Sahara, as to be deemed of importance to
the happiness of life." The nut, he stated, grows
on a large and broad-leafed tree, that bears a pod
of about eighteen inches in length, in which are
enclosed from seven to nine nuts. Their colour
is a yellowish green, they are about the size of a
chesnut, and are also covered with a husk like
that fruit. The Fezzan merchants at that time
purchased these nuts at the rate of twelve shillings for one hundred pods. The account which
the Ashantees give of the nut is, that it grows
spontaneously, and does not require cultivation.

Clapperton says that the Hausa merchants
deal in gora nuts, the produce of Ashantee
and its vicinity; and that they are chewed by all
people of consequence, on account of their agree-

able bitter taste, not unlike that of strong coffee, and their supposed virtue in curing a common complaint. Among the imports of Sackatoo, (Sakatú,) he enumerates gora nuts brought from the borders of Ashantee ; and in the narrative of his journey to that town from Bornou, he very frequently speaks of those nuts as the presents which he gave and received. The extent to which the trade in this article is prosecuted, may be inferred from the fact, that the large caravan which Clapperton met with at Kiama was chiefly laden with it. His own words are : " The principal part of the cargo of these Hausa merchants consists in gora or kolla nuts, which they receive in exchange for natron, red glass beads, and a few slaves, principally refractory ones whom they cannot manage." Lander also states, that, when leaving Kulfu, after the death of his master, he met with a company of merchants going to Ghunja for gora nuts.

It may be remarked, in passing, that it is not very improbable that the first intelligence respecting the expedition to the Niger, after it shall have passed through the Delta of that river, may be received by way of Ashantee. From the accounts which have been published of the recent voyage of Captain Becroft up the Niger, it appears that he reached, within a very few miles, the ferry of Komi ; and should any of the caravans, at the time of the arrival of the expedition in that neighbourhood, be met with proceeding from Bornou and Hausa to the borders of Ashantee, a good opportunity will be afforded of forwarding letters to Coomassie, (Kumási,) from which place a messenger would take them to Cape-Coast Castle in a few days.

The principal export of Ashantee (As-hánti) is, the precious metal from which the neighbouring coast takes its name. It is partly obtained by washing the soil. Mr. Swanzy, in his evidence, speaking of the Gold Coast, says, the gold is procured "from every part of that country; it appears more like an impregnation of the soil than a mine." At that time, in the year 1816, he supposed, that the Gold Coast produced one hundred thousand ounces of gold annually. In like manner the soil of Ashantee yields a large amount, and one stream is mentioned, (the Barra,) on which alone eight or ten thousand slaves are employed, for two months in the year, in washing for gold. The gold is also contained in mines; the richest of which are said to be in the province of Gaman, about nine feet from the surface. The gold from these pits is of a very deep colour, mixed with red gravel and pieces of white granite. It is sometimes carried to Coomassie in solid lumps, imbedded in loam and granite, weighing together probably fourteen or

fifteen pounds; of which mass, one pound or one
pound and a half is gold. The gold obtained
from the mines is denominated rock-gold; and
Mr. Dupuis is of opinion, that some of the lumps
which he has seen suspended as ornaments at the
wrists of the caboceers, would weigh as much as
four pounds each. The Rev. Mr. Freeman also
speaks of the large size of several of the masses of
pure gold worn in the same way by caboceers
when he was first introduced to the king. The
amount of the precious metal which might be
obtained is, however, incalculable; for many of
the richest mines are dedicated to the national
deities, and are thus protected from violation,
by the powerful influence of the popular superstition.

A small portion of the gold obtained in Ashantee (As-hánti) is sent down to the coast, and
exchanged there for European manufactures.
Another part is exported to Yahndi and Kong,
and other neighbouring places, where it is manufactured into trinkets. The artists of Dagumba
are especially celebrated for their workmanship.
The remainder is sent to Jenneh and Timbuctoo,
(Tumbuktú,) and from thence it is transported
across the Great Desert to the countries on the
shores of the Mediterranean.

Between Ashantee and Tumbuktú there appears to be considerable intercourse maintained

by means of the traders. Bowdich expressly
states, that most of the sojourners, who were at
Coomassie (Kumási) during his mission to that
capital, had visited Tumbuktú. And a Moor from
that place gave a circumstantial account of Mungo
Park's death at Búsah, of which himself had
been witness. The narrative of Abú Bekr, moreover, clearly shows that there is a constant communication between Tumbuktú, Jenneh, Kong,
and the borders of Ashantee.

The exports of Ashantee to Dagumba are
not confined to gold, but include iron, and
a small quantity of European merchandise obtained from the coast. Many thousands of the
Ashantees also obtain a livelihood by catching
fish in the lake Búro, and drying it, for sale in
the markets of Dagumba. Fishes of a large size,
and of delicious flavour, are said to be conveyed
alive from this lake to Salgha.

The northern provinces of Ashantee (As-hánti)
abound in elephants, the hunting of which is one
of the chief occupations of the people. The
natives of Yobati are said to be such expert
hunters, that they alone, if required, could
furnish the market of Coomassie with one
hundred loads of ivory in the space of a
month.

The native productions exported from the Gold
Coast are gold-dust, ivory, and palm-oil. A

species of ground-nut, which grows spontaneously, is at present attracting the attention of the merchants; it being found to yield an excellent oil for the table, which also burns beautifully in the lamp. This nut is a common product in all that part of Africa, and is now extensively cultivated in the neighbourhood of the Gambia.

In adverting to the languages or dialects of Ashantee (As-hánti) and the Gold Coast, it may be remarked, that language is a subject of interesting scientific inquiry as well as of practical utility. It is one of the most satisfactory indications of the affinities and relations of a people to other tribes and nations; and a valuable guide in the attempt to trace the streams of human emigration, in their various meanderings, to their common source or head.

The knowledge which Europeans have obtained of the languages of Africa, is very limited and imperfect; but Dr. J. C. Prichard, in his researches into the physical ethnography of the African races, is of opinion, that such *data* are extant as render it extremely probable that all the idioms of Africa, including the language of the ancient Egyptians, are so allied—not, however, in the manner or degree in which Semitic idioms resemble each other, but by strong analogies in their general principle of structure—as will go far towards the proof of a common origin. Such a common source is also indicated by the traditionary notion prevalent in Ashantee, as well as in the northern parts of the African continent, that the original influx of population into Africa came from the east, some time after Misraim, the son of Ham, founded the empire of Egypt. By the aid of the Rev. W. B. Boyce's Kafir Grammar,* Dr. P. believes that he has discovered one of the analogies to which he refers between that language and the Coptic, or ancient Egyptian. The general conclusion to which he leans respecting the affinity of the African languages, and their derivation from a common source, is not materially affected by the fact, that —as appears from a brief outline furnished by the Rev. Mr. Isenberg, of the Church Missionary Society—the language of the Gallas, a people dwelling in Shoa, or the southern part of Abyssinia, is, while partaking of the Semitic, evidently of Japhetic origin. Nor will it considerably alter the question, should the theory of Mr. D'Eichtal, respecting the Malayan origin of the language of the Foulahs,† be established. All general rules admit of exceptions; and although intermixtures of races have taken place, it may nevertheless be true, that the languages of Africa in general are

* See Note B.   † See Note C.

related to each other, and may truly claim a common parentage.

The idioms of Western Africa, from Senegambia to the Delta of the Niger, are divided by Dr. Prichard into ten classifications of language. The Ashantee (As-hánti) and Fantee (Fánti) are of the Inta race; and are so nearly alike, that they can hardly be considered as two distinct dialects. Natives of these two countries, as the writer has had the opportunity of observing, converse together without any apparent difficulty. One difference between the two languages appears to consist in the substitution of one letter, or letters, for others, in the orthography of certain words, as for instance, the syllable *ti* in Ashantee is sometimes *chi* in Fantee.

On examining the grammatical structure of the Fantee language, it will be perceived that it has not the articles *a* and *the*. Neither has it any terminational variations, like the Greek and Latin languages, to express the accusative, vocative, and ablative cases of nouns. The nominative and accusative, or objective, cases are alike; and the possessive is distinguished by an abbreviation of the relative pronoun affixed to it, or by placing first the word implying possession. The Fantees would not say, "The queen of England;" "A leaf of a tree;" "The shining of the moon;" but, Abrukíl hĭmá, "England's queen;" Idwía áhatau, "Tree's leaf;" Bŭsúm ĕfíl, "Moon's shining."

The plural is formed by prefixing *im* or *in* to the singular; and in this respect the Fantee (Fánti) also exhibits a degree of similarity to the Coptic, which abounds in prefixes. The following are examples :—

> Bĕnin ....Man.
> Im-bĕnin...Men.
> Tabu.........Board.
> In-tabu ...Boards.

Sometimes, however, changes take place in the initial letter of the singular, for the sake of euphony or brevity; thus, im-benín is often pronounced im-menin; and idu, "a tree," is in-dua in the plural, instead of in-idua.

It may be remarked, that there are two words in Fantee for *man*, bĕnin and bĕrima, nearly equivalent in meaning to the Latin *homo* and *vir*, bĕrima, like *vir*, being only used to distinguish a brave and illustrious man.

The adjective is placed after the noun; as,—

> Edán *kĕsi*......House *large*.

It is compared thus :—

> Edán awsuɳsin ....House larger.
> Edán awsuɳsin *ninăra* ...House larger *than all others*.

The personal pronouns are declined thus :—

FIRST PERSON.

Singular.		*Plural.*	
I	Emi	We..........	E-yen.
Mine	Midia	Ours	Ye-re-di-a.
Me	Mada	Us	I-yĕn-ă-da.

SECOND PERSON.

Thou	Ewu	Ye or you.	E-wŏn.
Thine	Wu-dia	Yours ...	Wu-re-di-a.
Thee	Wada	You	E-wŏn--ă-da.

THIRD PERSON.

He and she ...	Aw-nu ...	They	Wŏn.
His and hers..	Nidia	Theirs ...	Wŏn-di-a.
Him and her .	Nada	Them......	Wŏn-ă-da.

The personal pronouns are used somewhat sparingly, the noun being often repeated where, in English, the pronoun would be introduced.

Like the adjective, the demonstrative pronoun follows the noun ; as,—

Bĕnin *i-yi*......Man this.
Bĕnin *awnu* ...Man that.

The conjugation of verbs, as in the Mandingo,* is effected principally by means of pronouns, and by the use of particles which are affixed to the root of the verb. The pronouns undergo certain changes to express the several tenses. Thus,—

* See Note D.

I love .... is.........Emi daw, or mi daw.
I loved ....Emi daw yi, or mi daw yi.
I shall love...............Maw daw.

In each of these instances it will be perceived that the verb itself, *daw*, ("to love,") remains unchanged.

In Fantee (Fánti) construction, the object does not, as in the Mandingo, precede the verb, but follows it.

The Fantee has some adverbs, although not so many as in the English language.

It has the preposition *from*, but not *to*. Thus the Fantees say, Mi re kor Mansu, "I going Mansu;" but when leaving, they say, "Mi re *fi* Mansu, "I going *from* Mansu."

A peculiarity in Fantee construction may here be noticed. In the latter instance only, the particle *re*, which contains the force of the participle, is expressed, and the verb *kor* ("to go") is omitted, in order to introduce it before the name of the place to which the individual is removing. Thus, Mi *re* fi Mansu *kor* Kumási: "I going from Mansu to Kumási."

It may be added, that the Fantee has conjunctions both conjunctive and disjunctive; as, ŏni, "and," and na, "but."

In this brief outline of the Fantee language, the vowels and diphthongs are to be sounded according to the scheme given in the Preface.

With regard to the general character of the language, it may be remarked, that, owing to the great number of vowels and liquid letters which it contains, it is soft and harmonious in its expression. But it is deficient in synonymes, and in words conveying various shades of meaning, while agreeing in one general idea. Thus a person, in denying the correctness of a statement made by another, has no feebler mode of expressing his dissent than to tell him that he *lies*.

It has been a topic of general remark by writers on the subject, that a considerable number of dialects are spoken on the Gold Coast; but William De Graft, whose vernacular tongue is the Fánti, observes, that he was able to make out, to a great extent, the meaning of the people in their own tongues, at all the places which he has visited, from Dix Cove to Accra (Akráh). He understood less of the Accra dialect than any other. Possibly that dialect, and perhaps some of the others, may have been derived from an earlier race of settlers than the emigration whose descendants now people that part of Africa. He at the same time confirms the remark of Meredith, that the Fantee language is generally known by the inhabitants, as well as their own dialects. Although he understood but little of the dialect of Accra, the people of that place understood him, when he preached to them in

Fantee. Owing to the ascendancy of Fantee, and the intercourse kept up with it by means of its traders, its language has become the general medium of communication along the coast.

A Vocabulary of Fantee (Fánti) words, obtained from Mr. William De Graft, and printed in the list of African Vocabularies, compiled for the use of the Niger Expedition, will be given in the Appendix.*

The natives of this part of Africa are remarkable for oratory, and will discourse fluently on a given subject for hours. When Aga, whose history has been given in an earlier part of the volume, was first brought to the notice of the king of Ashantee, (As-hánti,) the speech which he made in defence of his master occupied three hours in the delivery. Bowdich says, (but the statement is ridiculed by Dupuis,) that the water of a small stream called the Bohmen is supposed to instil eloquence, and that a number of Ashantees annually visit it to drink the inspiring draught. Whatever virtues may be ascribed to this water, oratory is certainly an accomplishment of that people.

A taste for music is also extensively cultivated.

* See Appendix II.

Various kinds of instruments are used. The large drum is made out of part of a tree, which is hollowed, and covered at one end with a skin. This instrument is carried on the head of one man, and beaten with sticks by another. The smaller drums are hung round the neck of the performer, or placed on the ground, and played with the fingers. The most martial instrument is the large horn, made of the tusk of the elephant. The sound of this is powerful; and as every caboceer has his own peculiar air, which is universally known, the respective positions of all the chiefs in the heat of battle are easily ascertained. Gong-gongs, made of iron, castanets, and rattles, are also in request. Among the most musical of the instruments is their flute, which is much larger than the kind used in Europe. The natives profess to be able to hold conversation through it with each other. The sankú, a specimen of which lies before the writer, consists of a hollow wooden box, perforated with holes, and covered with a skin, to which is attached a long stick or neck; and it has eight strings, in two rows, supported perpendicularly by a bridge. This instrument, though somewhat resembling a violin, is played with the fingers like a guitar, and produces a soft and soothing tone. Some of the native songs are a kind of dialogue; and the parts are sung by individuals of each sex,

alternately rising from the ranks of the perform-
ers, who are ranged, with their sankús and other
instruments, in opposite lines. The musical taste
of the people is evidenced by the native band
at Cape-Coast Castle, which plays admirably,
by the ear, several of the most popular English
tunes.

CHAPTER VII.

National Character especially to be estimated by Reference
to Religion—Knowledge of a Supreme Being in
Guinea—Remarkable Tradition—Subordinate Deities,
or Fetishes—Rivers, Lakes, Mountains, Trees, and
some Animals, supposed to be Residences of Fetishes—
William De Graft and the Crocodile at Dix Cove—
Worship of Flies—Of Images—Classification into
national and domestic Fetishes—Fetish-Houses and
sacred Groves — Fetishes supposed to be spiritual
Beings who sometimes appear in White—Universal
Notion of a future State—Soul or Spirit likened to
Wind—Firm Belief in Apparitions—Good and evil
Spirits—Persons supposed to live over again, in another World, the Lives they led in this—Belief in the
Existence of the Devil—Annual Ceremony of driving
him out of the Town—Traces of the Sabbath—Time
divided into lucky and unlucky Days—The Priests
and Priestesses—Supported by the Offerings of the
People—Principle on which their Influence rests—
Means used by the Fetishmen or Priests to maintain
their Influence—Council of Fetishmen in Privacy
of the Forest—Disagreement of two—Fetishmen
study Medicine.

AMONG the causes which contribute to the
formation of national character, a principal place
is to be assigned to religion. Religion is indeed
the mould of character, and never fails to give a
peculiar expression to those distinguishing features

of a people, which other causes may have originated. Were this important consideration to be overlooked in the effort of philanthropy to elevate a dark and barbarous nation, painful disappointment would be the inevitable result. It would be found that many of the irrational and inhuman customs which were expected to disappear, on being contrasted with the enlightened practices and pursuits of civilized strangers, are too firmly interwoven with the religious system of the people to yield to any other means than the introduction of a purer faith. Under the impression of these views, it will be attempted to describe the prevalent superstitious practices of the natives of the Gold Coast, and of Ashantee, (As-hánti,) and, at the same time, to trace them to the principles on which they rest for support. And it may be observed, that a delineation of the religious system of these people will afford a view of the superstitions which, under various modifications, extensively prevail among the other Negro tribes and nations of Western and Central Africa.

It is a remarkable fact, that the notion of a Supreme Being lies at the very foundation of the religious system which it is proposed to describe. He is called *Yankumpon*,* from *yanku*, "friend,"

---

* His name in the dialect of Accra is *Numbo*.—Isert.

and *pon*, " great," or rather, " very great ; " for
the word is used in a superlative sense. The
meaning of the appellation thus appears to be
" very great," or " greatest friend." To this
name the Fantees sometimes prefix *Nănah*, that
is, " grandfather," or " father of us all."

Another name used by the Fantees, recognises this Supreme Deity as the creator of man.
It is *Yehmi*, compounded of *yeh*, " to make," and
emi, " me ; " and the idea intended to be conveyed by it is, " He made me." The Ashantees,
moreover, ascribe to him everlasting existence,
by giving him a title, written by Prince William
Quantamissah, *Titiquarfrarmuah*, which literally
signifies, " He endures for ever."

How the polytheism of the natives is engrafted
upon this doctrine of a Supreme Being, will
best appear from the tradition respecting the
creation, which has prevailed among them, with
some variations, from the earliest period of their
history. It is believed that, in the beginning
of the world, God, having created three white
and three black men, with an equal number of
women, of each colour, resolved, in order that
they might be left without complaint, to allow
them to fix their own destiny, by giving them
the choice of good and evil. A large box or
calabash was, in consequence, placed upon the
ground, together with a sealed paper or letter.

The black men had the first choice, who took the calabash, expecting that it contained all that was desirable; but, upon opening it, they found only a piece of gold, some iron, and several other metals, of which they did not know the use. The white men opened the paper or letter, and it told them everything. All this is supposed to have happened in Africa, in which country, it is believed, God left the Blacks, with the choice which their avarice had prompted them to make, under the care of inferior or subordinate deities; but conducted the Whites to the water-side, where he communicated with them every night, and taught them to build a small vessel which carried them to another country; from whence, after a long period, they returned with various kinds of merchandise to barter with the Blacks, whose perverse choice of gold, in preference to the knowledge of letters, had doomed them to inferiority. Is this notion of the judicial degradation of the Blacks traceable to the curse pronounced upon Ham? And is this again confounded with the result of man's probation in Paradise? These are interesting questions; but, however they may be decided, it is certain that in this tradition is to be found the source of those superstitions which enthral millions of the Negro race.

The appellation which has been given by

Europeans to the divinities of the Blacks is *Fetísh,*
or *Fetísche,* from the Portuguese word for witchcraft; but the native name, used by the Ashantees
and Fantees, is *Bŏsum,* or *Suman,* implying
sacredness; and the Ashantees employ the word
Tăno also in the same sense. *Juju,* it appears,
is the corresponding term in the languages spoken
in the Delta of the Niger.

These deities are identified with many of the
most striking objects of nature. They are
supposed to inhabit rivers. The river Tando
is a favourite fetish among the Ashantees.
So is the Adirai. Thus, one of the Ashantee
warriors, while extolling the power of the king,
and showing how difficult it was for his
enemies to escape his vengeance, exclaimed, " If
they run to Adirai river, it is the king's fetish,
and will kill them. They cannot pass Tando
river." The Prah is another of their divinities,
and is denominated Bosumprah, or the sacred
river. This river issues from a large gaping rock
about half-way up the side of a mountain, near a
little croom, called Samtasu. There the special
presence of the god is supposed to abide; and
sacrifices are consequently offered. On the
northern bank of the river, at the place where
it is crossed on the path leading to Cape-
Coast Castle, there is a fetish-house or temple,
where the Ashantee travellers make oblations

to the deity of the river, before they venture to plunge into the stream. The Sakúm, a small river about four miles westward from Accra, (Akráh,) is regarded, by the inhabitants of that place, as a great fetish. Its name is ever upon their lips, and to it the praise is ascribed when benefits are obtained, or evil averted. So greatly is this fetish esteemed at Accra, that it would be dangerous to speak disrespectfully of it in the hearing of the inhabitants.

Lakes, as well as rivers, have a share of the public veneration. Thus the lake Echui is worshipped as the guardian-deity of the capital of Ashantee (As-hánti). At Cape-Coast town, two ponds, called Papratah and Buakún, enjoy the honour of deification. The former is especially esteemed, because it has not failed to supply the inhabitants with water when besieged by their enemies.

Remarkable mountains and rocks are also regarded with religious veneration. The cliff on which Cape-Coast Castle stands is the supposed residence of a great fetish, called *Tahbil;* and, when the sea breaks loudly against it, the natives say, "The god is firing." Some kinds of trees are also esteemed as fetishes, and are always left untouched when the ground on which they stand is cleared for cultivation.

The animate creation, moreover, furnishes other

objects of superstitious veneration. Some animals (as leopards, panthers, and wolves) and dangerous reptiles (as serpents) are believed to be the messengers of the gods; and others are worshipped as the living incarnations of certain deities. At Dix Cove, the crocodile has obtained divine honours. It is kept in a large pond near the fort; and any person, going ashore at that place, may obtain a sight of it at the expense of a white fowl and a bottle of ardent spirits. The fetishman takes the fowl and the liquor, and, proceeding to the pond, makes a peculiar noise with his mouth, on which the crocodile comes forth, and receives the fowl as his share of the present. When Mr. William De Graft resided at Dix Cove, he frequently witnessed the fetishman calling the crocodile out of the pond, to gratify the curiosity of Europeans. On leaving the water, the animal would run to the fetishman, who, as it approached within two or three feet, would throw the white fowl into its mouth, and then pour out a little of the rum upon the ground. And he has frequently observed, that when there was any delay on the part of the fetishman in presenting the fowl, the crocodile would immediately make towards any person or persons present who were dressed in white, and pursue them until the fowl was thrown in his way. Some years ago, Mr. Hutchinson and Captain Leavens were exposed to considerable risk; for the fowl having escaped out of the hand of the fetishman into the bush, the crocodile pressed them so closely, that had not a dog crossed the path, of which the animal made a repast, one of them would, most probably, have fallen a victim to its rapacity. The voracious creature frequently carries off sheep and dogs from the neighbourhood of the pond, and will also attack children. On his first going to Dix Cove, William De Graft was cautioned by a native merchant to beware of approaching the crocodile, which had recently seized his daughter, and would undoubtedly have devoured her, had not the means of rescue been at hand. The crocodile which formerly received divine honours at Dix Cove was much larger than the present one; but he grew so tame, that he was accustomed to leave the water of his own accord, and proceed to the houses of the fetishman and the king, to receive his offering of a white fowl.

In Fantee, (Fánti,) there is a place called Embrotan, whose inhabitants might be imagined to have descended from the ancient worshippers of Baalzebub; for they carefully preserve a number of flies in a small temple, and honour them as fetishes.

To the various deities, furnished by the

animate and inanimate creation, artificial representations are added. Some of the images, to which religious offerings are presented, are made of wood, rudely carved, so as to resemble the human form, birds, and certain beasts, and covered with red ochre and eggs. Others are made of various materials, and of arbitrary forms.

This vast assemblage of objects of worship is capable of a regular classification. Some may be regarded as the tutelar deities of the nation at large. Such is the great fetish at Abrah, in the Braffo country, which from time immemorial has been venerated in this character. Others have under their care particular towns. The inhabitants of Cape-Coast town congratulate themselves that they enjoy the protection of seventy-seven fetishes. Every town has one fetish-house or temple, often more, built of mud or swish, in a square or oblong form, and thatched over; or constructed of sticks or poles placed in the ground in a circular form, and then tied together at the top and thatched. In these temples several images are generally placed. Like the ancient Canaanites, the people always plant a grove, where they build a place of idol-worship; under the shade of which grove their superstitious rites are celebrated. Every fetishman or priest, moreover, has his private fetishes in his own house. William De Graft describes one of those private collections which he had the opportunity of examining, as consisting of images of men, one of a bird, stones encircled with strings, large lumps of cinders from an iron furnace, calabashes, and bundles of sticks tied together with strings. All these were stained with red ochre, and rubbed over with eggs. They were placed on a square platform, and shrouded by a curtain from the vulgar gaze. Then there are the domestic fetishes ; for, like the Romans, the natives have their *penates*, or household gods. These are, in some cases, small images, in others a stone, about a foot square, with a bamboo string tied round it, or a calabash containing a string of beads. And, whatever may be the form or the materials, red ochre and eggs are invariably the covering. These household fetishes are sometimes placed on the outside of a house, by the door, but most frequently in a corner of the room within, covered by a curtain.

While contemplating this extensive pantheon, it must, however, be noticed that the natives do not appear to regard the material objects themselves as deities. The fetishes are believed to be spiritual, intelligent beings, who make the remarkable objects of nature their residence, or enter occasionally into the images and other artificial representations, which have been duly conse-

crated by certain ceremonies. It is the belief
of the people, that the fetishes not unfrequently
render themselves visible to mortals. Thus the
great fetish of the rock on which Cape-Coast
Castle stands, is said to come forth in the night
in human form, but of superhuman size, and to
proceed through the town, dressed in white, to
chase away the evil spirits. This serves to explain
the fear manifested by the king of Ashantee
when, supposing the moving figures of the magic
lanthorn to be fetishes, he laid hold of Dupuis,
and appeared afraid to be left alone with them in
the dark. Further evidence will be subsequently
given on this point; but it may here be remarked,
that the notions entertained by the natives of
spiritual beings are, after all, very incongruous.
They believe that these fetishes are of both sexes,
and that they require food, as though they possessed an animal nature.

The notion of a future state universally prevails.
It is believed that, at death, the soul passes into
another world, where it exists in a state of con-
sciousness and activity. And it is worthy of
remark, that although the native term for
ghost or soul—*sunsum* or *saman*—does not, like
the Hebrew word for the spirit or soul of man,
—*ruach*,—in its primary meaning, denote the air
or wind, yet the natives conceive of the soul under
that similitude. They say it is like the wind, and

that it can come into a room when the doors are closed, and there is no visible entrance. They firmly believe that the spirits of dead persons frequently appear to the living. The Rev. Mr. Thompson, a clergyman, who spent some time on the Gold Coast nearly a century ago, although evidently not disposed to be over-credulous upon the subject, mentions the following circumstance, which he had from good authority. "A caboceer, walking one day to a neighbouring croom or town along the sea-sands, saw a man before him coming forward in great haste, whom he was well acquainted with; and as he drew near, being still intent upon his speed, he called to him to stop a little. The other, making signs that he was in a hurry, ran past him, and continued his pace. When he came to the town, finding a concourse of people in the market-place, he asked the reason of it, and was told, that such a man's head had just then been taken off. He said, it could not be, for he had met him in the way, and spoken to him. But the answer was made, that it was so; and if he questioned the truth of it, he might see the parts of him, and be convinced by his own eyes."

The people believe that the spirits of their departed relatives exercise a guardian care over them; and they will frequently stand over the graves of their deceased friends, and invoke their spirits to protect them and their children from harm. It is imagined that the spirit lingers about the house some time after death. If the children be ill, the illness is ascribed to the spirit of the deceased mother having embraced them. Elderly women are often heard to offer a kind of prayer to the spirit of a departed parent, begging it either to go to its rest, or, at least, to protect the family, by keeping off evil spirits, instead of injuring the children or other members of the family by its touch. The ghosts of departed enemies are considered by the people as bad spirits, which have power to injure them. The gloom of the forest is supposed to be the haunt or abode of the evil spirits; and travellers into the interior have mentioned, that, when overtaken on their journey by the night, their native attendants have manifested great fear, and have made the forest resound again with their shouts and yells, uttered with the intent to drive the evil spirits away.

But although the natives have some notion of the spirituality of the soul, they have other opinions, utterly incompatible with a correct idea of its immateriality. They suppose that their friends live over again, in the other world, the lives which they led on earth; and that they eat and drink, live in the same state, and engage in the same pursuits, as when they were in the present world.

This belief exerts a powerful influence upon the minds of the natives, and leads to the most tragic results. If their friends are to resume in another world the state they maintained in this, then it is deemed necessary to send after them their wives and attendants; and thus the death of an individual becomes the signal for the whole-sale murder of his household.

It may be further remarked, that while the natives entertain notions inconsistent with a correct idea of the spirituality of the soul, they do not appear to have a just conception of its immortality. William De Graft says that, when he resided at Winnebah, he witnessed several instances of the Heathen digging up the bones of persons who had long been dead, and burning them; under the idea, that so long as any of the bones were left in an undecayed state, the spirits of the former possessors of the bodies were able to injure them, but that when the bones were consumed, there was an end of them and their power.

The existence of the devil is also an article of Negro belief. He is called by the Fantees and Ashantees, *Abonsum*, or *Aiyen*. This evil being is supposed to be ever at hand for purposes of mischief; for when a person rises from his seat, his attendants are accustomed immediately to lie down upon their side, to prevent the devil from slipping into their master's place. Whatever may be the case in other parts of Africa, it does not appear that the devil is worshipped by the Fantees and Ashantees; on the contrary, he is annually driven away on the Gold Coast, with great form and ceremony. This custom is observed at Cape-Coast town, about the end of August. Preparation is made for the ceremony in the course of the day; as the hour of eight o'clock in the evening draws nigh, the people are seen collecting in groups in the streets, armed with sticks, muskets, and other weapons; at the instant when the eight-o'clock gun is fired from the castle, a tremendous shouting, accompanied with the firing of muskets, breaks forth from all parts of the town; and the people rush into their houses, and beat about with their sticks in every corner, shouting and hallooing with all their strength. This sudden outburst of all kinds of noises often alarms Europeans who have recently arrived, inducing them to suppose that an enemy has attacked the place. When it is imagined that the devil is excluded from all the houses, a simultaneous rush is then made out of the town, and the people in a body pursue the invisible enemy, with lighted flambeaux, shouts, and the firing of muskets, until it is concluded that he is completely routed and put to flight. After this achievement, they return; and, in some of the towns, the women proceed to wash and purify their wooden and earthen vessels, to prevent the devil from returning to their houses.

To call another " devil," is a very great insult; and should the person who has thus been abused shortly after die, his death is ascribed to the influence of the evil spirit in the person who insulted him. When such a circumstance occurs, painful results generally follow; for the friends of the deceased do not fail to seek satisfaction.

Some traces of the sabbath are found in this part of Africa. The natives reckon time by moons; and the arbitrary division of weeks, which can only be satisfactorily accounted for by the original institution of the sabbath, was evidently known among them before they had an opportunity to learn it from Europeans. The names of the days in the week, in the several branches of the Inta or Ashantee (Ashánti) language, are native terms; and may be traced in the national customs backward to remote antiquity. The same day of the week is not, however, universally observed as the sabbath. When Mr. Freeman preached at Fómunah, and explained the Decalogue, Korinchi afterwards referred to the Fourth Commandment, and said he had entertained the belief, that God had appointed for each nation its own sacred day;— that he had set apart one day for the Ashantees, another for the Fantees, a different one for the

Wassaws, and others for other people. He could not, of course, support his belief by any show of argument : he had received it by tradition ; and referred Mr. Freeman for proof to the wonderful old fetishman in the interior, who is supposed to know all things, and to be able to do all things. But the apprehensions expressed by several who were present at the discussion, that they would expose themselves to great danger, should they substitute the Christian sabbath for their own weekly fetish-day, is evidence of the influence which their superstitions exert on their minds.

In all the countries along the coast, the regular fetish-day is Tuesday, the day which is observed by the king of Ashantee (As-hánti). Other days in the week are held sacred in the bush. On this weekly sabbath, or fetish-day, the people generally dress themselves in white garments, and mark their faces, and sometimes their arms, with white clay. They also rest from labour. The fishermen would expect, that were they to go out on that day, the fetish would be angry, and spoil their fishing ; and, in the interior, should a man go into his plantation on the sabbath, and by chance see a panther or leopard there, it would be concluded, that the fetish, who knew his intention to labour, had sent its messenger, to prevent him from carrying his purpose into effect.

The people, moreover, regard their natal day

with a kind of religious veneration; and honour the day of the week on which they were born with some of the observances practised on the fetish-day, or sabbath.

Time is further distributed into lucky and unlucky days and weeks; but every nation appears to have its own peculiar mode of division. In Ahanta, they divide time into periods of three weeks. The first week, named *Adai,* is regarded as the "good week;" and in this week much work is done. Traders then visit the market more frequently than at any other time; believing that every thing they do during its continuance must assuredly prosper. The second is *Ajamfo,* or "the bad week," in which no trade is carried on; as the natives are persuaded, that whatever is undertaken in that week will certainly fail. The third is the "little-good week," called *Adim,* in which they both work and trade, but not so much as in the first, or Adai, week. In some countries, the great fortunate time lasts nineteen days, and the lesser, seven days. Between these two periods, is an interval of seven evil or inauspicious days, on which they neither travel, till their land, nor engage in any business of importance. The people of Aquambú, it has been said, would not so much as accept any presents on those days, but either returned them to the owner, or left them in a separate place, until the arrival of the fortunate days, before they made use of them.

In Ashantee, (As-hánti,) the number of good or lucky days, it has been estimated, is about one hundred and fifty or sixty in the year; and, during the evil days, councils cannot be held, nor can troops either march, or engage the enemy. Incredible time is thus spent before any national concern can be undertaken; for, all the preparatory religious mysteries can only be celebrated on the particular days of the week or month which are deemed auspicious. Some months contain a greater number of fortunate days than others. September, for instance, is a more highly favoured month in this respect than the preceding. Ashantee couriers, travelling with despatches in September, will go from Coomassie (Kumási) to Cape-Coast Castle in twelve days; but they have been known to spend thirty days of the month of August in this journey, in consequence of the interruption occasioned by the more frequent recurrence of inauspicious days.

The priests and priestesses of the national superstition—the fetish-men and fetish-women—constitute a numerous order. One class are attached to the public fetish-houses or temples, at some of which a very considerable number are placed. At the house or temple of the prin-

cipal fetish of the Ahanta country, upwards of
fifty superior priests are said to be resident;
and the great fetish at Abrah also, it is known,
has a numerous attendance.

Another class of fetishmen itinerate through
the country, remaining six or twelve months at
a place, according as their services may be in
demand by the inhabitants.

The priestly office may, in some cases, be hereditary, but it is not uniformly so; for the children of fetishmen sometimes refuse to devote
themselves to the pursuits of their parents, and
engage in other occupations. Any one may
enter the office after suitable training; and
parents who desire that their children may be
instructed in its mysteries, place them with a
fetishman, who receives a premium for each.
The order of fetishmen is further augmented by
persons who declare, that the fetish has suddenly
seized, or come upon, them. A series of convul-
sive and unnatural bodily distortions establishes
their claims.

The revenue of the fetishmen is derived from
the liberality of the people. A moiety of the
offerings which are presented to the fetish
belongs to the priests; and this is very considerable in amount. The king of Ashantee's offering
is said to be generally ten ounces of gold; and
that of his subjects in proportion to their respect-

ive ranks. The denial of protection to run-away slaves is another source of emolument. It is the acknowledged privilege of a slave to forsake his master, and devote himself to the service of the fetish; and, in Ahanta, when a slave has once reached the fetish-house he is safe; for his proprietor would consider that the death of all his family would be inevitable, were he to take him back from the sanctuary. But in Ashantee (As-hánti) and other places, the priests have relaxed the strictness of this rule; and, on receiving a fee of two ounces of gold and four sheep, they will deliver up the fugitive slaves to their master, and absolve him from all the evil consequences which might be apprehended from their return into his family. The income of the fetishmen varies according to the dignity and reputation of the fetishes to whose service they are devoted. It has been remarked by Meredith, that the great oracle at Abrah was inaccessible to the poor and indigent. In consequence of its acknowledged superiority, the required amount of offerings was so great, that it could only be approached by the more opulent classes of society.

The influence of the fetishmen rests upon the universally-received principle, that whatever evils afflict men are produced by supernatural means, and can only be counteracted or removed by supernatural agency;—in other words, that evils

can only be removed, and desired benefits conferred, by the fetishes; and that their friendly
interposition must be sought through the medium
of their servants or ministers. This doctrine, it
will be perceived, puts the people completely into
the power of the priesthood, and wholly abandons
them as victims to its rapacity.

To keep up the delusion, and maintain their
influence, the fetishmen have recourse to a
variety of means. They exert themselves to
obtain all kinds of information. With this
view, they employ agents in various parts of
the country, who make them acquainted with
all that is passing within the range of their
observation. The fetishmen themselves, also,
when on their travels, industriously collect the
news as they pass along; and when one of them
enters a town, with a view to practise his profession there for a time, his first business is, to shut
himself up for a few days, until he ascertains by
secret inquiries what subjects are engaging the
public attention, who are sick, and what is the
private history of the principal inhabitants. In
these ways, the fetishmen acquire such an
amount of information as serves to astonish their
dupes, and to strengthen the popular belief in
their supernatural powers.

The success of the fetishmen is further promoted by their acting in concert. They commu-

nicate to each other the information they respectively collect, and agree upon the line of operations which they shall pursue. A short time since, a person residing at a croom, in the neighbourhood of Salt Pond, was hunting in a very secluded part of the bush, when he came upon a company of about twenty fetishmen; who had retired thither, to lay their plans for promoting the interests of their craft, at the public expense. He listened for some time to their conversation, unperceived, and might probably have kept their secret, had not his superstitious fears been partly dissipated by the subsequent application of the truths of the Gospel to his mind. At Djuquah, likewise, two fetishmen were lately overheard in a violent dispute, when one threatened, that unless the other would lend him a sum of money, he would make an exposure of the plans by which he had assisted him to deceive and fleece the people.

The fetishmen apply themselves, moreover, to the study of medicine; and the knowledge which they acquire of the properties of herbs and plants, it will be seen hereafter, powerfully contributes to strengthen their influence with the people.

CHAPTER VIII.

THE POPULAR SUPERSTITIONS—CONTINUED.

In proceeding to notice the ceremonies, in the
celebration of which the national deities receive
religious homage, and their counsel and aid are
sought, it may be proper to remark, that not only
are the deities themselves called fetishes, but the

religious performances or acts of worship : the
offerings presented are also spoken of as fetish, or
sacred, because they are performed and offered in
honour of those deities.

The daily household-worship of the people, in
itself, furnishes no mean proof of the constant
pressure from their superstitious notions under
which they act.   In the morning, the master of
the house will take water in a calabash, and,
pouring it upon the ground, before the door of his
house, will pray to the fetish, to the effect that he
(the fetish) is to wash his face, that he may be
better prepared to watch over the household on
that day, and may discern more clearly what will
be the best for them.

Sometimes an offering of a fowl is made.
When Mr. Dupuis was on his journey to Coomassie, (Kumási,) he was aroused from sleep one
morning at an early hour, at the place where he
had stopped for the night, by the entrance of a
man, whom he discovered to be the master of the
house, with a present for his tutelary god, which
in this case happened to be a tree, growing at the
door of the apartment where he (Dupuis) lodged.
The offering, which consisted of a white and
speckled fowl, and a small calabash containing a
little corn and plantain, steeped in a fluid looking
like blood, was, in the first instance, placed on the
ground, close by the tree ; but afterwards, the

members of the fowl were severed from each
other, and suspended by a piece of cotton-yarn
upon one of the lowest branches. A blackish
fluid, contained in another calabash, was then
poured out at the root of the tree as a libation,
during the recital of a prayer which Dupuis did
not understand. The washing of the stem of the
tree, with a colouring made from grey and white
clay, concluded the ceremony.

Previous to going abroad in the morning, it is
not unusual that a person endeavours to fortify
himself from some special evil, by having recourse
to other fetish practices. One morning, when Mr.
Hutchinson called on Apóko, this distinguished
caboceer began to consult his fetish, by a number
of strings, having various ornaments on one end,
to denote their good or evil qualities. These were
mixed promiscuously together; and, taking them
in his right hand, he put them behind his back,
and drew out one by one with his left. This was
repeated about twenty times. A wicker-basket
was then brought, on a small stool, covered with
a silk cloth. It contained two lumps, like pin-
cushions, made of eggs, palm-oil, and other
ingredients. Taking the stool, he turned it
upside down, and, making three holes in it with
an instrument resembling a shoemaker's awl, he
drove in an equal number of pegs with a stone,
muttering to himself all the time, and waving

each string round his right ear. An egg was
then brought in, broken at one end, which,
having been placed alternately on the lumps in
the basket, was crushed upon the stool where the
pegs had been inserted. The whole of this
ceremony, Apóko said, he repeated every morning, for the express purpose of keeping him out
of bad palavers all the day.

With such superstitious ceremonies and practices the day begins; and during its progress,
no food is taken without a recognition of
the claims of religion. Before eating and
drinking, a little of the liquid, and a portion of
the food, are thrown upon the ground for the
fetish, and the spirits of departed relatives.

Application is made to the fetishes for counsel
and aid in every domestic and public emergency.
When persons find occasion to consult a private
fetishman, they take a present of rum and
gold-dust, and proceed to his house. He receives
the present, and either puts a little of the rum on
the head of every image, or pours a small quantity
upon the ground before the platform, as an
offering to the whole pantheon: then taking
a brass pan with water in it, he sits down with
the pan between himself and the fetishes; and the
inquirers also seat themselves to await the result.
Having made these preparatory arrangements,
looking earnestly into the water, he begins to

snap his fingers, and, addressing the fetish, extols his power; telling him that people have arrived to consult him, and requesting him to come and give the desired answer. After a time he is wrought up, like Virgil's Sibyl, into a state of fury; he shakes violently, and foams at the mouth. This is to intimate that the fetish has come upon him; and that he himself is no longer the speaker, but the fetish, who uses his mouth, and speaks by him. He now growls like a tiger, and asks the people if they have brought rum, requiring them, at the same time, to present it to him. He drinks, and then inquires, why they have come, and for what purpose they have sent for him. If a relative is ill, they reply that such a member of their family is sick; that they have tried all the means they could devise to restore him, but without success; and that, knowing he is a great fetish, they have come to ask his aid, and beg him to teach them what they should do. He then speaks kindly to them, expresses a hope that he shall be able to help them, and says, " I go up to see." It is imagined that the fetish then quits the priest; and after a silence of a few minutes, he is supposed to return, and gives his response to the inquiry.

But what is this "going up to see?" The people believe, that the fetish has four eyes, and conclude that, therefore, he can see better than mortals, who have only two ; and some understand that the fetish goes up to the sky to look around for the cause of the disease, and for the cure. But the fetishmen themselves, when arguing with William De Graft in defence of their system, have insisted, that the fetish goes up to Yankumpon, the Supreme Being; and they have urged this as a reason for refusing to embrace Christianity. Their argument has been : " As the fetishes derive all their power and wisdom from God, why forsake them ? " Latterly, however, as they perceive that the people, under the teaching of the missionaries, are disposed to reject this mode of reasoning, and go to God at once, the priests do not appear to admit so freely the dependence of their deities upon a higher power.

When a principal chief is ill, or when any public calamity has taken place, the inhabitants of the town repair to the public temple, or fetish-house, to propitiate the fetish, who is supposed to be angry because his offerings have not been duly presented ; and who has therefore either himself appointed the afflictive visitation, or has allowed some evil spirit to inflict it upon them. The illness of the chief, however, is shrewdly traced up by the priests to his neglect of the prescribed customs for a departed relative, or some other similar offence.

On these occasions, the drums belonging to the

temple are brought forth. These are made of large calabashes, one end being cut off, covered with goat-skin. The persons who play them sit upon the ground under the shade of the grove, and beat them with their hands. All things being ready, the priest selects and commences a fetish song, which the people sing; while they beat the drums, and the attendant fetishmen dance with all their might. While thus engaged, the priests are often excited into a state of frenzy, which is regarded as evidence that the fetish himself has entered into them; and at the end of the song the fetish is supposed to speak in the priest, and give intimations of his will to the people. Previous to his beginning to speak, the priest lays his hand upon the drums, and silence ensues. Having ended his communication, he commences another song, and the former scene is renewed. After a length of time, perhaps when fatigued, the priest dances very slowly, and delivers his oracles to the people as he passes softly by them. On some of these occasions he will rush out of the circle, and run into the house of a principal person, to tell him what to do in order to avert some evil which he foresees is coming upon the family; and for such intimations he does not fail to receive the usual present.

It has been stated, that some of the fetish-houses are built in a conical form, with long sticks or poles placed in the ground, tied together at the top, and thatched. When a fetish dance takes place before one of these, a priest places himself at the entrance, to prevent the people from looking in. They are told, that when the fetish comes down to his temple, they will see it move. And verily they do. As the drumming, singing, and dancing proceed, the temple begins to rock backward and forward, which the people are led to believe is effected by the fetish, who has descended, and is dancing upon the temple. This deception is managed by a fetishman, who, before the people come together, places himself on a cross-seat in the building, near the top, where he is able to shake with ease the whole fabric. The stationing of another fetishman before the door, is to prevent the people from discovering the true cause of the phenomenon which they witness.

Sometimes the town-fetish does not wait to be consulted, but summons the inhabitants to his temple. On such occasions, the priests profess that the fetish has come upon them. They run about the town like frantic persons, eating raw eggs, using the most extravagant gestures, and telling the people that the fetish has a communication to make to them. On this, the inhabitants take the accustomed presents, and hasten to the fetish-house; and the usual scene of drumming, singing, and dancing, is exhibited.

In cases of great difficulty, the oracle at Abrah is the last resort of the Fantees. This has always been held in the highest estimation. Previous to the Ashantee (As-hánti) war, there was in the neighbourhood a deep and almost impervious dell, inhabited by a number of aged fetishmen, whom the people believed to be immortal, and to have lived there beyond all memory, in intimate converse with the fetish, and with the departed spirits of the aged and the wise. Adoko, the chief of the Braffoes, frequently consulted them, either in his own person, or through his head fetishman; and the Fantees afterwards attributed the success of the Ashantees, and their own defeats and misfortunes, to their disregard of the injunctions of the oracle. Abrah is now in ruins; but the fetish maintains his reputation; partly by the influence of the fetishmen in the country, who advise the people to go thither in cases of great emergency, and partly by means of the information conveyed to Abrah by the agents of the oracle. Frequently, when inquirers go from a distance, they are surprised to find that the fetishmen are already acquainted with many of their own private affairs; and often it happens, that, on the strength of the secret information which they have obtained, the priests send such messages to persons living in remote places as tend to cherish and confirm the popular impression, that they possess supernatural means of obtaining knowledge. The people throughout the country would be afraid, were they disposed, to speak disrespectfully of the Abrah fetish; for they believe that he would hear them, catch them up into the sky, and make them drawers of water, or would inflict upon them some other severe punishment.

This notable oracle is always consulted at night. It is not allowed to visit, during the day, the sacred thicket from which the response is given. Any of the natives, rambling within the precincts of the enclosure, would be severely fined; and if an European were seen approaching, the fetishmen would endeavour to dissuade him from entering it. When the inquirers arrive at night, they find a large fire made upon the ground; and the presents which they have brought they place in the hands of the priests, who are in attendance. But sometimes they are told, that they shall have the honour of giving them to the fetish himself. They are then directed to elevate their presents above their heads, and to fix their eyes steadfastly upon the ground; for should they look up, the fetish, it is said, would inflict blindness upon them, for their sacri-

legious gaze. Who or what it is, in the overhanging branches of the trees, that receives the
presents, will be readily conjectured. The visit-
ants are then instructed to sit down, and look
into the fire, without turning their heads aside, or
speaking to each other; and two or three priests
go round the company, and receive their applications. After a time, the oracle gives a response,
in a small, shrill voice, intended to convey the
idea, that it proceeds from an unearthly source;
and the inquirers, having attained the end of
their visit, then depart.

All possible precautions are used to inspire the
people with awe and fear, in order to deter any
persons from visiting this oracle from motives of
mere curiosity. It is inculcated, that, should any
one go thither who is not a devoted believer in
the fetish, he would be immediately discovered,
and summarily punished; and the fate of one
unbelieving and irreverent visitant is dwelt upon
with great solemnity. It is stated, that when he
arrived, and sat down by the fire, a chain came
down from the thicket, and dragged him up to
the skies, where he is now employed in drawing
up water from the sea, which the fetishes send
back to the earth, in answer to the applications
made to them for rain.

What are the remedies prescribed by the fetish?
—or what are the means which the inquirers are

directed to use for the attainment of their object?
—becomes now a subject for inquiry.

In cases of bodily affliction, a medical preparation is ordered for the patient. It has already
been noticed, that the fetish men and women
apply themselves assiduously to the study of the
healing art, and acquire such a knowledge of the
properties of herbs and plants as enables them
to effect the cure of many complaints. And this
knowledge is artfully employed to foster the public superstition. In administering medicine, they
invariably tell the patient, that it has not been
found out by their own skill, but that the fetish
has taught them how to make it strong, so as to
meet his case. It is backed, moreover, during the
healing process, by occasional fetish practices;
such as the binding of strings round the knees
and other joints of the patient, the ends of the
strings which hang down after the knots are tied
being covered with a red vegetable application.
And the professed object of this is, to strengthen
the operation of the medicine, and, at the same
time, prevent the evil spirits from handling the
sick person, and increasing his complaint by their
injurious touch.

If the malady of the patient does not appear
to yield to such applications, the fetish is again
consulted; and, in some cases, as a further expedient, the priest takes a fowl or cat, and ties

it to a stick, by which operation it is barbarously
squeezed to death. The stick is then placed in
the path leading to the house, for the purpose
of deterring or hindering the evil spirits from
approaching it. When the patient is known to be
a rich man, a present of gold-dust is required, and
sheep are directed to be offered. Mr. Bowdich
states, that during the illness of his native guide
at Coomassie, (Kumási,) several sheep were sacrificed, and that he was fetished until the last moment, and died amidst the howls of a number of
old fetish-women, who continued to besmear, with
eggs, and other ingredients, the walls, door-posts,
and everything about him, until he had ceased to
breathe. The sickness of persons of the highest
order is frequently attended with more serious
consequences than the slaughter of sheep and
fowls. During the illness of Osai Tutu Quamina,
it is stated that young virgins were regularly
sacrificed to the fetish on certain days in the
week, for the recovery of his health.

For the purpose of fortifying the applicant
against any apprehended evil, some kind of fetish
preparation is made, which he is directed to wear
about his person; and should it fail to accomplish the desired end, the blame is invariably
thrown upon the wearer. It is alleged that he
has neglected some necessary condition, or in
some way or other offended the fetish; and the

fetishman escapes without censure. However greatly the predictions of the priests may be falsified by the event, or whatever may be the failure of the measures to which they resort, their own credit is maintained with the people. The case of the fetishman at Gaboon will serve for the purpose of illustration. This individual, who declared himself to be invulnerable, was solicited by a credulous young man, to endue him with the same miraculous quality. The request, enforced by a handsome present, was favourably entertained by the fetishman; and the applicant having been duly fortified by the performance of the requisite superstitious rites, confidently exposed himself to the fire of a musket. His arm was shattered by the ball; but the fetishman adroitly threw all the blame of the miscarriage upon the wounded dupe. He stated, that at the moment when the gun was discharged, it was revealed to him by the fetish, that the young man had, on a former occasion, violated one of the fetish regulations. The sufferer was not prepared to maintain that he was faultless; and the people continued to regard the fetishman with undiminished veneration.

The measures prescribed to ensure success in war afford a striking proof of the direful influence exerted by the national superstitions. It has already been stated, that human victims were daily sacrificed by the king of Ashantee (As-hánti) at the commencement of the war with the British. A few years previous to that period, when entering upon the Gaman or Buntuku war, in 1817, he was employed in religious preparations during a period of several weeks. Not only in the capital, but at several other places, the king presented fetish offerings in furtherance of the undertaking. According to the account of those transactions which Dupuis received from a native, it appears, that the monarch, in the first instance, collected together his priests, and proceeded to consult the gods by a succession of human sacrifices. After fifty persons—thirty-two males, and eighteen females—had perished, the royal council decided that the answers returned by the priests were unsatisfactory. The king was then directed to make a custom at the sepulchres of his ancestors; and when the blood of many hundreds of human victims had been shed, the priests announced that the wrath of the adverse deities was appeased, and that they were at length disposed to favour the arms of the king. A certain composition was then prepared by the priests, which they delivered to the king, with a strict injunction to burn it daily in a consecrated fire-pot within the palace. On no account was the fire to become extinct in consequence of neglect; for, so long as the sacred flame should continue to destroy the com-

position, the king, it was alleged, would not fail
to triumph over his enemies.

Encouraged by the assurances which he received, the king prepared to join his army, and
committed to his eldest sister, at that time the
governess of the empire, or queen of the
females, the task of watching over the sacred
mystery; informing her that both his crown and
his life depended upon her vigilance. To assist
her, he selected three of his favourite wives, who
were to attend by turns, and prevent the fire
from being extinguished. To this trust, however,
the sister proved unfaithful. After the king
had been some time absent, she formed a connexion with a chief of Bouromy, whose ambition
led him to aspire to the throne of Ashantee
(As-hánti). Seventeen of the king's wives and
their families are said to have joined in the conspiracy; when the mysterious flame was extinguished, the fire-pot was broken to pieces; and
the rebellious chief openly began to arm his followers in maintenance of his claims.

With this state of things, the king, it was
believed, became acquainted by supernatural
means. Surprised at the severe checks which he
received in the early part of the war, he caused
an incantation to be performed over a certain
talisman, for the purpose of ascertaining why the
results of the campaign proved so contrary to

those which he had been encouraged to expect; when he is said to have obtained an insight into what was going on in his own capital. The fetishmen who were with him in the camp, had doubtless received private information from Coomassie, (Kumási,) which they communicated to the king as though it had been revealed by the oracle. The sequel may be briefly stated. The king immediately despatched Ossu Kujoh, with a body of troops, who speedily and effectually crushed the rebellion. When the king himself returned victorious, at the end of the war, he summoned a council to deliberate upon the punishment to be inflicted upon the offenders; and it was finally decreed, that the offending wives should suffer death by decapitation; but, to avoid the profanation of spilling royal blood, the sister of the king was ordered to be strangled, (her younger sister being elevated to her office of governess of the females,) and the chief, her paramour, and all his party, were doomed to undergo the most cruel deaths, at the grave of the king's mother. By the execution of these sentences, which were promptly carried into effect, it is said, seven hundred individuals perished.

In their preparations for war, the Ashantees have recourse to the Moors, who visit or reside at the capital, as well as to their own fetishmen.

Enormous prices are sometimes paid for the fetishes or charms, manufactured by those followers of the Prophet. The king, it is stated, gave for the fetish- or war-coat of Apóko, the value of thirty-seven slaves; and he paid, according to the same scale, for the war-dresses of several other chiefs, varied only with respect to the rank which they respectively sustained. For a small fetish, consisting of six lines of writing, enclosed in red cloth only, which the king presented to Mr. Bowdich's linguist, he gave six ackies * of gold. Sometimes the fetish is cased in gold instead of cloth. A single sheet of writing-paper is sufficient for a great number of charms; as a very small slip only will contain the mystical sentence.

To these cabalistic preparations the most extraordinary virtues are ascribed. The Ashantees firmly believe, that they greatly contribute to make them invulnerable in war; that they paralyze the hand, and shiver the weapons, of the enemy, and divert the course of the balls. Several of the Ashantee (As-hánti) captains seriously offered to allow Mr. Bowdich to fire at them; and such is the confidence which the warriors of that nation generally repose in these mystical defences, that they rush fearlessly and headlong

---

* Sixteen ackies make an ounce.

into the midst of the greatest dangers. In the praises of one of the great captains, proclaimed on a public occasion by the bards, this was the climax of the song: "He is invulnerable; his fetish no man can look upon, and live."

In the course of a war, the Ashantees use additional means to fortify themselves against evil, and to obtain fresh inspirations of vigour and courage. Several of the hearts of the slain enemy are taken out by the fetishmen who attend the army; and, having been cut to pieces, are mixed with blood and various consecrated herbs, while the accustomed ceremonies and incantations are performed. All who have never before killed an enemy, eat of the preparation; it being believed, that if they did not, their energy would be secretly wasted by the haunting spirits of their deceased foes. The smaller joints, bones, and teeth of the most distinguished among the slain, are worn by the victors about their persons. It has already been shown, in the narrative of the war in which he fell, that such was the end of the unfortunate Sir Charles M'Carthy. His heart was eaten, and his bones were worn as fetishes or charms, by his savage conquerors.

It serves to place in a strong light the character of the national deities, that, in ordinary or every-day life, an individual as easily obtains their aid to injure his neighbours, as to avert evils from himself and his family. If a revengeful or malicious design is formed, recourse is had to the fetish, for the purpose of carrying it into effect. During Mr. Hutchinson's stay at Coomassie, (Kumási,) a person was executed for an attempt upon the life of his brother, who was a caboceer, or nobleman. The criminal was presumptive heir to the property, and his object was to obtain possession of it, by the removal of his brother. To effect this, however, he did not use any personal violence, but only employed the fetish incantations which are resorted to for such purposes.

On another occasion, the keeper of the royal cemetery having been imprisoned for some offence, his wife was shortly after charged by the council with using fetish to turn the king's head. In her defence, she admitted that she had had recourse to fetish; but alleged that she meant no more than to dispose the king to think better of her husband. If this was really her motive, she was only imitating the king himself; for he made fetish with the view that the heart of the king of England might be favourably disposed towards him; and to attain this object, he sacrificed six men and nine women to his household gods. Her explanation, however, was not admitted. She was condemned for having invoked the fetish to make the king mad; and she paid the penalty of the alleged offence with her life.

Such facts as these sufficiently explain the alarm which the Rev. Mr. Freeman's presence excited on one occasion. He had obtained permission to visit Bantama, a small town connected with the capital by a street, about a mile in length. This town is regarded as sacred, because it contains the fetish-house, which is the mausoleum of the kings of Ashantee (As-hánti). Europeans are very rarely allowed to visit it; and Mr. Freeman was informed, that he was the only white man who has been there during the reign of the present king. Even the inhabitants of Coomassie are prohibited from going there except when the king is present, who regularly visits the tombs of his ancestors every forty days. The conduct of Mr. Freeman, it appeared, was narrowly watched on the occasion; for, after he had passed, on his return, under the magnificent banyan trees which grow in this place, three men, belonging to the chief of Bantama, ran after him, and requested him to stop. Mr. Freeman had looked attentively at some beautiful parasite plants which grew upon one of the trees; his interpreter, moreover, had raised his hand, to protect his face from the twigs and leaves, as he passed beneath the trees in his palanquin; and it was concluded, that some leaves had been plucked, by Mr.

Freeman's direction, for the purpose of poisoning the king. The three men appeared satisfied with the explanations which Mr. Freeman offered; but immediately after he had got back to his quarters at Coomassie, (Kumási,) he deemed it proper to communicate to Apóko what had happened, expressing at the same time his regret, that he had been the object of unworthy suspicions.

Now, as Mr. Freeman was regarded at Coomassie as a great fetishman, it was doubtless supposed that he intended to make a fetish preparation of the leaves, for the purpose of effecting his supposed malevolent object,—the destruction of the king. It is not improbable, that one reason why such dread is entertained of the fetish practices which are made to injure others is, that they are often followed by the death, or serious injury, of the individuals marked out thereby for destruction. Secret poisoning is practised extensively among the Negroes of Guinea, as one of the most recent publications on that part of Africa (Laird and Oldfield's Narrative) sufficiently shows; and, by means of this fatal science, the fetishmen can effectually ensure the success of their mystical preparations.

The invocation of the aid of the fetish to kill or injure others, appears to be considered as a different offence from what is more strictly called

witchcraft. If any one in angry contention with
another is heard to wish he were dead, and that
person shortly after dies or becomes seriously ill,
the person who uttered the evil wish is accused
of bewitching the sufferer. It is imagined, that
when the wish is uttered, the evil spirit, or devil,
goes out of the speaker, and, seizing upon the
victim, inflicts upon him sickness and death. In
such cases, the mischief is supposed to be produced not by the fetish, but by the devil. These
offences are generally visited with severe punishment. On one occasion, William De Graft, and
others who accompanied him, were instrumental
in rescuing a poor old woman, whom they discovered secretly confined in irons, and who most
probably, but for their interference, would have
lost her life on a charge of witchcraft.

The practice of appealing to the fetishes by
taking oaths is a striking feature of the national
superstition.

The common "oath-draught," consisting of
water poured into a brass pan, containing a
bead, or some other material possessed of fetish
influence, is administered on various occasions.
Sometimes an individual is thereby sworn to
maintain silence on a given subject; at other
times, to tell all he knows. During the Gaman or Buntuku war, the Ashantee (As-hánti)
traders, before they set out from Coomassie,

were laid under the obligation of this oath, not to divulge anything which might be prejudicial to their sovereign, while they should remain at the settlements on the coast; and, on their return to the capital, the oath was again administered to them for the purpose of binding them faithfully to report every circumstance of a political character which had come within their knowledge while they were absent.

It appears to be the usual practice, before any important negotiation is commenced, to administer the oath to the linguists and interpreters, enjoining them, under the penalty of death, and the vengeance of the gods, to give a faithful interpretation of the words and sentiments of the speakers. In the negotiations between the Ashantees and the British, this was invariably attended to as a necessary preliminary to the commencement of the business; and the binding character of the oath, and the dread which it inspires, may be inferred from the fact, that Dupuis's interpreters were so terrified at the thought of taking the oath-draught, that they urged him, by the most moving entreaties, to prevail upon the king to exempt them from compliance.

The oath is administered also at the conclusion of a negotiation, in ratification of engagements which have been entered into.

William De Graft has heard his father state, that when the surrounding people deserted from the Ashantees, and joined the British under Sir Charles M'Carthy, the Fantee (Fánti) chiefs required them all to drink the oath-draught, binding themselves utterly to renounce their allegiance to the king of Ashantee, and be faithful to their new allies.

Oaths are also administered to criminals on public trials. In Ashantee (As-hánti) these are of various kinds. There are the oath by the king's foot; the oath by his father; and the oath "by Acromanti and Saturday." The latter is the great oath of Ashantee, and originated in the calamitous death of Osai Tutu the Great. It has already been stated, that this monarch, and his principal ministers and officers, were surprised and destroyed by a detachment of the enemy, as they were proceeding to join the Ashantee army which had gone against Asín. Many of the enemy who made the fatal attack were natives of a town called Acromanti, and the whole detachment had been sheltered there during the preceding night. The consequence was, that the town was doomed to utter destruction by the main body of the Ashantee army, and was burned to the ground; while all the living creatures which it contained, men, women, cattle, and fowls, except such as were conse-

crated to the fetish, bled in expiation of the great
offence.

This work of extermination took place on a
Saturday; and, ever since, that day has been
placed, in the calendar, in the list of days stig-
matized by the Ashantees as days which forebode
evil, and which are consequently dedicated to
expiatory and propitiatory sacrifices; and no man
will commence on Saturday the most trivial
undertaking. From that time also, the phrase
which, in the native language, awakens the recollection of " Acromanti and Saturday," has been
regarded as an oath of the most fearful import.
The words themselves are deemed too sacred to
be uttered, unless in a whisper between friends;
and this terrible oath is most commonly taken by
inference only in the use of some such expression as, "The dreadful day," or, "The day of
God's chastisement." Dupuis states that he has
had the opportunity of observing at court, that
the mere utterance of these expressions has
instantly clouded every brow, and stamped the
expression of woe on every countenance, from
that of the king himself to that of the slave;
that some who were not men of influence at
court, or who were involved in litigious palavers,
and had especial cause to dread the royal displeasure, have immediately rushed out; and that
others, who have remained, have covered their

faces with both hands, uttering, at the same time, an invocation to the patron gods to protect them from the ominous import of those words, and the direful effects of the king's wrath or sorrow.

The oath chiefly administered in criminal cases is Adúm.   The draught is an infusion of the bark of a tree, called by that name, in about half-a-gallon of water.   The person charged with crime is required to drink the nauseous mixture ; and it is believed, that if he be innocent, his stomach will reject it, but if guilty, it will not make him sick. But let the reader mark the principle which is here involved.   It is supposed that the fetish goes down with the water into the man's stomach, and looks about in his heart for the guilt; that if he discovers the prisoner to be innocent, he comes back with the draught which is vomited up again ; but that if he finds the alleged guilt, he remains in the stomach with the water to inflict upon the culprit the merited punishment.   Bosman remarks that the draught, under the supposed influence of the fetish, was expected to cause the criminal to burst, especially when the offender was a woman who had been required to take it as the test of her guilt or innocence on a charge of adultery.   Has this custom originated in the Jewish law for trying suspected wives ?

When the innocence of the accused has been

established by the vomiting up of the water, powdered chalk is put upon his head, shoulders, breast, and back ; he is clothed in a white dress, and led round the town in triumph. In this procession, muskets are fired, and proclamation is made that the innocence of their friend, who was charged with crime, had been established by the fetish.

To administer Adúm is the most valued mode of trial. Witnesses may be called to substantiate the charge ; but this is regarded as a tedious mode of proceeding. It is deemed better to make the prisoner drink Adúm at once, because then the fetish himself goes into the man, and is sure to find out the truth !

The binding character of oaths, and the extent to which they are used, may be further proved by an occurrence which took place while Mr. Hutchinson was resident at Coomassie (Kumási). One morning, a slave, belonging to the house-master, swore, by the king's head, that the king must kill him that day. A great uproar immediately ensued. Some put the man in irons, and others hastily brought out the family-stools ; fowls and sheep were sacrificed, and the blood was poured upon the stools to turn away the wrath of the king from the family ; and a formal notification was then made to the king of what had happened. The person who took the rash oath had been guilty of an offence, and apprehended that he should be put to the torture; to avoid which, and to ensure speedy death, he swore that the king must shoot him with eight muskets. According to Ashantee (As-hánti) custom, the king was bound to perform the oath; but he determined that the man should not have the benefit which he anticipated from that mode of execution, and ordered that small shot should be put into the musket so that he might not be killed outright, but left to die a lingering death. As the oath, however, happened to be taken on the fetish-day of the king, he had it in his power to postpone the execution, and some weeks elapsed before it actually took place.

This delay was the occasion of fresh troubles and alarms. One day, a nephew of the king called to see Mr. Hutchinson: but he was afraid to pass the man in irons, lest he should swear that, when the king killed him, he must kill his own nephew also; and had the man sworn to that effect, the king would have been under obligation to put him to death. To enable the prince to avoid the presence of the criminal, Mr. Hutchinson let him out of the house by a private door; and, on a subsequent day, he afforded the same friendly privilege to Apóko, who had called upon him for some medicine; and who also dreaded a sight of the man in irons.

At length, as the king resolved to reserve the criminal for execution at the Adai custom, he was removed to a more retired place of confinement, as very few persons of rank dared to visit Mr. Hutchinson so long as he remained upon the premises.

One of the revolting barbarities inflicted upon human victims, previously to their being sacrificed, results from the dread which is entertained of oaths. In the descriptions which have been given of the great Ashantee festivals, the victims are represented as appearing in the procession with knives thrust through their cheeks and lips; and this is a precaution to prevent them from uttering rash oaths. When a person is selected for execution, he is suddenly thrown down, and his mouth is at once skewered up with a knife to hinder him from swearing the death of any person or persons whom he might be disposed to mark out for destruction.

CHAPTER IX.

THE POPULAR SUPERSTITIONS—CONCLUDED.

The religious Customs to be classed among the darkest Features of the national Superstition—Immolation of Prisoners taken in War required by the Gods—Two Thousand Prisoners destroyed on royal Death-Stool—Fetish Practices at Birth ; and Interrogation by Priest after Death—Funeral Ceremonies—Sacrifice of human Beings at Funerals—Wives buried alive with dead Husbands—Wives of King of Dahomy destroy themselves—Horrifying Funeral Scenes in Coomassie—Celebration of annual Yam-Custom—Catching Deer for Fetish at Winnebah—Yam-Custom in Ashantee accompanied with most revolting Practices—Scenes of Blood at Adai-Custom—Remarks on Nature and Tendency of the popular Superstition—Its baneful Effect upon the public Morals—It is the Source of the inhuman Practices which so extensively prevail—Son of Dinkara—The Influence of the popular Superstition in fostering the two great Evils of African Society, Slavery and Polygamy.

THE great Religious Customs, which are to be classed among the darkest features of the national superstition, yet remain for consideration. The immolation of prisoners taken in war is one of those revolting practices ; for it is presented to our notice, not as the effect of the ungovernable passions of the conquerors, breaking loose from the restraints and obligations of religion, but as an expression of pious zeal and devotion. It results from the principle recognised by the king of Ashantee, (As-hánti,) in a conversation to which reference has been previously made: that "the fetish makes war for strong men, because they can then pay plenty of gold, and proper sacrifice." To obtain a supply of victims for their altars, is thus a principal end for which the national deities are supposed to promote war; and the sacrifice of their prisoners consequently becomes a religious obligation on the part of the people. Dreadful are the scenes of barbarity which are exhibited after a victorious campaign. After the Gaman war, full two thousand prisoners were destroyed, by the most refined tortures, over the royal deathstool in Coomassie, (Kumási,) in honour of the fetish, and of the shades of departed kings and heroes; and at the commencement of the war which brought the Ashantees into hostile collision with the British, when the Asíns were overthrown near the Prah, the horrid work of sacrificing the prisoners went on at the little temple on the banks of the river, by night as well as by day, until thousands had perished. In the national songs which celebrated the latter victory, the principle which requires the sacrifice of prisoners was distinctly recognised; and the bards exultingly sang that " a river of perjured blood flowed from

Miasa to the Prah, and *propitiated the wrath of the river-god.*"

The customs for the dead may be prefaced by an account of the practices which are resorted to on the birth of children; for the purpose of connecting, in one view, the influences which superstition exerts upon the Negro, from his entrance into the world to the time of his leaving it. In some places, as soon as a child is born, the fetishman is sent for, who binds certain fetish preparations around his limbs, using, at the same time, a form of incantation or prayer. This is done to fortify the infant against all kinds of evil. Circumcision is practised by some people; but if inquiry is made respecting the origin or design of the custom, they are unable to assign any other reason for it, than that it has come down to them from their ancestors.

In Fantee, (Fánti,) the child usually receives his name at the time prescribed by the Levitical law for the practice of circumcision. On the eighth day after the birth, the father of the child, accompanied by a number of friends, proceeds to the house of the mother. If he be a rich man, he takes with him a gallon of ardent spirits, to be used on the festive occasion. On arriving at the house, the friends form a circle around the father, who delivers a kind of address, in which he acknowledges the kindness of the gods for giving

to him the child, and calls upon those present also
to thank the fetishes on his account. Then,
taking the child in his arms, he squirts upon him
from his mouth a little of the ardent spirits, and
pronounces the name by which he is to be called,
—usually the name of some relative or friend,—
at the same time offering a prayer that he may
live to be old, and become a stay and support to
the family, and may have the protection of the
departed spirit of him after whom he is named ;
or, if the friend be still living, that he may prove
worthy of the name which has been given to
him ; upon which, the friend referred to advances
towards his infant name-sake, and hangs round his
neck a trinket of gold, or a valuable bead ; and
continues afterwards to manifest a peculiar interest in the child, by sending him occasional presents, and showing him other special attentions.

A second name which the child usually takes,
is that of the day of the week on which he was
born. The following are the names of the days
in the Fantee (Fantí) language, varied in their
orthography according to the sex of the child :—

	MALES.	FEMALES.
Sunday	Quĕsi	Akosúa
Monday	Kújoh	Ajúa
Tuesday	Quábĭna	Abínaba
Wednesday	Quáku	Ekúa
Thursday	Quáhu	Abá
Friday	Kŭfí	Efúa
Saturday	Quámina	Ama

It is frequently the case that children **are** specially devoted to the service of the fetish before they are born ; and even death is not **an** immediate deliverance from fetish practices and ceremonies.   When a native departs this life, inquiry is instituted as to the cause of his decease, and particularly if it were somewhat sudden and unlooked for.   To ascertain this point, the dead person is himself interrogated. According to Bosman, persons are appointed **to** take the corpse upon their shoulders, when the priest enumerates the supposed causes of his death, and requires to know which was the real one ; it being believed, that when that is mentioned, the persons supporting the corpse will be constrained, by some secret power, to bend forwards towards the priest.   The object of this examination is not to ascertain whether the individual has died of natural disease, and what was the malady ; but whether he has not been poisoned by the secret practices of some one ; or whether his friends have not neglected, during his illness, to make suitable offerings to the fetish for his recovery ; or whether he himself had not been guilty of neglect of his duty to the fetish. The answer obtained is always that which is best calculated to promote the designs of the priest, or to further the plans which he had previously arranged with some of the friends of the deceased.

Such serious *palavers*, however, frequently resulted
from these *post-mortem* interrogations, that the
British authorities have endeavoured to discoun-
tenance them among those of the natives who,
since the Ashantee war, have been led to depend
upon England for protection.

In Fantee (Fánti) the preparations for a
funeral commence by washing the corpse, array-
ing the dead person in his best garments, and
adorning him with his trinkets and beads. He
is then laid on a sofa, in a room, the walls of
which are covered, either wholly or in part, with
red cloth. A silk umbrella is fastened to the wall
over the head of the corpse, and a table is placed
near it, covered with viands and wine for the use
of the departed spirit. The family then commence a loud wailing, which attracts the neighbours to the house, and the females generally join
in the lamentation.

Every party of relatives or friends coming from
a distance to join in the Custom, bring a suitable
present, and are accompanied with drums and
muskets. On their arrival, they give their
presents to the individual having the charge or
direction of the funeral, who is usually one of the
principal persons of the family of the deceased.
They then fire their muskets, and begin to
beat their drums. The director of the funeral-
custom takes a regular account of the presents

received, in order that a similar compliment may be returned, when the head of the family of the donors may be removed by death.

After a few days, the dead person is buried in his own house, or, if he be a young man, in the house of his father. And on the principle that individuals assume, in another world, the state which they maintained in this, the head of a family is interred in his best clothes and ornaments; gold-dust is also put into his grave; and sheep and cattle, at least, are slain on the occasion. Drumming, firing, dancing, wailings, shoutings, and other extravagant proceedings, take place when the soil is thrown upon the corpse; and food and drink are placed upon the grave.

If the deceased was rich, the Custom is continued, perhaps for a month, until the family are nearly reduced to want; as they are obliged to support all the parties who attended the funeral from a distance, so long as they remain. A funeral is usually absolute ruin to a poor family. Whether they can afford it or not, the Custom must be observed; and the survivors are obliged to find money to meet the expenses. The practice of persons borrowing money of others, and engaging to remunerate the lender by their future services, (a practice which cannot be regarded without suspicion, as liable to great abuse,) is very much promoted by funeral-customs. Many poor persons, on the death of the head of their family, have been obliged to become "pawns" to others, in order to obtain sufficient money to meet the unavoidable expense.

The funeral-custom is renewed at the end of twelve months, when sheep and cattle are killed in honour of the deceased. Every year, after this, a little rum and food is placed upon the grave by the relatives; and even if the house has gone to decay, or has been pulled down, they will not fail to repair to the spot with the accustomed annual offering.

Up to a comparatively late period, human sacrifices were publicly offered at funeral-customs in the immediate neighbourhood of the coast. Bosman mentions one at which he himself witnessed eleven persons put to death; among whom was an individual who, having endured exquisite torture, was then delivered up to a child of six years of age, by whom his head was, after much difficulty, finally sawed from his body. Meredith states, that, in the year 1800, when a king of Apollonia died, one or two human beings were sacrificed every Saturday, until the great-custom took place, which did not happen until six months after his decease; when upwards of fifty persons were sacrificed, and two of his youngest wives were put alive with his corpse into the grave, wherein was deposited a considerable quantity of gold, and several rich cloths. The lid of the coffin was covered with human blood, on which gold-dust was sprinkled. And Dupuis says that he himself has known many unhappy victims sacrificed in the last few years, within gun-shot of the castles. He mentions expressly the case of two men and two women, who were butchered, with the greatest barbarity, under the very walls of the fort at Accra; and adds, that at Tantum, Apollonia, Dix Cove, Succondee, and Chamah, the same class of murders was perpetrated with impunity. In a recent letter the Rev. Mr. Brooking mentions, that a person had just perished under the sacrificial knife at Dutch Accra. Since the Ashantee invasions, the power of the Fantees has been so greatly broken, and their numbers are so much reduced, that the British government, to which they are obliged to look for protection, has been enabled to put down these inhuman practices within the sphere of its immediate influence.

In the independent States in the interior, the funeral-customs of the rich and great exhibit spectacles of the most horrifying barbarity. In some cases many of the wives, and in others a great number of slaves, are, on these occasions, sent after the deceased, to enable him to maintain his proper rank in another world. At the instant

when a king of Dahomy dies, a dreadful scene
takes place in the palace. The wives of the
deceased monarch begin to break and destroy
his ornaments, and everything valuable belonging to themselves, and then to kill each other.
When Adahunzun died, two hundred and eighty
of his wives thus perished, before his successor
could arrive at the palace and put a stop to the
carnage; and, at the funeral of the deceased
king, all these victims were buried in the same
grave, with six of the remaining living wives.

In Ashantee, (As-hánti,) when a person of distinction dies, the slaves immediately rush out of
the house, to hide themselves in the bush; as a
slave or two are instantly sacrificed in order to
attend upon the spirit of the deceased until the
custom shall take place. It has been stated,
that the king of Ashantee, in his last battle
with the British at Dodowah, whenever it was
announced to him that any of his captains had
been killed, immediately caused slaves to be immolated to accompany them into the other world.

When Mr. Bowdich was at Coomassie, (Kumási,) he had the opportunity of witnessing a
funeral-custom for the mother of one of the
principal caboceers; and he states, that, as soon
as she had breathed her last, the king, her son,
and another of the nobles, each sacrificed a
young girl, that the deceased might not be alto-

gether without attendants, until the Custom
should take place.   The relatives and adherents
of the family then presented contributions of
gold, powder, rum, and cloth, to be expended at
the funeral; but the king, as the heir of all his
subjects, sent a larger present than any other,
except the nearest relative who succeeded to the
stool and the slaves.   He also sent a sum of gold,
and some valuable cloths, to be buried with the
deceased.

On the day of the funeral, an extraordinary
scene presented itself.   Walking out about noon,
Mr. Bowdich and his friends saw the vultures
hovering over two headless trunks, scarcely cold;
and were passed by several troops of women,
from fifty to a hundred each, who danced along
in a movement resembling skaiting, lauding and
bewailing the deceased in the most dismal strains.
Other women carried on their heads rich cloths
and silks, and other valuables which had belonged
to her.   All these women were profusely
daubed with red earth, in barbarous imitation
of those who had succeeded in besmearing
themselves with the blood of the victims.
The rush of the crowd was most tumultuous;
and the noise of the horns, drums, and muskets,
with the yells, groans, and screechings, which were
heard in every direction, produced a stunning
effect.   Now and then a victim was hurried along

at full speed, by persons, the savage delight of whose countenances gave them a fiend-like appearance; and the chiefs and captains arrived in rapid succession, their approach being announced by the peculiar flourishes of their horns, and the firing of muskets. Presently the king's arrival in the market-place was made known; and the crowd rolled impetuously towards it; but the sabres of the soldiers, which were freely used, hewed a way for the procession. The son of the deceased led the van, dancing from side to side like a bacchanal, and appearing as though he was intoxicated with the adulatory praises which were bellowed forth by his attendants. He looked upon the victims, who had large knives passed through their cheeks, with a savage joy, bordering on frenzy; while they regarded him with indifference or apathy. The other chiefs and captains, adorned in all the splendour of their fetish dresses, followed in the train.

On arriving at the market-place, the king was seen seated with his usual attendants and state-display. Thirteen victims, surrounded by their executioners, in black shaggy caps and vests, were pressed together by the crowd at his left hand. The troops of women already described, paraded on the outside of the circle, vociferating the dirge, and the utmost powers of the horns and drums were called forth. A discharge of musketry then took place near the king, which spread round the circle, and was continued without intermission for an hour. The soldiers kept their stations; but the chiefs, after firing their muskets, bounded once round the area with the gesture and extravagant behaviour of maniacs, followed by their sycophants, who waved flags over their heads and roared forth their "strong names." The head fetishwoman of the family was at the same time observed rushing through the ranks as the muskets were fired, and screaming as though in the greatest agonies. The firing having somewhat subsided, rum and palmwine were copiously drunk; and the principal females of the family, many of whom were described as being very handsome, and of elegant figures, came forward to dance.

A present of sheep and rum having been exchanged between the king and the son of the deceased, the drums announced the sacrifice of the victims, who were visited by all the chiefs in turn. The executioners struggled with each other for the bloody office, the victims looking on, meanwhile, with marvellous apathy. At length an executioner, snatching a sword, lopped off the right hand of one of the victims, who was then thrown down and had his head sawed, rather than cut, from the body. The remaining twelve were, in like manner, mangled and butchered upon the spot; and others, principally females, were provided, to be sacrificed in the bush where the body was interred. Slaves, however, are not the only victims on such occasions; for it is usual to "wet the grave" with the blood of at least one respectable freeman. The heads of all the slaves who have perished having been placed in the grave, several of the retainers of the family are called in a hurry to assist in lowering the coffin; when, just as it touches the heads which pave the bottom of the grave, one of the freemen is stunned by a violent blow, a deep gash is cut in the back part of his neck, he is rolled in upon the body, and the grave is instantly filled up.

After this, the firing, drinking, singing, and dancing were kept up during several days; and it was understood that, had not the approaching war with Gaman enforced the necessity of economizing powder, there would have been eight Great Customs for the deceased, instead of this one; at the last of which the king himself would have fired. On the last day of the Custom, all the females connected with the family paraded round the town, singing a kind of grateful acknowledgment of the services of those who had assisted at the Custom.

The funeral-customs for kings and members of the royal family are conducted on a scale corresponding with the rank of the deceased. The okras, who are slaves peculiarly devoted to the king, and distinguished by a large circle of gold suspended from the neck, amounting in number to more than a hundred, are always sacrificed, with many women, on the tomb of the king. When Osai Quamina died, the funeral-custom was repeated every week for three months, two hundred slaves being sacrificed, and twenty-five barrels of powder being fired on each occasion; but when the king's brother died, during the invasion of Fantee, the king devoted three thousand victims, two thousand of whom were Fantee prisoners, and nearly one thousand more were furnished by various towns; making, in the whole, about four thousand human beings who perished at the grave of this royal personage.

When the king dies, Ashantee is, in fact, one vast Aceldama; for all the customs which have been made for deceased subjects during his reign, must be repeated by their families, simultaneously with the custom which is celebrated, in all the excess of extravagance and barbarity, for the departed monarch himself. During the first two or three days after the death of the king, scarcely any one is safe; for the relatives of the king, bursting forth with their muskets, carry havock and death around; and few persons, even of the highest rank, dare, for a time, to stir from their houses. The funeral-customs of the kings of Ashantee are frequently repeated; and Bantama, the royal sepulchre, is ever and anon made to reek with the blood of newly-slain victims.

The annual Yam-Custom furnishes another exhibition of the true character of the national superstitions. This festival is celebrated about the end of the month of August, or the beginning of September, when the yam is ready for use; and the feast is intended as a public acknowledgment, on the part of the people, of the kindness of the fetishes in preserving them through another year, and permitting them to see the new yam.

In Fantee, (Fánti,) all the inhabitants of the towns assemble under the shade of the grove adjoining the fetish-house or temple; when a sheep or a number of fowls are killed; part of the flesh of which is mixed with boiled yams and palm-oil, and a portion of this mixture being placed upon the heads of the images, the remainder is thrown about before the temple, as a heave-offering to the deities. When the heave-offering has been presented, the fetishmen receive from the people the offerings of rum which they have brought; and, after placing a little upon the heads of the images, and pouring out a small quantity upon the ground before the temple, they invite all the fetishes to come and partake of it, saying, " When people eat, they need to drink also."

In this invitation, all the fetishes of the place are mentioned by name, which, as in the case of Cape-Coast town, where there are seventy-seven guardian-deities, is sometimes a tedious enumeration. And it is worthy of special remark, that the name of *Yankumpon* is, occasionally at least, placed at the head of the list. The remainder of the sheep and fowls, not used in the offering to the fetishes, is made into a kind of soup, of which no persons but the priests and priestesses are allowed to eat; but the people also partake of the residue of the rum. When the priests have finished their repast, the people begin to beat the drums, and sing fetish songs, to which the priests dance; and the festivity is often prolonged throughout the night.

The celebration of the Yam-Custom at Winnebah is attended with one peculiarity. The principal fetish at that place, it is believed, will not be satisfied with sheep, but he must have a deer brought alive to his temple, and there sacrificed. Accordingly, on the appointed day, every year, when the Custom is to be celebrated, almost the whole of the inhabitants, except the aged and infirm, go out into the adjoining country, which, studded with clumps of trees and bushes, has a park-like appearance; and, while the women and children look on, the men proceed to strike the thicket with sticks, at

the same time beating drums, and hallooing with
all their might. While thus engaged, sometimes
a leopard or panther starts forth; but it is usually
so frightened with the noise and confusion, that it
scampers off in one direction as fast as the people
run from it in another. When a deer bursts out,
the chace begins, and the people attempt to run it
down. At length it is perhaps tumbled upon the
ground, by the sticks which are thrown at its
legs, when the people seize it, and exultingly
carry it off to the town, with shouting and drumming. On entering, they are met by the aged
persons with staves; and, having gone in procession round the town, they proceed to the
fetish-house, where the animal is sacrificed, and
partly offered to the fetish, and partly eaten by
the priests. The catching of the deer is described
as an animated scene; and European gentlemen
not unfrequently go from Annamaboe (Anamabú)
to witness it. In 1839, the people succeeded in
catching two deer, which were both offered to
the fetish.

The annual Yam-Custom is continued during
several days; and is followed or closed by what
the English have termed the " Black-Christmas,"
when the people put on their best clothes, and
visit each other. On entering the house, they
shake hands with all the inmates, congratulating
them, and wishing they may live to see another

year. On this occasion, the chiefs bring out their large umbrellas, and all make the best display which their circumstances will afford. In about three weeks after this, the ceremony of turning the devil out of the towns takes place, and the people conclude that they have then made a promising commencement of the year.

At the time of the Yam-Custom in Ashantee, (As-hánti,) there is a great national assembly in the capital. All the caboceers, and the tributary sovereigns, or their representatives, are required to be present, except those who have been sent to a distance on urgent public business; and it is at this annual festival that suspected chiefs are usually placed upon their trial. During the whole of the festival, the greatest licentiousness and immorality prevail, and both sexes abandon themselves to their passions without restraint.

At a Yam-Custom which Mr. Bowdich saw, there was a display of the same barbarous splendour which is witnessed on all state-occasions; and this was made on the largest possible scale, seeing that there was present a full representation of all the power and wealth of the empire. Spectacles the most appalling were also exhibited on the occasion. Every caboceer, as he arrived, sacrificed a slave at the gate of the capital by which he entered; and, in the procession of the first day, all the heads of the kings and caboceers who had been conquered, from the reign of Osai Tutu down to that time, with those who had been executed for rebellion, were carried by two parties of executioners, each consisting of upwards of a hundred individuals. In the skulls were inserted sprigs of thyme, to prevent the spirits of the deceased from troubling the king; and as the bearers of those horrid trophies passed along in an impassioned dance, they clashed their knives upon the skulls either with the most frightful gestures, or with an expression of indescribable irony and ridicule. The festivity was kept up during the greater part of the night; and on the following morning, which happened to be the Christian sabbath, the king ordered a large quantity of rum to be poured into brass pans, for the use of the people, in various parts of the town. A most beastly scene resulted; for, in less than an hour, excepting the principal men, not a sober individual was to be seen. Towards the evening, another splendid procession took place. The third day was chiefly occupied with state-palavers; and on the day after, (Tuesday,) the assembly broke up, and the caboceers took their leave.

In the course of these proceedings, about one hundred persons were killed at various places in the capital. Several slaves were also sacrificed at the royal sepulchre of Bantama, over the enormous brass pan which is used there for

sacrificial purposes; and the streaming blood of
the victims was mingled with various vegetable
and animal matter, partly fresh and partly putre-
fied, for the purpose of making the most powerful fetish. All the chiefs, likewise, killed several
slaves, and caused their blood to flow into the
holes from which the new yams were taken; and
those who could not afford to kill slaves, took
the head of one already sacrificed, and placed it
upon the hole.

In about ten days after the Custom, the king
attends in the market-place, and the whole of the
royal household eat new yams for the first time.
On the day after, the king and his principal captains, followed by almost all the inhabitants of the
capital, set out early, for Sarasú, to perform their
annual ablutions in the river Dah. The king is
attended by his suite at the river; but he laves
the water with his hands over his own person,
his chairs, stools, gold and silver plate, and the
various articles of furniture used especially by
himself. One sheep and one goat are sacrificed
at the time; and several brass pans, with various
fetish preparations under them, are placed on the
ground, covered with white cloth. Twenty sheep
are also dipped in the water, and reserved to be
sacrificed on the return to the palace. Their blood
is poured upon the door-posts and the stools; and
all the doors, windows, and arcades of the palace,

as well as the stools of the several tribes and families, are profusely besmeared with a mixture of eggs and palm-oil. On entering the palace, the fetishmen walk first, with attendants, carrying basins of sacred water, into which they dip branches of trees, and sprinkle the water over the chiefs and principal persons, some of whom run to have a little poured upon their heads, and also upon their tongues. The king and all his attendants wear white clothes on the occasion; and three white lambs are led before him, intended to be sacrificed at his bed-chamber.

It has already been shown, that, in the interior, time is divided into periods of three weeks, and that the first of the three is regarded as the good week, and is called Adai. The Ashantees honour its return by a religious festival, termed "the Adai-Custom;" and this is distinguished again as "great" or "little," for reasons which have not been fully ascertained. The great and the little Customs, however, appear to alternate with regularity, so that one of each is celebrated every three weeks. At the setting of the sun on the evening previous to the Custom, the great death-drum, which stands at the gate of the palace, is struck with much force; on hearing which signal, all the persons connected with the royal household shout, and their exclamations are echoed by the people throughout the capital. Music and firing are continued through the night; and on the next morning, the king proceeds to the fetish-house, opposite to the palace, and offers in sacrifice several sheep, whose blood is poured on the golden stool, which is regarded as the palladium of the kingdom. There is then a numerous assemblage of all ranks in the palace-yard. A great display takes place; and it has been calculated, that the king, on every such occasion, makes presents to the superior captains and others, amounting in value to the sum of four hundred pounds sterling.

This Custom, also, is frequently accompanied by scenes most revolting to humanity. Mr. Hutchinson remarks, that the greatest sacrifice of human life which took place while he resided at Coomassie, (Kumási,) occurred on the eve of the little Adai-Custom. He had a friendly caution given him respecting it, from a quarter which he did not feel himself at liberty to name. "Christian," said his kind monitor, "take care and watch over your family: the angel of death has drawn his sword, and will strike on the neck of many Ashantees. When the drum is struck on Adai-eve, it will be the death-signal of many. Shun the king if you can, but fear not." As the time approached to beat the drum, and Mr. Hutchinson sat meditating on the horrors of the ensuing night, he suddenly received a message to attend the king. This was a somewhat startling summons, as obnoxious caboceers are frequently thus sent for on such occasions, ostensibly to talk a palaver, but, on entering the palace, they are seized and led to execution. Mr. Hutchinson, however, waited upon the king; and, while he remained with him, the officers appointed to attend the sacrifices came in with their knives, and other weapons of destruction.

The design of this sacrifice was, to propitiate the fetish, and secure its assistance in the approaching war with Buntuku. The bones of the king's mother and sisters were, in the first place, taken out of their coffins, and bathed in rum and water; and after having been wiped with silks, they were rolled in gold-dust, and wrapped in strings of rock-gold, aggry beads, and other most costly materials. Those against whom the king had any cause of complaint, were then sent for in succession, and immolated as they entered, in order that " their blood might water the graves" of the royal personages, whose bones had been exhumed. During the whole of the night, the king's executioners traversed the city, and all whom they met were dragged away for execution; but the intended massacre having by some means become known, the king was disappointed in securing many of the most distinguished individuals, who had been marked out as victims. Next morning desolation seemed to reign over the capital, and no persons appeared in the market-place, but the king and his attendants. When the day closed, the human sacrifices were again renewed; and during the night, the bones of the royal deceased were removed to the sacred tomb at Bantama, accompanied by a splendid procession. The chiefs and their attendants were all habited in their military costume; the stools, and all the ornaments used on great occasions, were borne by the proper officers; the human victims, in chains, with their hands tied behind them, preceded the bones; while at intervals, the chanting of the war-song indicated the eagerness which prevailed to march against the enemy. When the procession returned, on the following day, the king proceeded to the market-place; his horns sounded the well-known "wow, wow, wow," interpreted, "death, death, death;" and the work of sacrifice was at once resumed. The king sat with a goblet of palm-wine in his hand, and every time the executioners cut off a head, he imitated a dancing motion in his chair. The terrors of the day ended when the king returned to his palace; and the chiefs, issuing from their places of concealment, paraded the streets, rejoicing that they had, for that time, escaped death.

A similar description is given of the little Adai-Custom, by Dupuis. The city, he remarks, exhibited the most deplorable solitude; and the few human beings who were courageous enough to show themselves in the streets, fled at the approach of a captain, and barricadoed their doors, to avoid being shot, or dragged to sacrifice. The doleful cries of the women vibrated from various parts of the city; and the death-horns and drums seemed to stupify the obnoxious prisoners and foreign slaves with terror, as clearly indicating the dangers to which they were exposed. It is a curious fact, that a number of elderly Negroes in Jamaica, when they heard the journal of the Rev. Mr. Freeman read to them by a Missionary, immediately recognised the names of places at which they had formerly been, and appeared to retain a most vivid recollection of the fear-inspiring sound of the great death-drum at Coomassie. The second day of the Custom exhibited a similar train of horrors; and human blood again flowed in torrents, at the dictate of this sanguinary superstition.

It would be an easy task to enlarge this horrifying picture. The religious customs of the neighbouring country of Dahomy, whose barbarous monarch paves the approaches to his residence, and ornaments the battlements of his palace, with the skulls of his victims,—and the gigantic fetish-tree at Badagry, the wide-spreading branches of which are laden with human carcases and limbs,—would alone furnish abundant matter for amplification. But further research is unnecessary. The reader will now be able to form a tolerably correct estimate of the nature and tendency of the popular superstition. The range of its influence, it is seen, is almost without limit. It holds its votaries in a state of perpetual thraldom. They cannot eat or drink without recognising its authority. They cannot cultivate their ground, undertake a journey, enter into any negotiation, or engage in any business, but in obedience to its requirements. And both the practice of medicine, and the administration of justice, being under its control, it regulates the proceedings in all questions affecting property, and life, and health.

The baneful effect which such a system must have upon public morals, especially demands attention. What, indeed, must be the morals of a people where unchastity in unmarried women is no disgrace; where prostitution is even regarded as a virtue; where the priesthood is employed in promoting and concealing the intrigues of faithless wives; and where religion sanctions instead of discountenancing crime, and even lends the aid of its influence to him who cherishes injurious intentions against the property and life

of another! Bosman, an accurate observer of
men and things, remarks that "murder, adultery,
thieving, and all other such-like crimes, are here
accounted no sins." And Meredith, whose testimony and opinion are equally deserving of respect,
says, "The religious system of the natives has no
tendency whatever to improve their morality. It
consists almost entirely in a superstitious dread
of suffering from some malign influence, and in
the faith they repose in the fetishes or charms
which are furnished by the fetishmen, or priests,
for the purpose of warding off the dreaded evil."
This is a correct view of the case. The practical
religion of the people does not consist in the
exercise of the moral virtues, but in a careful
performance of fetish practices and ceremonies.
According as a person attends to or neglects
these, he is regarded either as a good or a bad
man; and it follows, that so far as the natives
refrain from the grossest acts of immorality, they
are influenced by other motives than those which
their religion furnishes.

A careful examination of the national religion
unfolds the true source of the barbarous practices which so extensively prevail. Was nothing
known of the superstitions of the people, it might
remain a matter of doubt, whether in the whole-
sale butchery of their enemies, they were not
merely indulging their own savage instincts, like

the wild beasts of the forest. In the absence of information on that subject, the interpretation of the following passages from Dupuis would be attended with difficulty.

"The wars of the king," says the writer, "were shortly after introduced as a subject of general discussion. That of Gaman was the favourite subject; and the king occasionally took up the thread of the narrative, or elucidated such events as were perhaps not generally known. As he caused the linguists to interpret to me the particular feats of himself, the king of Banna, and Apóko, his eyes sparkled with fiery animation; and at one period, he threw himself into a sort of theatrical attitude, which appeared to be unpremeditated and unaffected. He then seemed to be wrapped up within himself in delightful cogitations; and at this crisis, some of the auditors, like the bards of olden time, rose to the hum of the war-song, and recited their parts in a pleasing mellifluous strain. The king enjoyed the scene in ecstasy, and frequently motioned with his body and feet, in cadence with the metre of the verse. This reverie and the recitation occupied many minutes, and were ultimately succeeded by irony and satire cast upon the memory of his fallen enemy. 'His skull was broken,' said the king, 'but I would not lose the trophy, and now I have made a similar skull of gold. This is for

my great Customs, that all the people may know
I am the king.'

"A slave was deputed to one of the apart-
ments of the palace; and as he returned, he deposited a chair which, His Majesty said, was the
regal seat of Dinkara. This piece of workmanship was studded all over with gold and silver
ornaments, and silver coin of different European
States. The slave again disappeared, and returned, bringing under his escort a son of that
unfortunate monarch, one of the few male survivors of the race of Dinkara. A pallid hue, if
so it may be termed, overspread the jetty features
of the youth, as he bowed trembling before
the king. The angry glance which marked his
reception excited the most painful apprehensions,
and the countenance of the young man spoke
woful agony, as he endeavoured to scan the
purport of the summons.

" 'Your father,' said the king, addressing himself to the prince, 'was a rebel; he was full of
pride, and wanted to be a great king; he forgot
when he was my slave. Is not this true? Then
he wanted Sarem to help him, and sent gold to
make friends. Is not that true, too? He forgot
I was his master; he killed my sword-bearers,
and sent me an insulting message. Now I have
his skull, and the jaw-bones of his captains. His
wives, and you, and all the people, are my slaves;

and when I tell you to die, you shall die as your brother did; but now you shall serve me.'

"The king then desired him to strip off his robe, and show me the wounds he had received in battle. The unhappy youth did as he was instructed, pointing to five or six honourable scars upon his breast, arms, and thighs, which had the appearance of gun-shot wounds. 'Now,' said the king to him, with a stern, sarcastic apathy, ' you know your father was a fool, and that I am the king; you did not know that before; and so now go home until I send for you again.' "

It is added that this unfortunate youth had been compelled, in the presence of the king, to join a chorus in the cruel *epicedium,* or "death-song," which preceded his brother's sacrifice:— an execution which was performed in his presence, with torture, and amidst the mockery and derision of the whole court.

The inquiry naturally arises, On what principle could such a character as that described in the preceding quotations be formed? What had produced the feeling which, from its settledness and malignity, indicated the demon rather than the man, and made the monarch appear as the very personification of infernal revenge? Was he remarkable for his natural ferocity and savageness of disposition? The reverse was the case. He was polite and affable in his general

manners; and especially characterized by his
tender and affectionate treatment of his children.
To his *religion* this fearful trait in his character
must be traced. That taught him to regard his
captive as an implacable foe, who would carry his
enmity beyond the grave, and of whom, as an
evil spirit, even after death he would have to
beware. That instructed him, moreover, to believe that the torture and sacrifice of an
enemy are peculiarly acceptable to the deities
whom he worshipped. " A Negro," says Dupuis,
" can hardly be persuaded that an enemy
might be converted into a friend; and, as he
naturally thirsts after his gold, if he is so far
successful, nothing can satiate him short of his
opponent's blood, which is esteemed the portion
of the spoil due to the tutelar gods, (and acceptable to the shades of his ancestors,) whose service
it is incumbent on him not to neglect, lest their
wrath should overwhelm him on a future day."
This solves the difficulty, and shows on what principle the most diabolical revenge is sometimes
combined in the same individual with great
natural affection. When once it is ascertained
that a people are thoroughly imbued with the
persuasion, that the deities, whom they regard
as the arbiters of their own fate, require human
sacrifices as the most acceptable offerings which
their votaries can possibly present; that those

deities, in fact, employ themselves in promoting and fomenting war, in order that their altars may continually reek with blood;—when once it is found that such a persuasion is the governing principle, the dreadful scenes which occur in Ashantee (As-hánti) cease to create surprise, as it is evident that such practices must naturally result from such deep-rooted and prevalent principles.

The popular superstition, it is moreover evident, gives an intensity of expression even to those features in the social state of the Ashantees and their neighbours which it may not have originated. To whatever cause domestic slavery and polygamy may be traced, religion has laid hold of both institutions, and stamped them with its sanction. And it may be confidently anticipated, that so long as it remains an article of the national creed, that persons assume the same state in the next world which they maintained in this,—and that, so far from its being an act of criminal barbarity, it is required by the gods, and is the discharge of an imperative duty to a deceased relative, and an expression of the tenderest regard for his memory, to send his wives and slaves after him without delay;—so long as this is steadfastly believed, the most formidable obstacles will be opposed to the abolition of two of the greatest temporal evils by which Africa is afflicted.

CHAPTER X.

THE STATE AND PROSPECTS OF CHRISTIANITY ON THE GOLD COAST AND IN ASHANTEE.

Humiliating Reflection that so little has been done by Christian Europe to introduce the Gospel into Guinea—Rev. Mr. Thompson—Native Chaplain at Cape-Coast Castle—Basle Missionary Society—Circumstances which led to the Rev. Mr. Dunwell's Appointment to the Gold Coast—Openings for Missionary Labour in various Places—Joy expressed on the Arrival of Mr. Dunwell—His successful Ministry—The Priests excite Opposition—A native Female openly burns her Gods—Mr. Dunwell's early Removal by Death—Stability of native Converts—Great Alarm of the Fetish Priests at Abrah—Rev. Mr. Wrigley—Death of Mr. and Mrs. Harrop from imprudent Exposure—Mr. Wrigley's Decease—Arrival of Rev. Mr. Freeman—Completion of large new Chapel at Cape-Coast Town—Murder of Governor Meredith at Winnebah—Mission Chapel built on the Spot where the Fort once stood—Alarm of Fetishmen at Salt-Pond—The consecrated brass Pan at Salt-Pond stolen, and the People laugh because the Oracle cannot tell the Thief—Number of native Converts—Number of Children in the Schools—Principal Mission Stations—Discomfiture of Akwah the Fetishman—Circumstances which shook the Confidence reposed in the Fetish by the Natives at Winnebah—The Fetish at Mankoh goes to great Fetish at Abrah, to complain that he is burnt out by the Natives.

IT is a humiliating reflection, that, although the maritime countries of Europe have had intercourse with the coast of Guinea for three centuries, until a comparatively late period but few attempts have been made to communicate to the native population the light and blessings of Christianity. In the year 1751, a clergyman of the Church of England, having spent five years in America, as a Missionary, under the direction of the Society for the Propagation of the Gospel in Foreign Parts, obtained permission from the Directors of that Society to proceed to the Gold Coast in order "to make a trial with the natives, and see what hopes there would be of introducing among them the Christian religion." * During the four years of his stay, he officiated as chaplain at Cape-Coast Castle; but was much discouraged in his endeavours to introduce a purer faith among the natives. His health having failed, he returned to England in the year 1756; and, previous to his leaving, he had sent home three native boys from Cape Coast, who were placed by the Society in a school in Islington under the care of Mr. Hickman, with whom they are reported to have made considerable proficiency in useful learning, and in the knowledge of the Christian religion.

* An Account of Two Missionary Voyages, by the Appointment of the Society for the Propagation of the Gospel in Foreign Parts : the one to New Jersey in North America, the other from America to the Coast of Guinea. By Thomas Thompson, A. M., Vicar of Reculver, in Kent. London, 1758." P. 23.

One of the youths, of the name of Quaque,
was afterwards sent to the University of Oxford,
and having completed his education there, he
received ordination, and returned to exercise the
Christian ministry in his native country.   He
was chaplain at Cape-Coast Castle for more than
fifty years; but does not appear to have been
instrumental in turning any of his countrymen
to Christianity.   Nor will this excite surprise,
when it is known that on his death-bed he gave
evidence that he had at least as much confidence
in the influence of the fetish as in the power
of Christianity.   The case of this individual
furnishes matter for grave consideration on the
part of those who are anxious to promote the
enlightenment and elevation of Africa.   It
yields no support to the plausible theory of
Christianizing Pagan lands, primarily or chiefly,
by bringing natives to this country for education with a view to their becoming the principal instructors of their countrymen ; and
shows that if, on their return, they are left to
their own resources, it is more likely that they
will sink down again to the level of their former
state than that they will prove the regenerators
of their country. Instructed natives may maintain
their consistency, and act a useful part, where
they are placed under the eye and direction of
European Missionaries ; but if they be thrown

back into Heathen society without such support, it ought not to excite surprise, should the result prove that the time and care bestowed upon their culture have been expended in vain.

Some English chaplains, who were sent after the decease of Quaque, successively died soon after their arrival at Cape-Coast Castle.

About ten years since, a mission was commenced by the Basle Missionary Society at Danish Accra, (Akráh,) and in the adjoining country of Aquapím; but this truly philanthropic undertaking does not appear to have been attended with the desired success. The Missionaries encountered opposition in quarters where they ought to have received encouragement and support; several of them were removed by death; and the last survivor of their number, the Rev. Mr. Riis, returned to Europe for the benefit of his health, in the same ship by which the Rev. Mr. Freeman came on a visit to England in the spring of last year.

It was in the autumn of the year 1834, that the Committee of the Wesleyan Missionary Society were induced to send a Missionary on a visit of observation to the Gold Coast. A few native youths, who had learned to read the English translation of the Bible in the excellent Government-School at Cape-Coast Castle, became so interested by the contents of the sacred volume, that they agreed to meet at regular times for the purpose of reading it together, and of inquiring carefully into the nature and claims of the Christian religion. The name which this association assumed was that of " A Meeting or Society for Promoting Christian Knowledge;" and they adopted for their guidance the following rule, which is copied literally from the Minutes of their proceedings : " That, as the word of God is the best rule a Christian ought to observe, it is herein avoided framing other rules to enforce good conduct; but that the Scriptures must be carefully studied, through which, by the help of the Holy Spirit and faith in Christ Jesus, our minds will be enlightened and find the way to eternal salvation."

The formation of this most interesting Society or Meeting took place on the 1st of October, 1831 ; and in the year 1833, Mr. William De Graft, one of the first who began to read the Scriptures privately in the spirit of prayer and inquiry, received at Dix Cove, where he was then residing, a request from his young friends at Cape-Coast town that he would engage some suitable person, who might be proceeding to England, to purchase for their use a number of copies of the New Testament. Shortly after, the late excellent Captain Potter, master of a merchant-vessel from the port of Bristol, arrived at Dix

Cove; to whom William De Graft applied as one
likely to execute with promptness and care the
commission for the purchase of the Scriptures.
He was surprised at receiving such an application from a native young man, and became so
greatly interested by the information which his
questions elicited, that he was led to ask whether the instructions of a Missionary would
not be highly appreciated by those native
inquirers after the true religion.   De Graft
replied in the affirmative, but appeared doubtful
whether so high a privilege was attainable.   Captain Potter next proceeded to Cape Coast, where
he saw the members of the Meeting; and, having
consulted President Maclean, he returned to England, resolved to exert himself, in order that, on
his next voyage, he might, together with copies
of the Scriptures, take out a Christian minister
who should "preach the word" to those who
were already united in seeking "the way to
eternal salvation," and proclaim the Gospel of
Christ to other portions of the Heathenish native
population of the Gold Coast.

Immediately after his arrival at Bristol, Captain
Potter communicated to the Wesleyan Missionary Committee in London his views as to the
promising opening for Missionary exertion in
that part of Africa, and generously offered to
take a Missionary with him on his next voyage,

who might make personal observation and inquiry
upon the spot; and, should he conclude that the
prospect was not such as to warrant his continuance for the purpose of commencing a mission,
Captain Potter engaged that he would bring him
back to England without any expense to the
Missionary Society. This noble offer met with
acceptance on the part of the Missionary Committee, and the Rev. Joseph Dunwell was
selected for the interesting service.

This devoted Missionary embarked with Captain Potter at Bristol, on the 17th of October,
1834. The entries in his private journal sufficiently indicate the views with which he entered
upon his arduous undertaking. Impressed with
the responsibility which attached to him, and
fearing lest the important mission might fail
through his incapacity, he studied daily, on his
voyage, the lives of eminent missionaries, especially those of Brainerd and Martyn, in order
that he might catch a larger measure of their
spirit, and propose to himself as an example the
zeal and self-denial by which they were characterized. On the 6th of December, the ship came
within sight of land near Cape Palmas; and a
few extracts from the journal of Mr. Dunwell,
illustrative of the character and manners of the
natives, at the several places where they touched,
as well as of his own feelings while contem-

plating their moral state, will be read with interest :—

"December 7th, 1834. At daylight we were seen by the natives; and in half an hour upwards of fifty men were on deck, the first of whom recognised Captain Potter, and appeared glad to see him. I observed immediately that they were most rapacious beggars. We shortly weighed anchor, it being Sunday, in order to secure greater quietness and tranquillity; but although we had a good breeze, a great number of canoes came off to us in the course of the day. These people are the most athletic and well-proportioned men I ever saw, and have most animated countenances. They seem exceedingly fond of Englishmen, and say they would be glad if I would stay and live with them, as there is no 'white man' at Sesters, Garraway, or Cape Palmas; all which places we passed to-day. The inhabitants appear numerous; but Christ has not been named among them. What Christian can witness their numbers, and their degradation, without deep feeling? I noticed that nearly all we saw could speak broken English. The country appears almost like a paradise, though every thing springs spontaneously. At dusk we anchored off Cape Town, (an American settlement,) which I intend to visit to-morrow, God willing.

"Monday 8th. At day-break I saw many canoes coming off. Numbers of people were soon upon deck, with rice, fowls, and ivory, which they exchanged for articles of English manufacture. About nine o'clock, the king, whose name is Freeman, came, with several attendants. He was dressed in a coat and trowsers of coarse blue cloth, and wore a three-cornered hat, with a red cockade. A coloured silk umbrella covered him from the rays of the sun. Upon entering the cabin, his attendants presented the treaty lately made between the Americans and himself, respecting the colony, (which is about twenty miles square,) in behalf of the Colonization Society. Having received a note from Dr. Hall, the governor, Captain Potter accompanied me on shore, and we were politely received by the doctor, and his secretary, Mr. Thompson.

" While I was there, I was introduced to a man who told me that he was a member of the Wesleyan-Methodist society, and that there are sixteen persons who meet together in Christian fellowship on a Sunday morning. The governor expects a Missionary shortly. He expressed a strong wish that our Committee should send one; indeed, I think there is a good opening for Missionary labour, as there is already a Christian society which stands in need of a shepherd, and there is a great number of the

Aborigines of the country in the town adjoining the settlement.

" Before we returned on board, we visited the king at his hut, where chairs were placed for us, and we were welcomed with much cordiality. No sooner were we seated, than a great number of natives assembled round us, in a state of perfect nudity; and when we took our departure for the boat, we were escorted by scores of them to the shore. Mr. Thompson, the governor's secretary, told me that the people were astonished at me, and said among themselves, that I was a 'god-man,' come to talk ' great palaver.'

" Tuesday, December 9th. To-day we have been visited by three kings, who all appear to be great men in their way. They have many under their control. Kavally seems to be next in importance to Cape Palmas. The news of a 'god-man' (as they term me) having come, appears to have gone like lightning down the coast. Cape Coast seems to be much envied, as these people also desire to have a Missionary. We asked one of their chiefs last night if he would wish me to come and live with him; and, to express his meaning, he laid himself down, and extended his arms at full length, and said, ' You be my father, my brother.' Several chiefs have brought their sons to me, and wished me to take them, and teach them ' *sensen.*'

"One native came to know when Christmas was, and why we called it so. When I told him, he seemed utterly astonished, and said, 'That be great palaver indeed;' and, striking his head, he added, 'Will keep that there good *sensen.*' Another came, and wrote on a slate, 'You come.' Upon examination, I found he could write his name, and read the alphabet; another could read words of one and two syllables. The quickness with which they learn is amazing. How great the harvest!—and the labourers, not few, but really *none!*

"I cannot doubt: I do believe that I am in the way of Providence, in coming with this vessel. If I live, I shall have an opportunity of visiting several hundreds of miles of this coast; and what I have seen of it I admire, and should not mind settling anywhere.

"December 11th. When I arose in the morning, I found that we were opposite the land of Drewin. The country still assumes the same appearance; but, to my surprise, I learned that few ships touch here, as the people are savage, and speak another language. Not many years ago, Captain Thomas Feebin, of the ship 'Union,' from Bristol, stopped here for the purposes of trade; but, for some reason or other, the natives murdered the captain and the whole of the crew. They ransacked and plundered the vessel; and shortly after, Captain Potter passed, and caught some of the natives on the wreck; but he was obliged to abandon it, in order to save his own life, and those of his crew. In the evening, as we passed along, we came in sight of a village named Kutro. Here the natives kindled a fire on the beach, as a signal for us to anchor; but as we did not stop, two canoes came off, with some plantains, bananas, and fowls, which we bought. These natives had a very different appearance from those we saw last, having nothing round their waists but a mere strap of cloth, instead of the Manchester cloths I observed round the others; and they were afraid to come on deck, and seemed distrustful of all of us in the extreme.

"Friday, 12th. Early this morning, we were opposite Pikanani Lahú, or Long-Jack's Place. Here the inhabitants appear exceedingly ignorant of religion or letters. If possible, they are worse beggars than I have seen before, as nothing seems to satisfy them. About one o'clock we arrived at Cape Lahú, and anchored. As usual, we had the decks soon filled with natives; among these were kings, chiefs, and counsellors, who all appeared exceedingly kind and familiar. They are athletic and well-proportioned; and their costume is nothing but a belt round their waist. Some wear their hair in large tufts, others curled, plaited, and braided.

"Saturday, December 13th. At five o'clock

this morning, or soon after, I could perceive the canoes making to the vessel. In a short time the decks were covered from end to end. To-day I embraced the opportunity of making some inquiries about this people and the place, as it is acknowledged to be one of great importance. The town appears to be divided into two districts, governed by two kings, namely, Peter and Antonio, both of whom I saw. Of the extent of these places I cannot speak positively; but the number of inhabitants certainly amounts to many thousands. The people appear to be possessed of gold; and I saw vast quantities of ivory. The country is low, but very fertile and pleasant, producing spontaneously every kind of vegetation necessary for its inhabitants. I very much wished to visit this people in their town, as they gave me several pressing invitations. King Peter told me he would build me a house, if I would go; and one of his sons made me a present of half an ackie of gold, patted me on the face, and said, ' Me like you face; black man do.' My friend, Captain Potter, told me, that if they got me there, most likely they would keep me several days, till they had all seen me. I felt a longing desire for the salvation of these people, and could have freely stayed with them, and given myself up into their hands, and spent my strength and life amongst them, for the glory of God.

"December 15th. I arose early this morning, and found we were opposite Pikanani Bassam. Here is a large population, exceedingly ignorant, and, at this time, engaged in war with what are called the Bush-men. This is also the case with two large towns which we have passed, namely, Jack Lahú, and Jack Jaques; so that we considered it best not to call here. In the evening we came to anchor at Grand Bassam, one of the prettiest-looking places I ever saw. The town stands about six miles up a noble river of the same name. It is a place of considerable importance. Old Kwosia, the king, is the greatest man we have seen. He possesses much wealth, and has a great number of wives. His influence is such, that nothing is done without his consent and approbation. We had not been here an hour, before he came on board. I was struck with his appearance; for although he is low in stature, there is something noble and dignified in his person. He is a complete man of business, and carries a large box of gold at his side, of no little value; yet he wears a mean cloth round his waist, and assists occasionally in rowing his canoe. If we have an opportunity of visiting his town, it is our intention so to do; and I believe I shall be the first Christian Missionary that ever set foot in this place.

"December 16th. About nine o'clock this

morning, the king sent messengers to say, that he could not visit us for ten days, as one of his wives, and a brother, had died last night. Upon inquiry, the messengers told us, that they had been bewitched; and that two persons would be sacrificed, as well as a thousand guns fired at the same time.

"December 17th. The roar of the guns, fired on account of the death of the king's wife, although at seven miles' distance, was like that of distant thunder. In the evening we took the boat, in order to ascertain whether we could land on the beach; but as we found that it was nearly perpendicular, and the swell very great, we did not attempt it; so I fear that our intended visit to Grand Bassam will be frustrated.

"December 20th. Another day has been on my part almost wholly unemployed. I cannot read for the continual noise on deck, much less think closely. The Africans are indeed a noisy people; but this is not all: they are ignorant in the extreme. To-day, while conversing with one of them, I introduced religion; but, alas! he was as ignorant as a brute; he neither knew who made him, nor anything else. All I could get from him was, 'Great devil talk angry:' signifying, that when it thundered, the devil was angry.

"December 23d. This day we got under weigh, and came to a poor, small town, called Half

Assinee. This place seems to have sprung up from one of the same name, destroyed by the king of Apollonia; who is a dreadful tyrant, carrying terror and destruction wherever he comes. Although the people at this place are poor in comparison with some of their neighbours, yet they are industrious. One young man who came on board, and calls himself 'Tom Coffee,' says he has been at Liverpool, and went to church. He appeared much surprised at what he saw and heard."

Leaving this place, they called at Dix Cove and Commenda, both which towns have since become mission-stations; and on the 29th of December, the vessel anchored off the Dutch fort of Elmina. At this place, within sight of Cape-Coast Castle, Mr. Dunwell wrote in his journal as follows: "What my feelings have been this day, I cannot describe. The place of my future residence is in view: it may prove the spot where I shall finish my earthly existence; and there the name of Jesus Christ may be honoured, or dishonoured, by me. But, in the strength of grace, I trust that whether my days may be many, or soon numbered, they will be spent in the service of God. All things appear to me to sink into nothingness, compared with the great work of my Divine Lord and Master."

While at anchor off Elmina, Mr. Dunwell

wrote a letter to President Maclean, at Cape-Coast Castle, respectfully informing him of his arrival on the coast, and stating the objects contemplated by the Wesleyan Missionary Committee, in sending him as a Missionary to that part of Africa. On his arrival a day or two afterwards at Cape-Coast Castle, he met with a kind reception from the President, who invited him to remain at the castle until he could provide himself with a suitable residence; and expressed his opinion, that there was a very favourable opening among the natives for Missionary exertions.

By the native young men who formed the Society or Meeting for reading the holy Scriptures, Mr. Dunwell was received with the warmest expressions of gratitude and delight. When the tidings reached Cape-Coast Castle, that there was a Missionary on board a vessel from England lying off Elmina, they hardly dared to give credit to such welcome intelligence; and one of them immediately proceeded to Elmina to satisfy himself by ocular demonstration that the report was true. They placed themselves at once under the care of Mr. Dunwell, who commenced his public ministry at Cape-Coast town on the first sabbath after he landed; which, from the entry in his journal, appears to have been January 4th, 1835. Speaking of the congregation to which he preached his first sermon, composed of the members of the Meeting, and a few others, Mr. Dunwell remarks: "The deepest attention was manifested; joy beamed on every countenance;" and adds, "Their gratitude is without bounds, and they say, 'We did never think of the Missionary's coming to teach black man.'"

One class of persons, however, the fetishmen, speedily took the alarm, and used their influence to prevent the people from attending public Christian worship; and many of their steadfast votaries employed ridicule and threats, for the purpose of deterring their friends and neighbours from listening to the truths of the Gospel; meeting them on their return from the public service, and saying, "What, you turn White? You know not, that God gave the Bible to White man, and fetish to Black man? How dare you go and forsake the religion of your forefathers?" But, in spite of such opposition, the people flocked to the ministry of Mr. Dunwell at Cape-Coast Castle, Annamaboe, and other places which he visited; and, under the divine blessing, the great doctrines of Christianity produced a salutary effect on many minds; and the number of those who were united together in church-fellowship steadily increased. Mr. Dunwell, in his correspondence at the time, mentioned, with much satisfaction, a striking instance of decision in the case of a woman, who brought out her household gods into the open air, and publicly burned them in the presence of her Heathen neighbours.

The mission soon assumed a most promising appearance. The large room in which public service had been held at Cape-Coast town proved too small; and a subscription was commenced among the natives for the erection of a suitable chapel. Mr. Dunwell had secured general respect among all classes of society, and was receiving applications to afford the benefit of his labours to distant places. But in the midst of the anticipations which this hopeful state of things inspired, he was attacked by fever, under which he sunk in a few days; and left the societies which he had been instrumental in forming, as sheep without a shepherd. The last entries in his own journal, and the notices furnished by Mr. Joseph Smith, the native master of the school at the castle, show with what feelings this useful Missionary met his death; far from his father's home, uncheered by the presence of mother, or sister, or other relative, and attended only by those to whom his generous qualities had endeared him in the land of strangers. On Sunday, the 14th of June, 1835, having mentioned that he had preached twice, although unwell, he added: "After the evening-service I had

a most violent head-ache, with some fever
and sickness, which continued till I retired to
rest. There appeared every symptom of what is
called the ' seasoning,' which so frequently proves
fatal; still I cannot describe the peace of mind I
felt. I feel that I am a most worthless sinner;
and have no hope, no plea beside, but that Jesus
died for me: were it not for this, I should be lost
for ever."

The day after, he used his pen for the last time,
and wrote: " I passed an exceedingly restless
night, having great pain of body, so that I rested
very little. Yet, O the composure of mind! I
believe I can say, ' In life or in death I am the
Lord's.' "

" On the 24th instant," Mr. Smith says,
" Mr. Dunwell sent for me this morning; and,
to my great sorrow, I found him worse than I
expected. On my first entering the room, he
called me by name, and, having conversed with
me for a considerable time on various subjects,
desired me to pray for him. I knelt by the side
of his bed, and engaged in prayer for about a
quarter of an hour: he also prayed himself. He
besought the Lord to let the cup pass from
him, as the sons of this part of Africa would be
left to grope in darkness, if he were removed
away by death. At this I was uncommonly
sorry; but he encouraged me to hope in the

Lord; for the debt of nature must be paid. He repeated the fourth verse of the twenty-third psalm: 'Though I walk through the valley of the shadow of death, I will fear no evil; for thou art with me; thy rod and thy staff they comfort me.' If I may use the expression, I would say, 'Let me die the death of the righteous, and let my last end be like his.' When it was now time to leave him, and attend the school, he said, with tears, 'Brother Smith, we have passed many agreeable evenings in conversing on instructive subjects; but I have to tell you I shall soon be absent from you, and be present with the Lord. I am going hence, and shall be no more seen; but watch over the flock, and strengthen them in the Lord, when I am gone.' About four o'clock in the afternoon I visited him again. He was quite insensible; the pangs of death had seized him, and every hope of his recovery was then lost: between eight and nine o'clock he expired." Thus died the Rev. Joseph Dunwell. No words of disappointment or regret escaped his lips, on account of his having so early sacrificed his life in the Missionary enterprise; but a quenchless zeal for the cause of his Divine Master sustained him to the last, and all the solicitude which he manifested was for the infant church formed by his instrumentality.

This afflictive dispensation produced the deepest

feeling among all who took any interest in the
mission.   On the following morning, a native
wrote, "Sad news in the town; the shepherd is
away! The poor Missionary is reported dead."
Great numbers of the native people, and the resident English gentlemen, attended his funeral;
and the governor having read the funeral-service,
that beautiful and appropriate hymn which is
numbered fifty-one in the Wesleyan Hymn-Book
was sung over the grave by the members of
the society.

On the day after the funeral, the bereaved
society met, to take into consideration the circumstances in which they were placed by the
afflictive dispensation which had overtaken them.
The artless manner in which a record of this
meeting was made in the minute-book of the
society, will best explain the conclusion which was
adopted: "I met the class on purpose to know
whether they would continue in the profession
they had recently entered into, or desire to return
to their former ways, in consequence of the death
of their Missionary.   They said, they would
remain in the new profession; for though the
Missionary was dead, God lives.   We commended
our souls in prayer to God, and separated at ten
o'clock."

A respectful letter was then addressed to John
Jackson and John Barr, Esquires, who had kindly

undertaken the administration of Mr. Dunwell's affairs, preferring a request that they would use their influence for the purpose of inducing the Wesleyan Missionary Committee to appoint another Missionary to Cape-Coast Castle; and those gentlemen obligingly communicated to the Committee in London the particulars respecting Mr. Dunwell's lamented death, and the earnest wish of the native members of the society respecting the mission. The Committee, unable to reconcile to their conviction of duty the abandonment of a work which had been so auspiciously begun, resolved to more than meet the application, by sending two Missionaries, on the principle that the interests of a mission in such a climate as that of Western Africa ought not to be left to the care of only one individual. It was further agreed, that the two Missionaries to be sent should be married men, in order that their wives might attend to the improvement of the native females.

The communication of the intentions of the Committee was received with unbounded satisfaction by the members at Cape Coast, who continued to hold their religious meetings with regularity, and were exerting themselves to raise subscriptions for the erection of a suitable chapel. When the Rev. G. O. Wrigley landed there, on the 15th of September, 1836, he found that the society had increased in numbers, and that the influence of Christianity was felt to a considerable distance inland. This was so manifestly the case, that the fetishmen at Abrah, in the Braffo country, had taken the alarm, and used means to counteract the spread of a system by which their own "craft" was so greatly endangered. It was announced, that the great fetish, Nănah Num, was highly offended with the caboceers in the bush, for allowing their people to renounce the gods of their fathers; and a man was sent to say, that he had been caught up by the fetish into the air, and had received a message for the people, to the effect, that if they did not immediately reject the new religion, the fetish would not send any more rain. By such means, Afo, the caboceer of Donási, was so alarmed, that he abandoned a school which had been established among his people. But another school, formed by George Amísa, son of the caboceer at Domonási, was still continued, in spite of the threats of the great fetish.

Mr. Wrigley commenced his varied labours with zeal; and a suitable place of worship having become indispensably necessary, he undertook, without delay, the erection of a commodious building, including a chapel and school-rooms; the expense of which was estimated at five hundred pounds sterling. Mrs. Wrigley also evinced her pity for her degraded sex by opening a school for native girls, where she instructed them in the English language, sewing, and other useful branches of learning; but they were deprived by death, in a few months, of their disinterested benefactress. Mr. and Mrs. Harrop, who had also been appointed by the Committee to the Cape-Coast Mission, landed there in January, 1837; when, owing to the injurious exposure of themselves to the effects of the sun in the middle of the day, they were almost immediately attacked by fever, which proved fatal to them both; and Mrs. Wrigley sunk under the fatigue which she experienced, while attending, with affectionate anxiety, by night and by day, to her suffering friends.

The shock which Mr. Wrigley received from this complicated bereavement was the more severely felt, as he himself was only just recovering from a bilious fever; but he soon applied himself anew to his various ministerial and pastoral duties, at the same time superintending the erection of the new chapel, and prosecuting the study of the native language, until the month of November, when he was taken ill as he was returning by water from Annamaboe, (Anamabú,) and in a few days died in the full triumph of Christian faith. The death of this truly excellent Missionary produced a great sensation; and his funeral was one of the most affecting scenes which had for a long time been witnessed.

The arrival of the Rev. Thomas B. Freeman, with Mrs. Freeman, early in January, 1838, once more revived the drooping spirits of the native society, who came from various parts to welcome their new friends. Mr. Freeman had zealously entered upon the duties of his mission, when he was attacked with the seasoning-fever; and while watching with solicitude his sick-bed, Mrs. Freeman was seized with a violent inflammatory complaint, which terminated her life in a few hours. The death of this valuable woman was a great loss to the native females, for whose benefit she had made some important arrangements; and her funeral furnished evidence of the respect which she had secured for herself from all classes of society. Mr. Freeman gradually recovered his health; and from that period, until the time of his visit to England in 1840, he was engaged in the execution of plans which have contributed greatly, under the divine blessing, to the enlargement and establishment of the Mission at the Gold Coast.

The completion of the new chapel was effected shortly after Mr. Freeman's recovery. In this work, the zeal of the natives had been strikingly manifested. During the rains, a large part of the

wall, which had been built of swish, was washed
down; but the native people and children carried
no fewer than four thousand pieces of stone from
the distance of a mile, for the purpose of repair-
ing the breach; and they fetched four thousand
bundles of a particular kind of grass from a place
six miles distant, for the purpose of thatching the
roof, which had been sent from England.   On
the 10th of June, 1838, Mr. Freeman had the
satisfaction of conducting the opening-service, in
a substantial place of worship, large enough to
accommodate from seven hundred to one thousand persons on the ground-floor.   Two commodious vestries are also attached to the chapel.
The first service was attended by President
Maclean and several other Europeans, and by
at least twelve hundred natives; for, those who
were not able to obtain admission within the
edifice crowded round the door and windows, and
there participated in the sacred service.   The
President and other English residents contributed
handsomely towards defraying the expenses of the
erection.

In noticing the several places to which this
mission has extended, Annamaboe (Anamabú)
first claims attention. This place, the name of
which has been rendered familiar by the attack
of the Ashantees, enjoyed the benefit of Mr.
Dunwell's labours, and of those of his successor,

Mr. Wrigley. A chapel was commenced here also ; but the walls having been brought down by the rains, another was built, on a larger scale, and opened for public worship on the 26th of May, 1839. The natives at this place emulated the zeal of the Cape-Coast people in their exertions to provide themselves with a suitable place of worship.

The inhabitants of Winnebah had their attention first called to the claims of Christianity by Mr. William De Graft, who went to reside there, and soon prevailed upon some of the natives to unite with him in religious meetings. The people of this place had unhappily acquired an infamous notoriety, by their violence and rapacity, and especially by their murder of Governor Meredith, in the year 1812. While walking in the garden of the fort, he was suddenly siezed by a number of persons, who hurried him away into the " bush," and there charged him with detaining a quantity of gold, the property of a native, which, as they alleged, a serjeant had delivered to him at the time when the Ashantees visited the neighbourhood ; at the same time declaring, that they would not liberate him until he gave up the gold. The serjeant had forgotten to whose care he had committed the property, until he consulted the great fetish at Abrah, and was told by the oracle, that he had consigned it to Mr. Meredith ; and, after this authoritative announcement, it was in vain that the unfortunate governor maintained the groundlessness of the charge, and that he knew nothing of the gold.

On being informed of the seizure of the governor, Mr. Smith, who had the care of the Tantum Fort, hastened to Winnebah, when he was immediately seized by a body of natives, and conducted to the place where Mr. Meredith was confined; and as it serves to indicate the obstacles which the character of such a people necessarily presents to the introduction of Christianity, Mr. Smith shall describe what he saw in his own words:—" After walking a mile and a half in the interior, escorted by a numerous body of people, I met with an assembly of the Pynims, seated on the ground. I was called, and desired to take my place in the centre; which after doing, I made inquiry into the cause of such outrageous conduct, and urged them to produce Mr. Meredith. After waiting half an hour, he was brought in, on a man's back; for so wearied was he, from the cruel usage he had received, as to be unable to walk. The situation he was first introduced in was a lamentable sight, and the wound it gave my feelings it is impossible to describe: so much affected was he, that tears would force their way. His face and clothes were covered with dirt, and his clothes were torn in half. He said, the treat-

ment he had experienced from these savages the
day before was so inhuman, that he had offered
them an order on the fort for the whole of the
property he was possessed of, in order to get
liberated from them; but this they refused, and
insisted on detaining him until he delivered up
the gold he was unjustly accused of having
received. He therefore requested that I would
do all in my power to compromise the business,
and release him from such a miserable situation.
Some time after, the mob retiring a short distance from us, he recited the particulars of the
treatment he had suffered. Whilst taking his
usual morning's walk in the garden, he was
surrounded by a number of the town's-people,
and hurried away as fast as possible. They
obliged him to walk some miles in the heat of
the sun; during which, they were guilty of many
outrages against him. The dried grass was set on
fire, and he was forced to walk close to the flame.
His shoes he was obliged to take off and put on
alternately, as it suited their caprice, and to walk
without them on the sharp stubble of the grass
which had been just burnt. He received blows
with a stick; and they twice made an attempt to
cut his stockings off, and put him in irons. They
extended his arms, by tying them to a stake,
which pressed hard on his throat; and at this
time, he said, he fully expected that they were

about to put a period to his existence. Indeed, the cruelty with which he had been used was such as to make him covet death, and he was perfectly resigned to his fate; they however spared him, to inflict more miseries upon him. After remaining a short time in one part of the bush, he was taken to another, and so on till night, when it was with great difficulty that he could prevail on them to allow a mattress to be brought him. He was obliged to sleep in the open air, surrounded by a number of his tormentors, who continued their abuse with noise and riot throughout the night, during which they forced him to send to the fort for tobacco and ankers of liquor, just as they thought proper to demand them. At day-break they carried him off again to some distance from the place where he had slept; and, on my arrival, he was brought back to the spot where I met the Pynims."

From the effect of these sufferings, Mr. Meredith died before any effectual means could be taken to extricate him from the hands of the natives; and his successor, Mr. James, having been blockaded in the fort, by the natives, for three months, application was then made to the Honourable Captain Irby, of His Majesty's ship " Amelia," who proceeded to Winnebah; and, the fort having been blown up, the place was altogether abandoned as a British settlement.

On the very spot where the Winnebah Fort once stood, a mission-chapel was commenced, chiefly through the exertions of William De Graft, in the month of July, 1838, which was opened for divine worship on the 2d of June following. A school has also been established, and a number of natives are united together in church fellowship.

The formation of a school at Domonási, by the son of the chief, has already been mentioned. The people at that place have erected, at their own expense, a small chapel, in which public worship was celebrated for the first time on the 25th of November, 1839.

The commencement of a chapel at Salt Pond occasioned considerable alarm to the fetishmen. Mr. Freeman, having obtained a piece of land from the chief of the place, had caused the ground to be excavated for the foundation; but when he accompanied the workmen to the place on the following morning, he found that a fetishman had placed in the hole, where the foundation-stone was to be laid, an idol image, for the purpose of deterring the people from proceeding with the work. Mr. Freeman, aware of the prejudices with which he had to contend, applied to the chief, requesting him to remove the image; but he declined to interfere. Mr. Freeman then appealed to him whether he had not bought the

land, and whether it was fair or honest to attempt
to deprive him of his purchase. The chief admitted, without hesitation, his claims, but still shrunk
from the task of dislodging the new occupant of
the property. At length, however, the Missionary
gained his point; the image was removed; and
the chapel which was then commenced has since
been opened for public worship under favourable
circumstances. When the first religious service
was held in the chapel, a large number of the
inhabitants, who were unable to obtain admission
within the walls, on account of the crowd, brought
their native stools and sat on the outside. The
school which has been commenced excites much
interest; and the people tell the Missionary, that
they send their children to him for instruction
because they believe that he has come among
them to do them good : and while the Mission is
thus rising in the public estimation, the cause of
superstition is rapidly declining. At the date of a
recent letter, the people were much amused with
the embarrassment of the priest, because some one
had stolen a brass pan consecrated to the fetish,
and the oracle was unable to name the thief.

At Commenda, and Abása, chapels have also
been erected. At British Accra, (Akráh,) a promising society has been formed; and a school
has been undertaken. At Mansu, also, a prosperous school has been established.

For the purpose of enabling the Missionaries to prosecute their labours among the natives with greater regularity and effect, three Districts or Circuits have been formed; in each of which, one or more English Missionaries are placed, with native agents as their assistants. The first of these Circuits is that of Cape-Coast town, the principal places connected with which are Commenda and Dix Cove; the second is that of Annamaboe, (Anamabú,) including Salt Pond, Domonási, Mansú, and Abása; the third is that of British Accra (Akráh) and Winnebah. To various other places, where there are openings for usefulness,—one of which is Djuquah, where Kujoh Chibbu, who took so prominent a part in the Ashantee war, and fifteen thousand of his people, are now located, —the Missionaries will direct their attention as time and opportunity serve. At the several stations which have been enumerated, between six and seven hundred natives have renounced the idolatry of their ancestors, and are now united together as members of the Wesleyan society; and nearly three hundred children are receiving a religious education in the mission schools.

Two schools, one at Annamaboe, and the other at Accra, were established by the assistance of President Maclean; and the Committee in London, by whom, under the Imperial Government, the affairs of the Gold Coast are conducted, laudably anxious to promote the sound instruction of the rising generation, kindly made a grant for the purpose of defraying half the expense.

A few anecdotes, illustrative of the process by which the native mind has been disenthralled to so great an extent from the influence of the superstition of ages, will not, perhaps, be unacceptable to the reader.

Shortly after the commencement of the Wesleyan mission, a fetishman, named Akwah, came from the interior to Cape-Coast town, who professed to be able, when he had bruised a bead to powder, to unite the particles together again, and make it what it was before.   Several persons put his skill to the test, and he contrived so adroitly to slip other beads into the places of the powdered ones, that the spectators were led to believe that he had really restored the broken beads to their former state.   He professed, moreover, that he could thrust his finger through a stone, and produced one with a hole in it, which hole he said was made by his finger; and he managed to obtain credit with the people for having done it, although they did not see the alleged feat performed.   He stated, moreover, that he had sufficient influence to call apes from the bush, and make them talk with the people; but he could not do this in the day-time, because he said the apes were timid, and shunned the light. He therefore took his dupes into the bush after dark, and they returned into the town perfectly satisfied that they had conversed with apes. By such exploits, he gained great renown, and considerable profit; and then proceeded to Elmina, and Commenda, and having convinced the people there of the great powers of his fetish, he returned to Cape-Coast town.

After his return, a native trader, possessed of some wealth, was taken ill, and consulted Akwah, who engaged speedily to restore him to health. The trader then expressed a wish to witness some of the great feats, of which he had heard so much, and especially desired to hear the apes talk. Akwah was quite ready to comply with his request; but, as the apes were still averse to the light, it was arranged that the meeting should be deferred until eight o'clock in the evening. The light of the gospel was, however, just beginning to exert sufficient influence upon the mind of the trader to awaken some doubt as to the powers of the fetishman; and he resolved to use every precaution to prevent himself from being imposed upon. He accordingly instructed his servant boys, who were to accompany him with a present of rum, to take care to ascertain who or what it was to whom they gave it; and, at the appointed time, taking four flasks of rum, containing about one gallon, he proceeded to the appointed place, near to the spot where the mission-house now stands. All things being ready, Akwah began to call for the apes, telling them that a man of distinction had come to hear them, and begging them to honour his fetish by obeying the summons. At length, a rushing noise was heard in the bush, and a small voice proceeded from it, saying, "We have come: give us some rum." The trader immediately sprung forward, saying, "I will give it to them;" but Akwah interposed, telling him, that it would be more consistent with his dignity to sit down, and allow his servants to perform the duty. Little, however, did Akwah suspect that the boys had been previously instructed as to the part which they should act, or anticipate the result which followed. The boys took the flasks, and thrust them into the bush whence the voices proceeded; and each, as he extended a flask in one hand, stretched out also the other, that he might be able to ascertain by feeling what was the recipient. It being quite dark, this manœuvre could not be perceived; and immediately one of the boys called out to his master, "My father, my father! it is not an ape; I have caught a boy's hand." "Hold it fast," replied the trader, "until

I come and satisfy myself;" but in the struggle which ensued, the captive gained his liberty; and the trader and his boys pursued the fugitives, and ascertained that they were a number of boys who had been trained by Akwah to personate apes.

On their return to the bush, the trader and his servants found that the fetish boys, in their haste, had left the bottles they had brought, into which to empty the trader's flasks for the use of their master; but Akwah himself had taken to his heels, and was never seen or heard of more at Cape-Coast town. This discovery broke the spell with which the popular superstition had bound the mind of the trader; and he soon after became a member of Christian society.

At a later period of the mission, the chief fetishman at Cape-Coast town had called the people together to "play fetish;" and, while he was dancing, a stone was thrown, which struck him in the face. At this he was very much displeased, and required that the people should find out the person who had thrown it; but they expressed their surprise at such a requirement; and told him, that if the fetish could not inform him who was the offender, it was in vain that they should apply to him for counsel and direction in their affairs. They then threw down the drums, to the sound of which he was dancing, and left the priest to his own meditations.

When William De Graft resided at Winnebah, a circumstance occurred, which tended to impress many of the people in favour of the new religion which he taught. A great scarcity of fish having occurred, it was proposed to send messengers to the great fetish at Abrah to "buy fish," that is, to prevail upon the gods to give them a good fishing-season. De Graft ridiculed the idea of their going into the country to buy fish, when they had only to put off into the sea in their canoes, and catch it for themselves. However, it was determined that the influence of the fetish should be sought; and the messengers carried up to Abrah a present for the fetish, amounting in value to £4 sterling. A promise of help was obtained; but two unfavourable seasons followed, in which little fish was caught; and the people were, in consequence, reduced to great straits. The cause of the failure then became the subject of much discussion. Some were of opinion, that the messengers had slept on their way back from Abrah, and that another fetish, who was angry that he had not been applied to, had embraced the opportunity of stealing away the fish which they had bought; but others acknowledged to De Graft, that their faith in the power of the fetish was greatly shaken.

On another occasion, a fire had taken place at Winnebah, and De Graft asked some of the Heathen inhabitants, who laughed when they met him in the street, why it was that they were so cheerful; they told him to go with them and see. He accompanied them to the ruins; found that the fire had burned down a fetish-house; and saw the fetish images lying in a half-consumed state. The people then said: " We laughed when we saw you, because we knew that you would tell us that we had better forsake the worship of gods which could not save themselves from the fire." De Graft embraced the opportunity of deepening the impression which he perceived was made upon their minds, and exhorted them to turn to the true God, who was alone worthy of their confidence. They admitted that it would be better to serve the God of the Christians; but they said they were not able, at once, to break off their customs. Several natives, however, from that time, became regular in their attendance at the public worship in the mission-chapel.

One more anecdote shall suffice: When William De Graft, and other native Christians, first visited some small crooms at the foot of a large hill, generally known by the name of the Devil's Hill, (although the natives call it Mankoh,) about five miles from Winnebah, they preached to the inhabitants on the goodness of God, and the freeness of the salvation of the Gospel; assuring them that they needed not take money and goods to the true God, as they did to the fetish. At length the people expressed a wish that they had heard those doctrines sooner; and gave the following account. They said that they had for two or three successive seasons employed themselves in clearing away the bush on the side of the hill, and forming plantations for the support of their families, when the priests at Abrah sent down messengers to inform them, that the fetish of the hill, Mankoh, had been to Abrah, and complained to the fetish there, that the people had cleared away, or burned up, the bush which had covered the hill; and that he was suffering much pain in consequence. The people were therefore required to send back by the messengers, two ounces of gold as a peace-offering, or the superior fetish would inflict upon them some terrible punishment for their offence; and as they had recently seen a number of wolves in the neighbourhood, whom they regarded as the messengers of the great fetish, they immediately paid the gold, to prevent the consequences which they seriously anticipated.

CHAPTER XI.

of the Mission to Ashantee—Important Bearing on
the Work of Evangelization of Africa generally—On
Civilization — Influence in promoting Peace — Arduous Nature of the Undertaking.

THE formation of native religious societies
is not, in itself, sufficient proof of the beneficial
effects of the exertions of the Missionaries ;
and evidence may be very fairly required to
show, that the conversion of the people to the
Christian religion does not consist in the mere
renunciation of one set of opinions for another, but that, with the adoption of a new faith,
they have imbibed the spirit and principles of
Christianity, and are exhibiting a corresponding
change in their character and conduct.   But
the writer is fully aware of the delicacy and
difficulty of the task of furnishing such evidence ;
and how easily, without the exercise of much
caution, he might subject himself to the charge of
exaggeration.   It is a fact, that travellers and
others, who have opportunity of personally
observing the proceedings of Missionaries in
Heathen lands, do not always sufficiently appre-
ciate the effects of their teaching.   An unfair cri-
terion is frequently adopted ; either the attainments of the native converts are compared with
the acquirements of Christians in enlightened and
civilized countries, or, in some other way, the
disadvantages of their condition are overlooked ;

and, as a natural result, all the benefits which have actually resulted from the instructions of the Missionaries are not perceived and acknowledged. Duly to estimate the change which has been effected by Missionary labours, the present state of the people whose benefit has been sought, should be contrasted with their former Heathen condition; and the comparison ought to be instituted under the full impression of the truth, that the elevation of a people from the depths of barbarism is not the work of a day. The writer is persuaded, that if this mode of investigation be adopted, the candid inquirer will find, that a very considerable amount of benefit has been produced by the instrumentality of the Wesleyan Mission at the Gold Coast.

The new class of religious observances which has been introduced, cannot fail to arrest the attention of the truly enlightened Christian observer. Instead of the superstitious fetish practices to which they formerly resorted at the beginning of the day, the natives attached to the mission now regularly assemble at the early hour of five in the morning, for the purpose of prayer, and of singing the praises of the true God. Every sabbath morning at six o'clock, public worship is celebrated in the chapel at Cape-Coast town, when the liturgy of the Established Church is read; and the decorum which is observed by the natives, who repeat the responses with an impressiveness superior, as William De Graft remarked, to what he has witnessed in any congregation in England, appears in striking opposition to the wild and irrational service which they formerly offered at the temples of the fetish. The scenes which the death-beds and funerals of the Christian natives present, are altogether new. In his last hours, the native convert is not now surrounded by fetish priests, practising their incantations for his recovery; but, freed from superstitious fears, he commends, with calm confidence, his departing spirit into the hands of his Lord and Saviour: and the funeral procession which accompanies his corpse to the grave stands out in such pleasing contrast to the revolting scenes which Heathen funerals exhibit, that many of the idolaters are led to acknowledge the superiority of the Christian religion over their degrading and inhuman superstitions.

An improvement in the morals of the native converts is equally observable. The case of one who was employed in conveying goods to an English vessel may be mentioned in illustration. Having returned to the shore, he found that he had accidentally overlooked a quantity of ivory, amounting in value to thirty pounds sterling; and he immediately put off again in his canoe, with

the intention of giving it to the captain. The
vessel, however, had proceeded so far, that he was
not able to overtake it: and on his return he
went immediately to the castle, and placed the
property in the keeping of the President of the
Council, to be restored to the captain on his next
voyage. The change of conduct in many of the
native converts is so manifest, that Heathen
parents are heard to say, " How is this? Our
children, who were formerly unkind and disobe-
dient, now treat us with respect and attention,
and take care of us in sickness and old age.
Surely the Missionaries have come amongst us to
do us good." And Heathen masters, seeing that
their domestics are now diligent and attentive to
their duties, adopt, in many cases, the same
conclusion as to the tendency of Missionary
instruction.

The change effected in domestic life is especially deserving of notice. Polygamy, one of the
greatest evils in African society, yields to the
influence of the Gospel. The Missionaries do not
allow any natives to become members of their
religious societies until they renounce polygamy
and concubinage. When this point is gained,
and a native has agreed to be the faithful husband
of the one wife whom he retains, a difficulty occurs
on the point of Christian marriage. English
ladies will smile at the reasoning of the African

husband on this subject: he is sometimes heard
to argue, that, should he be united to his wife
by a tie which nothing but death can sever, he
would not be able to keep her in due subjection;
because he could no longer employ the threat,
once so availing, that if she does not please
him he would put her away. Encouraged, however, by the Missionaries to hope, that religious
motives will operate more beneficially upon the
mind of the female than threats and menaces,
the husband, in numerous instances, has ventured
to unite himself, in the bonds of an indissoluble
union, to the wife to whom Heathenism so loosely
attached him.   Many domestic circles now
pleasingly exhibit the change which Christianity
effects. The husband no longer lives alone, and
sends to the wife her meals in a separate house,
when he has finished his own repast; but both
now dwell in the same habitation, and, with
their children, eat together at the same table.
The husband does not now devolve upon the
wife the heaviest burden; but himself labours
for the support of the family, and she devotes
her attention to domestic duties.   A taste for
the decencies and comforts of European life has
been introduced; and many native families have
adopted the English mode of dress, and furnish
their houses in English style.

While on this point, the want of female schools

may be properly noticed. Many of the other sex are obtaining a decent education; and when this is completed, the untaught and degraded females are wholly unfit to make them suitable companions for life. The wives of the Missionaries, it is true, have exerted themselves with laudable industry to instruct the youth of their own sex; and the mission-school at this time contains several interesting girls, who are making considerable proficiency in useful attainments; but the want of a more extensive provision is greatly felt, and the writer ventures to express his deep conviction, that there are few works of greater charity to which British females could extend their aid, than the promotion of a comprehensive plan for the education of the females of the Gold Coast.

The spirit of industry, and desire for general improvement, which have been excited, are strikingly evidenced by the fact, that many of the Christian natives applied to Mr. Freeman to obtain for them, while he was in England, the means of introducing an improved method of agriculture, and such other assistance as would enable them to advance more rapidly towards a state of civilization. An extract from a Report on this subject, drawn up by Mr. Freeman during his visit to this country, will be read with interest. After expressing a decided opinion of the practicability of Sir T. Fowell Buxton's plans for the instruc-

tion and elevation of the natives of Africa, he
proceeds :—

" It is with great pleasure I state, that many
of the natives of Fantee, with whom I have had
frequent intercourse, and who have already laid
aside their Heathen errors, and embraced Christianity, are very anxious to engage in agricultural
pursuits ; and have requested me to render them
some assistance, by taking out for them, on my
return to Africa, a supply of seeds, implements of
husbandry, and anything that would be useful
to them in cultivating their native soil.   At
Domonási, a small Fantee town, about twenty-
five miles in the interior, there is a little
band of Christians, about sixty in number, with
the young Chief of the district at their head,
who are now anxiously awaiting my return
with a supply of the above-mentioned things.
There are also many of the natives of Cape
Coast and Annamaboe, (Anamábu,) who have
small plantations in the bush, at a distance of
from three to ten miles from these towns, who are
now turning their attention, more fully than they
have ever before done, to the cultivation of the
soil.   These requests on the part of the natives
have impressed our minds with the importance
of establishing, at the earliest opportunity, two
model-farms in the interior of Fantee (Fánti) ;
that we may thereby have the means of teaching

them the best methods of culture, and of showing them the very great capabilities of the soil. One of these farms will be established at Domonási, and the other at Mansu, formerly the great slave-mart, and still a considerable town and district, about fifty miles on the road to Ashantee (As-hánti). In each of these places, a residence for a Missionary is now being prepared; and we hope that, in the course of a few months, both these posts will be occupied; when one of the great objects of the Missionaries will be, that of instructing in the practical science of agriculture all those natives, whether Christians or Heathens, who may feel disposed to turn their attention to it.

"The moral improvement which has already taken place in Domonási, is beginning to have a powerful bearing on the social condition of the people. Their houses are kept more clean and decent than those of the Heathens; and they are imbibing a taste for those many domestic comforts and conveniences, which are to be found in an European cottage. Several of them are also beginning to wear European clothes, and have requested me to take them out a fresh supply, on my return from England. The effects produced in the mind of the Heathen in the surrounding neighbourhood, by these salutary changes, are also becoming strikingly manifest. They begin to admire the improved social condition of their Domonási neighbours, often calling their town a 'white man's croom;' and, as a natural consequence, they are now feeling, in some measure, at least, a respect for that religion which has been the cause of such a beneficial change."

The following fact is illustrative of the frankness with which the Heathen generally acknowledge the good effects of the mission. A native, who had married the daughter of a chief, having become a Christian, soon manifested a desire to improve his condition; and carefully hoarded the fruits of his industry, until he was able to purchase European clothing for his wife and himself. The first day on which they arrayed themselves in their new attire, they paid a visit to their Heathen father, who was so much surprised at their appearance, that he rose up to receive them; and expressed his wishes, that the God in whose service they had become so respectable would continue to bless them, and do them good.

The testimony of the principal chief on the coast, who is dignified with the title of king, may also be adduced. When Mr. Freeman, on the eve of his embarkation for England, called upon Agri to bid him farewell, he acknowledged, as he had frequently done before, that Christianity was effecting a great deal of good in the country.

On Mr. Freeman's expressing his regret that he should not be able to inform his friends in England, that Agri had embraced Christianity, the chief replied, that although that was not the case, many of his people had become Christians; and he hoped that Mr. Freeman could give a better account of the people on the coast than many travellers had done, who had generally described them as turbulent and unmanageable. He hoped that the Missionaries could testify, that they were not so now.

Evidence more conclusive, as to the salutary effects of Missionary instruction, cannot, however, be brought forward than the fact, that instances are not wanting of fetish priests having embraced Christianity, and applied themselves to honest and industrious pursuits.

The case of Domonási having been submitted to Sir Thomas Fowell Buxton, Baronet, and by him to the Committee for the Society for the Extinction of the Slave-Trade, and for the Civilization of Africa, that Committee liberally met the request of the chief, by voting the sum of One Hundred Pounds, to be laid out in the purchase of various agricultural implements for the use of himself and his people, Mr. Freeman engaging to employ his influence and personal exertions for securing the right appropriation of the grant. Matthew Foster, Esq., generously added to the grant

of the Committee another sum, for the purchase of ploughs and of harness for oxen. Thus
furnished, Mr. Freeman returned, with the con-
fident hope, that a very great improvement will
ere long be effected in the social condition of
the people at Domonási. His expectation is,
that the chief will be persuaded to let out the
land in small farms, for a fixed annual rent;
and, this principle once admitted, the independence of the people will be secured, and domestic
slavery will entirely pass away.

The influence of the mission, it may be observed, is steadily exerted in promoting the cause
of rational freedom. The Missionaries constantly
inculcate on the chiefs the Christian doctrine,
that all souls are of equal value in the sight of
God; and that a subordinate station in society
does not stamp him who fills it with an essential
inferiority. When Mr. Freeman has heard, that
any chief to whom he has become known has ill-
treated a slave, he has not failed to send a messenger to expostulate with him, and to enforce
the great principles of religion and justice; or,
if the chief was within a moderate distance, he
has personally visited and reasoned with him;
and these appeals have generally produced the
desired effect. A single case may serve as an
illustration. A native, whose services Mr. Freeman had hired, complained to him, that he had

received some ill-treatment from an old chief. Mr. Freeman immediately sent for him, and reasoned with him on account of his conduct; but for some time he remained unmoved, and asked, " What did it matter? the man was only a slave." At length, however, he admitted the force of Mr. Freeman's arguments, and acknowledged that he was wrong; and Mr. Freeman remarked, that he was at a loss to say which most delighted him, the becoming manner in which the chief offered an apology, or the truly Christian spirit in which it was accepted by the complainant. By pursuing such a course, the Missionaries have the gratification to perceive, that juster views are finding their way into the public mind on the relations which one man sustains to another in society. And it is only in this way that any effectual change can be accomplished in the social condition of the people. It is due to President Maclean to remark, that so far as British influence extends, it is employed by him in protecting the weak against the strong; but beyond the range of that influence, none but moral means can produce the desired improvement in the condition, as well as in the character, of the natives.

Interesting as this mission appears, when viewed in its beneficial effects upon the natives of the

Gold Coast, it, however, rises in importance when regarded as the means by which a way has been opened, it is hoped, for the introduction of the Gospel into Ashantee (As-hánti). Its establishment has served to excite more particular attention to the circumstances and spiritual wants of the people of that country; and has created facilities for bringing the claims of Christianity under the consideration of their sovereign.

In contemplating the commencement of a mission to Ashantee, the attention is arrested by one of those coincidences which it may not be presumption to regard as arrangements of Divine Providence in preparation for the spread of the Gospel in Heathen countries. The mission to the Gold Coast was undertaken, after a long and desolating war, or rather succession of wars, when peaceful intercourse had but recently been restored between that coast and Ashantee; and two youths of the royal family, Quantamissah and Ansah, whom the king had sent as hostages to Cape-Coast Castle, were among the first who enjoyed the advantages of Missionary instruction. Under the faithful ministry of Mr. Dunwell, they both became convinced of the truth and excellence of the Christian religion; the public profession of which they have since assumed in England;—Quantamissah receiving in baptism the name of William, and Ansah, that of John. These two interesting youths— having completed their education, under the direction of the African Committee, by whom the British Government now conducts the affairs of the Gold Coast; and having visited the principal places in Great Britain and Ireland, under the care of the Rev. Mr. Pyne, a clergyman of the Established Church—are now returning to the Gold Coast, with the Niger Expedition, followed by the best wishes of all who are interested in the cause of Africa.

Shortly after the formation of the Cape-Coast mission, Christian worship was introduced into the capital of Ashantee, by some of the native Christians from the coast; and one individual, especially, obtained the favourable notice of the king himself. On the 17th of October, 1836, Mr. Wrigley, in writing to the Wesleyan Committee, remarked :—

"The present king of the Ashantee nation, I have learned, is a far more tolerant man than his predecessor; and a Missionary might, with perfect safety, reside at Coomassie, the capital of his kingdom. A young man is now resident there as the king's writer, or secretary, under the direction of the President of Cape-Coast, who formerly was a member of our society here; and who continues, as far as I can learn, to maintain a moral and steady character, and is steadfast in his religious attachments."

On the 11th of January following, Mr. Wrigley again wrote as follows :—

"I have just seen, at our preaching this evening, one of our members, who has resided at Coomassie for some time past. He states to me, that in the house where he dwelt, he has several times had the sons of the king of Ashantee (As-hánti) with him at prayers; and that, on Christmas-day, the king requested their attendance at the palace, when he, in conjunction with one or two others, had singing and prayer in the presence of the monarch."

To this important field for Missionary enterprise the attention of Mr. Freeman was naturally directed; and he resolved to embrace the first favourable opportunity for exploring it.   At length, having completed the erection of a chapel at Cape-Coast, and made the necessary arrangements for the arduous undertaking, he placed the mission-house and societies under the care of Mr. William De Graft, and on the 29th of January, 1839, set out for Coomassie, (Kumási,) with his interpreter and attendants; among whom were two native soldiers, provided by President Maclean, to whose kindness he was also indebted for a letter of introduction to the king of Ashantee (As-hánti).   The zeal manifested by the native converts on this occasion deserves especial notice. As Mr. Freeman was the only English Missionary on the coast, it was no ordinary sacrifice on their part to relinquish the benefit of his services for a period of several months; but, in addition to this, they liberally contributed nearly sixty pounds sterling, to meet in part the expenses of his journey. This noble instance of self-denial and liberality, in behalf of the people who had for a length of years been the bitterest foes of their own country, is striking evidence, that an element altogether new had been introduced by Christianity into the African character, in which a feeling of kindness and compassion for enemies had not previously had a place.

The day after crossing the river Prah, Mr. Freeman reached Quísah, the first town in Ashantee Proper; and here he was informed, that he could not proceed any further without the consent of the chief of Adansi, who resided about a mile distant, at a neat little town called Fómunah. As it was then evening, and he had the unexpected pleasure of meeting with several Fantee traders there, who were members of the Wesleyan society at Cape Coast, he resolved to take up his quarters at Quísah for the night, and proceed to Fómunah in the morning. On the following day, the chief Korínchi received him with the etiquette generally observed on such occasions;—sitting under his large umbrella, in the front of his house, supported by his captains on the right hand and on the left. After the usual salutations had been exchanged, the chief inquired what object Mr. Freeman had in view, in visiting Coomassie; to which he replied, that he had nothing to do with any palavers, nor was he engaged in any kind of trade; but that his sole object was to explain and recommend the Christian religion, as the best means of promoting the highest interests of both the king and his people. The chief then expressed a desire to hear the Gospel for himself; and Mr. Freeman, in compliance with his wish, explained to him the scriptural doctrine of the One true God, and gave a summary of the leading truths of Christianity.

On the following day, which was the sabbath, Mr. Freeman, accompanied by the chief of Quísah, again visited Fómunah, at the request of Korínchi, who wished to have further information on the subject of the new religion. About five hundred persons assembled, and a regular religious service was held; during which the native members of the mission from Cape Coast, who were then on a trading excursion in the neighbourhood, united in singing the praises of

Almighty God. Great seriousness was manifested while Mr. Freeman discoursed on an appropriate passage of Scripture; and frequently the truths which he delivered were assented to by an audible "Yes" from many of his hearers. At the conclusion, the chief and the captains said it was "a good palaver;" and Korínchi said he was anxious to hear more; and wished to be particularly informed what *Yankumpon* ("God") liked, and what he disliked. He appeared much pleased, when Mr. Freeman expressed his readiness to preach to him again; and both he and his captains were evidently disposed to infer the excellence of the Christian religion, from the zeal which had prompted the Missionary to make such great sacrifices, merely for the purpose of doing them good.

In a day or two, the Chief sent for him again; and an officer arrived from Coomassie, (Kumási,) with a present for him from the king, of nine ackies of gold, in value two pounds, five shillings, and a friendly message, informing him, that he should be invited to proceed in a few days, during which time the messenger would remain with him. Mr. Freeman then accepted the offer of Korínchi, to remove to Fómunah, and await there the final determination of the king; and he was once more strictly interrogated as to the object of his visit, in order that the king might have the fullest possible information upon the subject. A messenger was immediately despatched to Coomassie, with the answers which were obtained; and Mr. Freeman embraced the opportunity of sending by him to the king the introductory letter which he had received from President Maclean.

While Mr. Freeman remained at Fómunah, he had opportunities of witnessing the effects of the popular superstitions. The fetishmen took the alarm at his coming, and attempted to excite the apprehension of impending evil; and on one occasion, he noticed, that the path leading from Quísah to Fómunah was strewed with a fetish preparation of eggs and other materials, for the alleged purpose of preventing the town from destruction by fire. The occurrence of two deaths about the same time was also the occasion of manifesting the sanguinary character of the false religion which enthrals the minds of the natives. On each of those events, a human being was sacrificed, with the usual ceremonies; and the entire indifference manifested by the people at the sight of the mangled victims lying in the streets, strikingly evidenced their familiarity with such scenes of horror. Mr. Freeman did not fail to remonstrate with the chief, on account of those proceedings; and the answer which he received, in extenuation of the drunkenness and rioting which took place at the funeral custom, afforded a striking verification of the apostolic description of those who " sorrow" for the dead as persons " which have no hope." Korínchi said, that they felt very unhappy when they lost their relatives and friends, and were then glad to have recourse to drunkenness, or anything which would drive away their gloomy thoughts. On the following sabbath, he and his captains manifested much excitement when Mr. Freeman discoursed to them on the Ten Commandments; and appeared to be painfully affected, on being assured, in answer to one of their questions, that the offering of human sacrifices is murder in the sight of God.

Six weeks having elapsed from the time of his arrival at Quísah, Mr. Freeman began to be very uneasy on account of his detention. The Christian societies on the coast needed his services; the rainy season was so nearly approaching, as to leave little more than the necessary time for the journey to Coomassie, (Kumási,) and back again to Cape Coast; and there was no fairer prospect of his being allowed to proceed, than on the first day of his arrival. Korínchi met all his inquiries with evasive answers, or fair promises which were not performed; and he at length packed up his luggage, and set out on his return. When the chief found, that the Missionary was really

gone, he became greatly alarmed; and sent two
or three persons after him, to assure him, that if
he would go back to Fómunah, he would without delay provide messengers to accompany him
to Coomassie. Not being satisfied as to the sincerity of the chief, he continued his homeward
course; when Korinchi applied to a Fantee trader,
then resident at Quísah, with whom Mr. Freeman
was well acquainted, begging him to follow the
Missionary, and entreat him to return. He,
however, still deemed it advisable to proceed, till
he came to a small croom, about nine miles from
Fómunah, and there remain till the following
morning. Scarcely had he halted, when several
other messengers arrived, stating that Korínchi
was very unhappy, and that their lives would be
in danger, should the Missionary leave the country. And it was the fact, that Korínchi was
thrown into such a state of apprehension, that
he made a " custom," and spent the whole of
that night in drinking and dancing, in order
to banish gloomy apprehensions from his mind.
The messengers, moreover, skilfully urged the
benevolent object of his visit; and told him,
that his kind intentions to promote the welfare of
their countrymen would be defeated, should he
now abandon his undertaking, and go back to
the coast.

Mr. Freeman was at length convinced, that the

chief did seriously intend to send him forward, without further delay, into the immediate vicinity of the capital, where he might remain until he received the king's permission to visit him. In in the morning, therefore, he returned to Fómunah; which place he had scarcely entered, when a messenger arrived from the capital, accompanied by two or three persons whom Korínchi had sent in haste, to inform the king that the Missionary would not wait any longer, but was determined to return home, unless he might immediately go forward to Coomassie (Kumási). The messenger brought a request from the king, that Mr. Freeman would proceed at once to the capital; and on the following day he commenced his journey.

The principal cause of the tedious delay which he experienced at Fómunah, was not the caprice or unwillingness of Korínchi, but the apprehensions of the king himself. Spies were placed at Fómunah, to watch his conduct; and messengers were frequently sent up to report his daily proceedings. The following dialogue between the king and one of the messengers, on his return to the capital, will sufficiently indicate the anxious fears which the barbarian monarch entertained:—

THE KING.—You have seen the fetishman? (meaning Mr. Freeman.)

MESSENGER.—Yes.

KING.—Had he plenty of drums with him?

MESSENGER.—I saw no drums.

KING.—Why! he is a fetishman : he must have drums with him.

MESSENGER.—I saw no drums. He has plenty of boxes ; but I cannot say what they contain.

KING.—Why did you not endeavour to learn whether the boxes contained drums or not?

At another time the king said, " Never since the world began has there been an English Missionary in Ashantee before. What can he want ? "—What an affecting scene is disclosed by such inquiries and remarks ! In the ineffectual endeavours of the king to comprehend the object of the missionary's visit, a striking proof is afforded that the human mind may be so darkened and depraved by the practice of idolatry, as to appear utterly unable, at first, even to form a conception of the disinterested compassion of the Gospel. To obtain time for the full consideration of the question respecting the probable object and tendency of a visit unparalleled in the annals of the country, was, doubtless, the principal reason for the delay which took place. The king was not willing to treat the white fetishman with discourtesy by sending him away; for who could tell the power of his wrath ? and, on the other hand, he did not

dare to allow him to advance to the capital until
he had pondered well the probable consequences
of his approach.   A somewhat similar feeling
of anxious curiosity was manifested by the people generally; for, as Mr. Freeman passed along
the path, all the inhabitants of the towns and
crooms crowded together to gaze at him; but,
whenever they saw him engaged with his attendants in religious worship, they immediately ran
away evidently in great alarm.

When he arrived at Esárgu, about nine
miles from the capital, he waited until he
should receive another message inviting him
to proceed. He spent the sabbath there without any summons, for the king had been made
aware that the Christian missionary did not
travel on that sacred day. Parties of soldiers,
however, were seen passing towards the capital;
and, during the whole of the ensuing night,
the tinkling of the little bells, attached to the
dress of the military, announced the approach
of successive detachments of troops, who were to
take part in the formalities of Mr. Freeman's public reception. On Monday morning, about eight
o'clock, he reached Franfraham, a little croom
which had been built for the accommodation
of persons travelling to Coomassie (Kumási);
and, while waiting there, under the influence
of feelings which none can fully comprehend

but the faithful minister of Christ, and oppressed by a sense of the solemn responsibility which attached to him, as the first herald of the gospel who had ever entered the dark and blood-stained capital of Ashantee for the purpose of offering to its monarch and his people the religion of purity and peace,—he united with his Christian native attendants in fervent prayer, that the blessing of the God of missions might prosper his pious enterprise.

About two o'clock in the afternoon a royal messenger arrived, requesting him to proceed; and, almost immediately after, three other officers, bearing gold-hilted swords, followed, for the purpose of hastening him. Preceded by the messengers, and by a party of soldiers carrying arms, he advanced nearly to the entrance of the capital; and there, in accordance with African etiquette, waited, under a large tree, for a further invitation from the sovereign. In a short time Apóko, the king's chief linguist, one of the most influential men in the kingdom, came in his palanquin, shaded by an immense umbrella, and attended by several officers, bearing gold-headed canes, who took charge of the travelling luggage, and conveyed it to the place provided for the temporary residence of the stranger. Another messenger, accompanied by an escort of troops, and by men bearing large umbrellas, then arrived, with an invitation to the visitant to meet the king in the market-place. As they entered the capital, Mr. Freeman noticed that he passed between two heaps of earth, newly thrown up, one on each side of the road; but it was well for him that he did not learn, at that exciting moment, what those heaps concealed; for they were the graves of two human beings who had been just buried alive, as fetish victims, with a view to avert any evil that might, without such precaution, result from his visit. This appalling fact, afterwards ascertained by his interpreter, a Christian native, whose veracity was above suspicion, tends to throw fresh light upon the cause of Mr. Freeman's long detention on the frontier; at the same time that it exhibits, in a striking point of view, the fearful character of those superstitions with which the Christian Missionary in Ashantee will have to contend.

On arriving at the market-place, the imposing scene which the court of Ashantee (As-hánti) presents, burst full upon his view. There sat the king, surrounded by his officers of state, his caboceers, and captains, and attended by a very large body of military, and many thousands of other persons without arms. The whole number present was estimated at forty thousand. A narrow path leading to the king was kept open, and Mr.

Freeman was occupied half an hour in saluting the caboceers as he passed along, before he reached the royal presence. Having paid his respects to the king, by whom he was graciously received, it then became Mr. Freeman's privilege, or rather task, to receive the salutations of the sovereign and his court in return. Attended by his own people, and by some respectable Fantee traders who happened at that time to be in Coomassie, he accordingly placed himself in a convenient situation, at a little distance. The caboceers successively greeted him, as they passed with their bands of music, umbrellas, and every variety of fantastic ornament. The king, whose immediate suite made an astonishing display of gold, followed by the war-captains, and the troops, closed this striking exhibition of barbarous splendour. It was a full hour and a half before the gorgeous pageant passed away, and left the Missionary to his meditations. What his reflections were, his own language will best declare :—

" I gazed on this concourse of Heathens with feelings of sorrow and joy. I sorrowed in the reflection, that most (perhaps all) of them were totally ignorant of the great Author of their being, without one ray of divine consolation to cheer them amid the changing scenes of this visionary world. Are they laid on a bed of languishing? They have nothing to comfort them, or buoy up their drooping spirits. Does death, which stalks through the land in horrid forms, rob them of their friends? Alas for them! they must sorrow as men without hope. They never hear the shouts of departing Christian friends, as they ascend the steep of the heavenly Zion, to join the church triumphant above. Neither do they see, with the eye of faith, the blood-bought throng standing in the presence of God, 'clothed with white robes and palms in their hands.' Does death stare themselves in the face, and ask the panting breath? Alas for them! they have no Christian hope beyond the grave, blooming with immortality! Is it not so? Tell it, ye murdered human victims, whose blood disfigures the streets, and whose putrefying bodies taint the air! Tell it, ye midnight revellers, who vainly strive to draw the anguish from your hearts by the fumes of intoxication! Tell it, ye carnivorous birds, and ye wild beasts of the forest, that feed on the mangled corpses of the thousands of victims of superstitious cruelty! And, lastly, tell it, ye human bones, that lie bleaching in the open day!"

On the third day after his arrival, Mr. Freeman was visited by the royal linguists, some of whom were heavily laden with golden ornaments. They had been sent by the king to obtain from the Missionary full information as to the object of his visit. " I gave them," says Mr. Freeman, " all necessary information ; but found much difficulty in making them understand me. And no wonder; for how can those who are buried in superstition, and who witness scarcely anything but scenes of cruelty arising from that superstition, form any just idea of the motives which stimulate the Christian Missionary to visit them ? "

The important negotiation was now suspended by one of those painful events which are ever and anon interrupting the course of affairs, and putting a stop to all business among these unhappy people. On the morning after this visit from the linguists, Mr. Freeman learned that one of the king's relatives was dead, and that already four human victims had been sacrificed, whose mangled carcases were lying in the streets ; and, in the course of the day, he received a message from the king, through Apóko, who had intimated the Missionary's anxiety to return as soon as possible to Cape Coast, requesting him not to go out into the town that day, as he was making a " custom " for a deceased relative, and he knew that Europeans did not like to witness human sacrifices. Apóko was attended by two officers, one of whom carried an immense golden sword, to which was fastened a decanter of the same precious metal, which would contain about a pint. He was, however, assured, that the king was now fully satisfied that the object of his visit was only to do good, and would see him upon the subject as soon as the custom was over. In the course of that day, twenty-five human victims were sacrificed in the capital and surrounding villages; the heads of those who were killed in the suburbs were brought into the town in baskets ; and the work of slaughter was renewed, at the sound of the death-drum, on the following day, when about fifteen more unfortunate creatures perished. The carcases, after having been exposed for some time in the streets, were thrown into a deep dell on one side of the market-place, from which a most intolerable stench proceeded, as Mr. Freeman passed the place on a subsequent day. In the midst of these scenes of horror, Mr. Freeman sanctified the Christian sabbath by conducting public religious worship at his own quarters, which was attended by many Ashantees, some of whom manifested deep attention.

Having received a handsome present from the king, consisting of a cow, a sheep, a pig, a quantity of palm-nuts, yams, and plantains, and one ounce and five ackies of gold-dust, (£5 currency,) with three ackies for his interpreter, and five for his other attendants, Mr. Freeman went to the palace to return his thanks for the present; but the business of his visit could not be entered upon until the funeral " custom " was over. In the meantime he employed himself in examining the capital, and visiting Bantama. His being permitted to see the royal sepulchre at the latter place, must be regarded as a decided proof of the favourable impression which the king had received respecting him; for the standing rule is, that no persons shall be allowed to go to Bantama, save when the king himself visits the tombs of his ancestors.

The " custom " continued for a whole week, at the expiration of which, Mr. Freeman, having walked out for recreation, passed the end of a street where a great number of persons were assembled, and a band of music was playing; and the horrifying exhibition of another human victim, weltering in its gore, presented itself to his view. Turning from the affecting sight, he passed on to the further end of the same street, where he also found a large concourse of people, among whom, seated under his umbrella, was the king, who had come out to drink palm-wine publicly with his chiefs, previously to a week's partial seclusion in the palace after the " custom " had ended.

In the course of this day, Mr. Freeman reminded Apóko of his anxiety to obtain an answer from the king respecting the establishment of schools, and other contemplated arrangements for the benefit of the Ashantee people; when Apóko said, " The king will speedily give you an answer; and we hope you will come to Coomassie (Kumási) again, and pay us another visit, and we shall be always glad to see you. The king believes that you wish to do him and the people good." On the second day after this conversation, Mr. Freeman, when in company with Apóko, adverted again to the approaching rains, which would render his speedy departure necessary; and Apóko, who is the only subject that possesses the privilege of visiting the king whenever he pleases, went immediately to the palace, and returned with a message to the effect, that the monarch had been so busily engaged throughout the morning, that he could not see him that day, but would make arrangements with him for his departure, on the morrow.

The following day, however, was the sabbath, on which Mr. Freeman again conducted divine service at his quarters; and a most encouraging scene was exhibited. A native of the interior, who had received instruction from some of the Christian Fantee traders, had applied for baptism, and was found to be so well acquainted with the doctrines of the Gospel, and manifested such a desire to become a disciple of Christ, that Mr. Freeman felt justified in admitting him into the Christian church by that sacred ordinance, which he did in the presence of many Ashantees. On the morning of Monday, Apóko, who had gone to the palace to remind the king, that it was necessary for Mr. Freeman to set out on his journey home, returned, accompanied by a great number of linguists and other attendants, with a present for the Missionary of two ounces and four ackies of gold-dust, (nine pounds currency,) and of a slave; and with two pounds currency for his interpreter, and other attendants. Apoko, at the same time, delivered the following message :—" His Majesty knows that you cannot stop longer, on account of the rains; and as the thing which you have mentioned to him requires much consideration, he cannot answer you in so short a time : but if you will come up again, or send a messenger, after the rains are over, he will be prepared to answer you."

In reply, Mr. Freeman engaged that either himself would return to Coomassie, or send a messenger at the time appointed; and he then repaired to the palace to take leave of the king, who sat surrounded by a great number of attendants; and who, on parting with him, politely requested him to present his (the king's) compliments to his Excellency, President Maclean.

About noon the same day, after an affectionate farewell from Apóko, who had acted throughout a most friendly part, he left Coomassie, preceded by an escort of soldiers, who accompanied him as far as Franfraham.

At this place, Mr. Freeman halted awhile to perform what he felt to be a pleasing duty, namely, to emancipate the slave which had been presented to him by the king. The history of this poor creature, though brief, was eventful. He had been sent down from the interior to Coomassie, and was placed among the slaves, about one thousand in number, whom the king keeps in irons to be ready for sacrifice. During the " custom" which had just taken place he had been twice brought out for execution, but as often his fetters had been placed upon him again, and he had been sent back into confinement; and on that morning, on which he was taken out to be presented to Mr. Freeman, he fully expected that the fatal day had at length arrived, and that he should then be sacrificed. Mr. Freeman is of opinion, that, as he was a well-proportioned, good-looking man, the king had reserved him as a more worthy present than a mean and ill-looking person would have been. After the joyous scene of his emancipation had taken place, the Missionary pursued his journey to Fómunah, where Korínchi, overjoyed to see him, threw his arms round his neck, and gave him the most affectionate welcome; and when, on parting again, Mr. Freeman told him that he should need his assistance in forwarding messengers to Coomassie, or in furnishing himself with aid on a second visit, he readily promised to do everything for him which might be in his power, and afforded at once a substantial proof of his kindness, by providing four strong men to assist him across the hills of Adansi, on his homeward road. On the evening of the 23d of April, Mr. Freeman arrived at Cape-Coast Castle, after an absence of nearly three months.*

The results of this important journey were as encouraging as could have been reasonably anticipated. The long delay of Mr. Freeman at

* Mr. Freeman's own Journal of his visit was published at length in the Missionary Notices of the Wesleyan Missionary Society, for the month of January, 1840 ; and also in the General Report of that Society for the same year. To that most interesting Document the Reader is respectfully referred for full particulars. The preceding abridgment of its contents it was deemed expedient to introduce into this volume, in order to furnish a brief, but complete and connected, view of the religious state and prospects of Ashantee, as well as to secure the sympathies, the prayers, and the continued and persevering liberality of the Christian and benevolent Public of this country, in behalf of the Wesleyan Missionary Society, which has had the truly apostolical honour of making the FIRST movement towards the establishment of one of the most needed, but most difficult and perilous, Missions of modern times.

Fómunah, however perplexing at the time, was doubtless productive of very beneficial effects. It tended to make him well known on the borders of Ashantee, (As-hánti,) and afforded him the opportunity of attaching to himself a considerable number of friends, among whom he can place himself with confidence, when he shall again go up to the capital. Fómunah will be a kind of advanced post, which will facilitate his future missionary arrangements with respect to the interior. It was at that place that he partially succeeded in producing a favourable impression upon the mind of the king himself, who was encouraged, by the frequent reports which he received as to his spirit and conduct, so far to renounce his superstitious apprehensions, as to give him a cordial welcome to the capital. The sovereign's personal intercourse with Mr. Freeman there, strengthened the good opinion of him which he had formed, and even produced a wish to detain him much longer than it would have been convenient for him to stay; for Mr. Freeman is of opinion, that the king would not have parted with him so soon, had it not been for the considerate kindness of President Maclean, who wrote to explain to him the danger to which the health and life of the Missionary would be exposed, should he not leave before the rains set in, as he had not made the necessary precautionary arrangements for spending the rainy season in Coomassie.

That Mr. Freeman was not deceived in his opinion, as to the good effect of his visit, was rendered apparent in a few weeks after his return to the coast; for he received a communication, stating, that the king was waiting to see him again, and was anxious that he should establish a school at Coomassie (Kumási). And his hope, as to the success of his future undertaking, was greatly strengthened by the circumstance that several Ashantees, who came down on business to Cape-Coast Castle, called at the mission-house to see him, and recognised him as an old friend. Among these was a brother of Korínchi, who presented to him that Chief's regards, and told him, that they should all be happy to receive from him another visit.

The impression of Mr. Freeman as to the character of the favourable opening into Ashantee, was considerably confirmed by the opinion of a very competent judge of African temper and character. Having submitted the journal of his tour to President Maclean, his Excellency, on sending it back, thus expressed his views :—

" I herewith return your narrative of your journey to Ashantee, (As-hánti,) which I have perused with very great interest.

" I would fain hope that, from the manner in

which you were received in your *avowed* character as a Missionary, throughout the whole of your arduous journey, there will not exist many obstacles to the accomplishment of the first object,— getting a *locus standi* in the country. Certainly I think there will be no *insuperable* obstacle.

"I hope and trust that the Wesleyan Missionary Committee will be satisfied, that there is such an opening as will justify them in pushing the advantage gained by your indefatigable zeal. I would almost go so far as to say, that, if they have the means, a serious responsibility will rest upon them, and on Christian England, if so glorious an opening into interior Africa, if so rich a harvest, be neglected. But I hope better things. And I do not despair of yet witnessing the peaceful triumph of the Cross, even in that stronghold of Satan, Coomassie.

"I expect that considerable advantages will arise from the Christian education of the two Ashantee Princes, now in England. If well supported, for all depends upon that, their influence in Ashantee will aid the good cause much. I shall not fail to take care that they be introduced to the Wesleyan Missionary Committee."

It is due to J. G. Nicholls, and W. M. Hutton, Esquires, leading members of the Committee for managing the affairs of the Settlements at the Gold Coast, to state that they had already kindly

introduced members of the Wesleyan Missionary
Society to the acquaintance of the Princes, and
that they have ever taken a lively interest in the
Society's Mission at the Gold Coast, as an
important means, in their judgment, for promoting the improvement of that part of Africa.

On the receipt of Mr. Freeman's Journal in
England, the question, " What shall be done ? "
became the subject of grave consideration on the
part of the Wesleyan Missionary Committee,
under whose direction Mr. Freeman acted. The
ordinary annual income of the Society was already
pledged for the support of existing missions ; and
yet the Committee dared not to take upon themselves the responsibility of refusing to *attempt*,
at least, the establishment of a mission in Ashantee. It was at length resolved, that Mr. Freeman
should be allowed to return home for a time,
partly for the purpose of recruiting his health,
but more particularly with a view to a special
effort being made, in order to raise the funds
necessary for the new undertaking ; and two Missionaries were immediately sent to relieve him,
for a time, from his laborious duties at the Gold
Coast. On the arrival of Mr. and Mrs. Mycock,
and Mr. Brooking, Mr. Freeman, therefore, came
to England, accompanied by Mr. William De
Graft, and was the bearer of a message from
the king of Ashantee, who requested that his

two nephews might be immediately sent home, —the contemplated establishment of a Christian school at Coomassie having rendered him very anxious to see them.

The results of Mr. Freeman's visit to several of the principal towns in Great Britain and Ireland have been of the most gratifying description. Members of the Church of England, some of whom are in the higher walks of life, and Christians of other religious denominations, as well as the members of the Wesleyan community, responded to the novel and deeply-interesting appeal; and, by these united exertions, the proposed sum of £5,000 was placed at the disposal of the Wesleyan Committee, to enable them to send with Mr. Freeman, on his return, Six additional Missionaries, in order to strengthen the existing establishments at the Gold Coast, and to commence a new mission in the kingdom of Ashantee. Arrangements were made in due season for their outfit and departure; and, at Mr. Freeman's suggestion, the Committee agreed so far to comply with the established African custom of offering presents, as to send for the king's acceptance and use a suitable carriage, which was noticed with approbation by Her Most Gracious Majesty and His Royal Highness Prince Albert, to whose inspection it was submitted by Mr. Sims, the builder. In the month of Decem-

ber, Mr. and Mrs. Freeman embarked at Graves-
end, on board the "Osborne," accompanied by
Mr. and Mrs. Hesk, Mr. and Mrs. Shipman,
Messrs. Watson, Walden, and Thackwray, and
Mr. William De Graft, whom the Committee had
received as a regular agent of the Society, to be
hereafter wholly employed in the work of the
Mission; and, after a few days, the party left the
Channel, followed by the best wishes and ardent
prayers of thousands who have become deeply
interested in their arduous enterprise.

CONCLUSION.

IN adverting to the probable results of the
projected Mission in Ashantee, it may be fairly
anticipated, that, should the Divine blessing
crown it with success, it will have an important
bearing on the work of the moral illumination and
social elevation of Africa; an object to which the
public attention is now so especially directed, and
for whose attainment such a combination of ener-
gies have been called forth, and so many ardent
prayers have been offered, by those who have
learned from the volume of inspiration, that,
without the benediction of God, "nothing is
wise, or strong, or good."

It is presumed that the preceding pages furnish evidence in support of the views so strongly expressed by that enlightened philanthropist, Sir T. Fowell Buxton, on the primary importance of Christianity. Great as is the stress which he lays on the application of subordinate means, such as the promotion of agriculture, and the introduction of a lawful and healthful commerce ; yet one of the principles, to which most prominence is given in his spirit-stirring volume, is, that the Gospel is the great civilizer of barbarous men, and that the exertions of the Missionary are therefore of indispensable necessity.* And can any one, possessed of a competent knowledge of the superstitions of Ashantee, hesitate to adopt this conclusion? Is an improved system of agriculture to be introduced? The visible representatives of the gods of the people are growing upon the very spot where the experiment is to be attempted. Are the natives to be taught to work the invaluable mines with which their country abounds? It will be found that the hills which contain the precious treasures are the imaginary residences of the national deities, and that superstition will deprecate the sacrilegious touch. Are the advantages of an innocent commerce to be recommended? Yes ; but the intervention of the numerous "unlucky days," and the

* " The African Slave-Trade and its Remedy," p. 502.

time necessary for the consultation of the Heathen oracles, before any important business can be undertaken, will retard, and often entirely defeat, the best-concerted arrangements. Are remonstrances to be addressed to the people, on account of their inhuman practices? The sacrifice of human victims is not inhumanity, in their estimation; but an act of piety most acceptable to their gods, and one of the best proofs which they can afford of their affection for departed relatives and friends. Even Osai Quamina, who lost his throne because he had ventured to abolish several other superstitious customs, did not dare to abandon the practice of human sacrifices at the graves of his relatives. Nor was such a reluctance an uncommon feeling. Very recently, the neighbouring king of Dahomy replied, to a gentleman from Cape-Coast Castle,* (who expostulated with him on the occasion of a public sacrifice,) that their religious customs rendered such offerings imperative, and that were he to forbid them, the dissatisfaction of the people would place his own life in jeopardy. It may, therefore, be considered as certain, that, whatever may be done by other means in the way of *facilitating* the introduction of the Gospel, the work of civilization will not be advanced to any consi-

* Thomas Hutton, Esq.

derable extent, until the superstitious spell by
which the people are bound shall be broken by
Christianity itself. When that, however, shall be
once accomplished, the happiest results may then
be expected to follow.

The influence which a successful evangelical
mission in Ashantee (As-hánti) cannot fail to
exert in promoting peaceful relations between
that country and the British settlements on the
coast, deserves especial notice. However it may
be regretted that, in the former war of the
coast, greater exertions were not made to meet
those demands of the Ashantee king which
possessed something of the character of justice, it must yet be obvious, that it will ever
prove a most difficult task to prevent misun-
derstandings with a people whose views and
principles of action are so remote from those
which prevail in civilized society ; and it may be
concluded, that, unless a revolution be effected in
the Ashantee character, little hope can be entertained of the continuance of peace. That such a
conclusion is not to be regarded as a mere theo-
retic opinion, unsupported by experience, will
appear from the following extract of a letter
addressed to the Rev. Mr. Mycock, on the 9th of
April last, by President Maclean :—

"I am truly glad," his Excellency remarks,
"that your Committee have taken up the subject

of a mission to Ashantee as they have done. The experience of every succeeding year convinces me more and more, that, even in a political point of view, the establishment of a mission, and of schools, in Ashantee, would be of infinite value; for these would eventually prove our truest and best safeguard against the revival of those quarrels and wars, betwixt the Ashantee and Fantee tribes, which, as matters at present stand, a very small spark might rekindle. Although our relations with Ashantee have certainly been, for the last nine years, on a better footing than during any former period in the history of the colony; yet they have been a constant subject of anxiety to me, knowing, as I do, the people with whom I have had to deal. I only hope, that as neither Mr. Freeman nor myself have ever attempted to undervalue or understate the difficulties which *must* be encountered in carrying Christianity and education into the interior, the Wesleyan Missionary Committee will not allow their zeal to be quenched, or their endeavours to slacken, when those obstacles come to be *felt*, and fought against."

Assuredly the Committee did not resolve upon attempting the formation of a mission in Ashantee, but under the deep and solemn conviction of the arduous nature of the undertaking. The formidable obstacle which an insalu-

brious climate opposes to Missionary labours in
every part of Western Africa, will prevail also in
Ashantee to a great extent; but that will not be
the worst feature of the case. Moral difficulties,
of the most appalling character, must be encountered. Let the situation of the Missionaries be contemplated, when, far from civilized
society, the almost every-day scenes with which
they must become awfully familiar will be
those tragedies of barbarity and horror, at the
bare recital of which the heart sickens; and when
frequently they must witness those outbursts of
superstitious fury, during which scarcely any
life is safe,—with the conviction, too, that themselves are peculiarly obnoxious to the priests,
the demons who direct the storm,—let these
circumstances be kept in view, and then it will
be understood how great an amount of moral
courage and of divine support they will require to
sustain them at the post of duty. And who can
tell to what an extent the indulgence of a barbarous caprice may not frustrate their exertions,
and for a while disappoint their hopes? Mr.
Freeman congratulated himself on having found
a friend in Korínchi, the chief of Fómunah; but
his aid cannot be anticipated; for Korínchi, having
given some cause of offence, has been destroyed
with deliberate cruelty,—the king having ordered
a certain stream to be diverted from its channel,

until a hole should be dug in its bed, in which that unfortunate chief was placed, and then left to perish in the returning waters of the rivulet.

In deliberating upon the formation of a mission in Ashantee, (As-hánti,) the Wesleyan Committee, the writer repeats, had a distinct conception of the formidable character of the undertaking. But unless they had renounced the first principles of our most holy religion, they could not avoid the conclusion, that it is the imperative duty of some section or other of the Christian church to send the Gospel even to Ashantee; nor did they dare to deny that the indications of Providence imposed upon the particular Society which they represent, a special obligation to make the attempt. Viewing the encouragement to exertion afforded in the success which had been vouchsafed to the labours of their Missionaries on the coast, where, in the short space of five years, upwards of Six Hundred natives had been united together in Christian societies, and several Coloured Teachers had been raised up, a specimen of whom they had before them in the person of Mr. William De Graft;—considering what facilities such a mission was calculated to afford for extending the gospel into the interior;—taking into account the fact, that the way had been partially opened by the successful visit of Mr.

Freeman to Ashantee, and that the king had expressed a wish that he should return and establish a Christian school in the capital;—and aware, moreover, that the Society had Missionaries at its disposal, who would not shrink from the peril of even such an undertaking ;—the Committee could not have justified themselves, nor would they, as the writer is persuaded, have been acquitted by the Christian public of Britain, had they resolved that they would not " at least attempt" to establish a mission in Ashantee.

In the prosecution of this great work, the most strenuous and persevering exertions will doubtless be necessary; for it is not to be expected, that the strong-hold of Heathenish darkness and superstition which the Missionaries have gone to assail, will be won in a day. Perhaps a long period may elapse before much visible impression may be produced. But if the necessary efforts be made and continued, in the spirit of prayer, and of humble dependence upon the Divine blessing, the promises of Holy Writ warrant the expectation of eventual success. In that *regenerated world* which is contemplated in the bright vision of prophecy, even Ashantee must be included ; and faith steadfastly anticipates the time when that vision shall become a delightful reality :—" For the mouth of the Lord hath spoken it."

NOTES.

NOTE A.—See page 31.

ABU BEKR, having obtained his liberty by the kind intervention of Dr. Madden, accompanied Mr. Davidson to Africa; when the caravan by which they were travelling from Wad-i-Nún to Tumbuktú, was attacked and plundered by a party of Arabs, and Mr. Davidson lost his life and property together. Since that catastrophe, which occurred in December, 1836, Abu Bekr has not been heard of; but his former benefactor, Dr. Madden, has prepared an advertisement to be sent into the interior by the Niger Expedition, generously offering a reward of one hundred dollars, to any individual who may give such information respecting him, as may lead to his liberation, should he have been reduced a second time to slavery.

NOTE B.—See page 161.

THE reduction of the Kafir language to a written form, was a work of considerable labour; and the first grammatical sketches of it were so imperfect, that in some cases the exceptions to the rules were almost as numerous as the instances in which the rules applied. The Rev. William Shaw, the principal Wesleyan Missionary in Southern Africa, at length obtained the clue which enabled his colleague, the Rev. W. B. Boyce, to trace out the principle on which the language is constructed. This has been termed the "Euphonic or Alliteral Concord;" and it operates so extensively, and with such regularity, as to secure the greatest *precision*, while effectually promoting the *harmony* of the language. Whether or not the analogy traced between it and the Coptic by Dr. Prichard, may be considered as a satisfactory indication of the origin of the people by whom it is used; it will be obvious to all who examine carefully the structure of the Kafir language, that it must originally have been the medium of communication among a people, who were possessed of a refinement and civilization altogether unknown in the extensive regions of Southern Africa, where the language, in its various dialects, is now spoken.

A second and enlarged edition of Mr. Boyce's Grammar, prepared by the Rev. J. W. Davis, is now in the press; and the Rev. H. Dugmore is compiling a Dictionary of the language. The Rev. James Archbell has also published a Grammar of the Sichuana, a kindred dialect. The Missionaries of the Society have translated into the Kafir language, and printed at the mission press in Graham's Town, nearly the whole of the sacred Scriptures; and the agents of the London and Glasgow Missionary Societies have also diligently applied themselves to the work of translation in both languages.

NOTE C.—See page 161.

THAT the Fúlahs of Senegambia were of a different origin from that of the Negro race, is not a novel opinion; that they are identically the same people with the Felatahs of central Africa, has been shown by Professor Vater, who, on comparing the Felatah Vocabulary which he obtained from Seetzen, with the list of Fúlah words given by Barbot, found that they were the same language; and recently M. Gustave D'Eichtal, in a paper which he read before the Academy of Moral and Political Sciences in Paris, has endeavoured to prove, that all these tribes are of Malayan origin. His opinion is founded on a comparison of the Fúlah language with the group of languages spoken in the Archipelago, to all of which it was found to bear many obvious affinities; while it most closely resembles the Java tongue, from which source he supposes, that the Fúlah derived a certain number of Sanscrit words, which it is said to contain. Their name Fúlah, signifies " white," in the Rotte dialect of the Archipelago; and M. D'Eichtal supposes, that they may have adopted that name in confirmation of the tradition which they cherish, that they are descended from a race of white men. With this opinion respecting the Malayan origin of the Fúlahs, the learned gentleman, however, appears to hold another, which is contradictory. He traces the settlement of the Fúlahs in Africa to a very remote antiquity, and suggests that they may be the same people, who are designated in the ethnological table of the Book of Genesis, " Phut," and placed after " Kush " and " Misraim ; " but if they are the descendants of Phut, then they are not of Shemitic origin, for Phut was the third son of Ham. (Gen. x. 6.)

NOTE D.—See page 164.

In prosecution of the philanthropic designs of Dr. Lindoe and his friends, in behalf of the Fúlah tribes in the vicinity of the Gambia, the Wesleyan Missionary Society sent the Rev. Robert M. Macbrair to M'Carthy's Island, for the purpose of reducing to grammatical form, one or more of the principal languages of that part of Western Africa. Finding that the Fúlahs generally understood the Mandingo tongue as well as their own, he prepared a Grammar of the Mandingo, and also made translations into that language, of the four Gospels, one of which translations—that of St. Matthew—has been printed by the liberality of the Committee of the British and Foreign Bible Society. With the view of giving further effect to the benevolent plans of Dr. Lindoe, the buildings of an Institution more especially designed for the education of the sons of native kings and chiefs, are now in the course of erection at M'Carthy's Island.

APPENDIX.

I.

DESCRIPTION OF A SLAVE WAR.

(See page 119.)

THIS narrative was written by Joseph Wright, a member of the Wesleyan society at Sierra Leone. He calls himself an Akú, the name by which natives of Eyeo, or Yarriba, are generally known. The Document was received by the writer from the Rev. Thomas Edwards, a Missionary of the Society, on his return from Sierra Leone; and no liberties have been taken with it except to expunge a few redundant expressions, and to introduce such slight grammatical corrections as may serve to make the meaning more apparent.

I WAS born Heathen in a Heathen land, and was trained up in my youth to the fashion and customs of that heathenish country; but the Lord, who will not have me to live to be old in that unhappy country, brought among us war and confusion as the wages of our sins.

I was born of respectable parents; but they were not very rich. My father was a member of council, and he had two wives, besides those of his father, which he left to him at his death, according to the law of our country.

My mother was the first wife my father had, and she bore five children unto my father. We were all boys except one, and we all were with our parents until this last tumultuous war, which is the cause of our separation. The war had been heard of long ago; but, at the time we heard of that war in a far distant land, we confidently thought, they will not come to us; but, alas! in space of about seven years after, they come to us unexpectedly, and besieged us round about. These people that raised up this war are not another nation. We are all one nation, speaking one language.

The war shut us up from all business; our enemies fighting us with all their strength, and we fighting against them with all our might, but not with hope of escape. In this miserable state we lived for about seven months, almost destitute of food. We had nothing to eat, in order to have strength to fight our enemies. In this hard case of ours, we had no real God to go to for help, but we were constantly sacrificing. There is a god which we call the public god; it is the god of man, and not of woman. No woman is ever allowed to go or pass by the mountain where they place that god. The name of that god was Korowah. To this we were all looking for help; and to another, by name Turbertaru. This is woman's god; the females often killing pigeons, fowls, and sometime bullocks, as sacrifice for their god. And these were to overcome the war which had besieged our city, besides thousands of private gods which the people kept in their houses. At last the famine overcame us, so that the chosen men of war could not forbear; and one night, in about seven months after the war had besieged us, they consulted together to go to another place, in order to buy us some food, to preserve us children of the land. And so they did; and in this band were my father and mother. They went to get us some food, too; for they pitied us, when they saw us perishing with hunger. At the time they left me and all my brethren, they knew not that they would never see us again in the flesh, or else they would never have left us, or they would have given us a final kiss, as dear children; but they knew not what would take place after they left us. Short time after, they were gone, with all the mighty men of war. May be, the enemies knew this ; so they got ready to take the city, before the people, who gone for food, should come back. The town had become very poor, for want of people to fight ; because the greater part of the people determined to go to seek food.

The city was in danger of being taken every day, because there remained but women, and young men, and boys, in town. In the night, before the city was taken, the people were trying to make their escape ; and many did escape. When I heard of this, I took my brethren with me, and we came to the gate of the city, to make our escape, if possible. The gate was quite crowded, so that the strong were treading upon the feeble. Doubtless, there were many trodden upon to death ; and had I and my brethren attempted to go over the wall, we should have been trodden upon, and we should have died, the wall builded round the city was so high and strong ; and besides, there was a large and very deep ditch dig round behind the wall ; so that there was no way to pass, except through the gate ; and we obliged to come back, to our father's house, there to remain, to see what would take place in the morning.

O sorrowful, sorrowful morning ! When the morning come, I and my brethren took a walk about in the town, to see what the people were doing. We found the city in sorrowful silence ; for many had fled, and many of the aged men had put an end to their lives. Among these was one in our house,—my father's near and very dear relation : he had put an end to his life, too. His name was Ahkarlah : but since he became the chief priest of Korowah, the public god of man, his name was changed to Aboreh ; for so they call the chief priest of the city. His manner of dressing was remarkable : the day when he was going to officiate, he would put on all white, white garment, white cap, he would put on all white. He would be attended by all the other ministers, and all those whose office was to attend the ministers of the said god ; and when they were about to come out from the closet of the priest, warning would be given to the women in the yard, to hide ; and also warning would be given to the market-women, to hide themselves, or bow down their heads beneath their knees, or cover their faces with their handkerchief; for they were not allowed to see the priest in his ministerial dress; for if they did, they would die for it. They always remained very long when they carried the bull to sacrifice. And when they were coming, in the night, one would go before, giving warning, as perhaps there might be some women remaining in the streets.

When this elderly relation of our father, whom we should have looked to for some guidance, had put an end to his life, of course, there remained no hope in ourselves. I brought my brethren back home. The enemy had fully taken the city. When I saw none of them pass by my father's house to take us for slaves, I then took my brethren with me. We came out into the street; and when we had walked about fifty fathoms from our house, we saw the city on fire, and before us were the enemies coming in the street. We met with them, and they caught us separately. They separated me from all my brethren, except one of my father's children, born to him by his second wife; I and this were caught together by one man. By the time we left the house of our father, I saw my father's mother pass the other gate: she and I had no hope of seeing her again in this flesh, because she was an old woman: doubtless, they would kill her. Many were killed. They killed our captain, Jargunor, by the river side. And they killed Barlah, in his gate. He was second to the king: he was a very high man in the city: nothing can be decided without his presence.

The city was taken about nine o'clock in the morning. There were two cities beside our own, that those enemies had besieged. The same day our city was taken in the morning, and the other two were taken in the afternoon, about two o'clock.

The enemies satisfied themselves with little children, little girls, young men, and young women. They did not care for the elderly, and old people: they killed them without mercy; and then father knew not the son, and the son knew not the father; pity had departed from the face of mothers. Abundant heaps of dead bodies were in the streets, and there was none to bury them ; suckling babes crying at the point of death, and there was none to take them up : the mothers looked upon them with neglect. These three cities were consumed in one day, and many of the inhabitants were taken as slaves by the enemies. One of our chief men of war they punished severely ; his name was Ofersapu. In this manner they punished him. They first cut him in tender parts; and after that, they put rope on his neck ; and then they dragged him about a quarter of mile, and put an end to his life. They took revenge on him, because he was valiant in fighting them. Very many of the chief men of war they punished more severely than I can mention.

I was brought, the same day the city was taken, to Imodo, the place which they make their residence. When I came to that place, the man who seized me in the city, took me, and made a present of me to the chief man of war, which commanded the band which he belong to ; for the custom was, when any one of their company went with bands to war, if he catch slaves, half of the slaves he would give to his captain. I was with them in the camp about ten days ; during the time, they used to send me for firewood. In one of the cities they took the same day they took our own, there I saw some people burned in the streets.

They dug out many dead bodies from their graves, in order to take off their grave-clothes to sell for money ; for the manner of dressing the dead in that part of the world quite differs from this country.

In this manner they dress the dead. If the dead person has been a man of fortune, the council would take all his valuable clothes, and dress him carefully, with all costly apparel; the dress would make him about four feet high from the ground. Perhaps there would be about twenty large pieces of costly cloths, besides those that he lived in. And then they would make a large coffin, about five feet high, and about four feet wide, and properly dressed with all fine and costly cloths. After that, they would send for king's drum, or band ; and about twelve or fourteen men would take the coffin upon their shoulders, and one would stand before, giving out country hymn, and followed by thousands of people, singing after them. They would go round the city with the coffin, and then come back to the place where the dead person lay. After all this, the relations of the dead person would give warning to the council when the body should be buried; and in the night, when the body was to be buried, the council's drum would beat. The market would be broken up in the evening, and they would come to the place where the body laid; and abundant of apparel would be prepared to line the bottom of the tomb, and plenty of money would be laid in bottom of the grave; and then they would lay the body of the dead upon these things, and cover him with dust. This is the way they bury the dead. We do not bury the dead out of the house, as they do in this country; we bury a person in his own room; but if the person has been a slave, we bury him in the square. The house where dead person is buried is not to be forsaken, but to be taken possession of by another person. A dead body may remain for many years and not spoil. This is the cause why the enemy dug out dead bodies in order to take the money, and the fine clothes with which the bodies were dressed; but this cannot be done unless the city is taken by the enemies. While I was with these enemies in the camp, I saw many wonderful instances, all which I cannot now mention. I saw a child of about eighteen months old, which was cast out of the camp because the child was too young, that nobody would buy him; and that poor orphan was there crying, at the point of death, for about two days, and none to pity or take him up. Another time I took a walk about in the camp, when I saw my own brother. I was not allowed to speak to him, although they knew him to be my own brother. Few days after this, the person whom I then belonged to sent me home to his wife for sale; and I was with his wife one day and a half. She sent for a trade-man to examine me. They stripped me naked. The man examined me all over. They then went aside from me to make a bargain; and in a few hours after that, the man came again, and my mistress told me to go with the man and fetch some rum. Just as I went out of her sight, the man stripped me of my clothes, and sent them to my mistress. Then I know that they only deceived me, by telling me to go with the man and fetch some rum.

Then I went with this man, who had just bought me from my mistress. The man tried to feed me and make me clean as possible, for the next market-day; one day out of six is generally market-day. One morning, at the cock-crow, the man started me, for the following day would be market-day; and when we come to the village near the place where the market was to be held the day after, we there slept; it was then a late hour. Early in the morning we came to the market, where many hundreds of slaves. We were put in rows, so that we all could be seen at one view by the buyers; and in about five hours another trade-man came and bought me, and put me in a canoe at once, and we were sailing all that night. Next morning we come to another slaves' market, by name Krodú, and there we remained the whole day; for the man wanted to buy more slaves. At the time of the evening, the canoe was quite loaded with slaves, and we sailed for his home directly; we arrived about twelve o'clock in the night. The town that we arrived at is Ikko, by name, the place where the Portuguese traded.

Early in the morning we were brought to white Portuguese for sale; after strict examination, the white man put me and some others aside; after that, they then bargained how much he would take for each one of us. After they were well agreed, the white man sent us to the slave-fold; and when we enter into it, the slaves shouted for joy for having seen another of their countryman in the fold. The articles which the Portuguese paid for slaves, were tobacco, rum, clothes, powder, gun, cutlasses, brass, iron-rod, and jaki,—that is our country money.

The inhabitants of Ikko are very cruel people; they would even sell the children of their own bosom. May God Almighty make bare his holy arm, in sending the Gospel to this benighted land!

I was there in the fold for about two months, with a rope on my neck. All the young boys have ropes on their necks in a row; and all the men with chains in a long row, for about fifty persons in row; so that no one could make escape without the other. At once the town took fire, and about fifty slaves were consumed; because the entry was so crowded that these slaves could not get out. During the time I was in that cruel place, their king was very sick; and the business of his attendants is to ask the diviner; and whatsoever he commands to be done, for the recovery of the king's health, is immediately attended to. During the time of the king's sickness, the slaves often met with a goat or a sheep sacrificed, and money put on the top of the sacrificed beasts, to appease the god of their land. This money the slaves always took as good luck; for the money generally amounted to two thousand jakis. This large sum of jakis they used to put upon the top of the sacrificed beasts; and this one jaki is worth as much as English halfpenny. Alas! the worthless prophets, with all their Ododowor and Obahtahlah, (for so they call their gods,) were not able to do any good for the king in regard to his recovery. Three days after his death, we came away over the river to prepare for shipping; for their custom was, when the king died, to sacrifice about one thousand slaves for the celebration of the king's death; for we supposed at that time, if we still remained in that cruel town, and if the king's slaves should not be enough for the celebration of the king's death, doubtless, they would ask our master for some slaves to make up the number. We all believed this was what induced our master to bring us over the river in haste for shipping.

The place that they brought us to it is Igayi, and we were all naked, both men and women; so that we hardly had any rest in the night, for we were very cold. Next day, early in the morning, we were all brought down close to the salt water for to be put in canoes. We all were heavy and sorrowful in heart, because we were going to leave our land for another which we never knew; and not only so, but when we saw the waves of the salt water on which we were just to enter, it discouraged us the more; for we had heard that the Portuguese were going to eat us when we got to their country. This put us more to despair; and when they began to place in canoes to bring us to the brig, one of the canoes sunk, and half of the slaves died. After they had done loading the brig, they stowed all the men at the bottom under the deck ; the boys and women were left on the deck. The brig sailed in the evening ; and one morning we saw an English man-of-war coming. When these Portuguese saw this, it put them to disquietness and confusion. They then told us, that these are the people which would eat us, if we suffered them to prize us ; and they also enticed us, if they should ask us how long it was since we sailed, we must say it was more than a month ; and they also gave us long oars, and set us to pull, (about ten men set on one oar,) and we tried to pull as we were able ; but it was of no avail. Next day, the English vessel overtook us, and they took charge of the slaves. We were very poor for water ; we were only allowed one glass of water a day ; and we were allowed only breakfast, no dinner. Many of the slaves were dead for want of water, and many were dead through confinement.

One day, as I sat by the fire-side, where they were cooking, boiling water was thrown on my head, and my head all peeled, and this pained me very much. All the slaves thought I should have died. But the Lord nourished me in that painful time, and I am not dead. Thanks be to his name for his tender care over a poor wretch like me !

We landed at Sierra Leone in about a month after we sailed from Igayi. It was great joy among the slaves that day ; for we had supposed we should never see land any more.

After we landed at Freetown, they sent us boys to York, in order that we might be instructed. There we were placed at school. We began at once to learn to read English books ; which books I have cause to praise God for, while I have life and breath ; for through the reading of those books, I came to know that high and glorious name of Jesus Christ the Saviour. But I have to acknowledge, that, although I read these books which taught me to know Jesus Christ the Saviour, I did not then believe in him as I ought to have believed.

In five or six years after I came to this country, I began

to learn to pray morning and even ; although I did it not from the heart, for I did not know the nature of prayer at the time. In the year 1834, I began to attend the Methodist chapel. I praise God, and I will have to praise him if I be faithful to the end, that I have joined the Methodists' society ; for they are not careless about my soul ; they do not only tell me that heaven is a happy place, but they do teach me the way to it. May God bless this body, and may the work of God prosper in this land ! When I joined with them, I begin to seek the Lord ; and from the time I obtained the peace of God, I go among my friends, telling them that the Lord is good ; inviting them to come and taste for themselves how good the Lord is. The Lord has blessed my endeavours ; and many of them do come, having found what I said to be true, and they are enabled to tell others of the Saviour they have found.........I find the work of God to be good work, and it hath been the delight of my soul. I pray God to assist me in doing this work, as saith the wise man, in the book of Ecclesiastes, "Whatsoever thy hand findeth to do, do it with thy might ; for there is no work, nor device, nor knowledge, nor wisdom in the grave, whither thou goest."

II.

VOCABULARY OF THE FANTI LANGUAGE.

(See page 161.)

Abandon, to, pa
able, tum
aboard, ehénum
abode, tinábu
above, asúl
about, hung
abrupt, awirefírim
abscess, sua
abscond, to, gwan
absent, nihór
absolve, to, firi
absolute, jawpe nouye
absorb, to, min
abstemious, enuéjin
abstinence, kin
absurd, omfokanum
abundant, pi-hi
abuse, to, yau
abyss, e-hi
accept, to, gi
accident, imusu
accompany, to, kang-wung
accomplice, buáfu
according, minonam
account, inkungtá
accurate, nenuarapé
accuse, to, kwatu
accustom, to, otaw
ache, e-youú
acid, yere-yerau
acknowledge, to, pemsi
acorn, ok-ama
acquire, to, ngya
acquit, to, yin
across, kwim
action, in-ji-é

Active, ahumál
add, to, fakang
admire, to, kángfu
admit, to, muko
admittance, akwanma
adopt, to, fa-hé
adore, to, abujin
adorn, to, hi-hé
adult, abenima
advance, to, tunchin
advantage, umfasu
advise, to, afutú
adze, sosau
affectionate, adoi
affirm, to, aúchisa
affliction, efúna
affront, kasam
afloat, ta-u
afraid, súro
after, akí
afternoon, inwíbil
afterwards, inkíri
again, ibbío
against, afim
age, ínfi
agent, yamafu
agree, to, ahim
ague, heim
aid, búam
aim, to take, susu
air, infráma
alarm, akumitú
alike, se
alive, nikan
alligator, denkem
all, ning-yinára

Alliance, yekul
allow, to, ma
almost, kekuma
aloft, asúl
alone, nanku
along with, kahung
already, sesé
also, susú
alter, to, sisang
alum, alum
always, denína, daba
amaze, to, ahungbu
ambush, antau
amiable, oyipapa
among, auwóm
amuse, to, anígi
anchor, síke
and, oni
angel, yami smafu
anger, ébufu
angry, eníbiri
animal, abua
ankle, nangua
ankle-ring, adechinan
answer, buan, gidu
ants, patakan
ant, white, imforchi
ant-hill, isu
antelope, adua
any, ebi, biara
apart, pem
ape, adópi
appear, to, fil
appetite, ekom
approach, to, pin
Arab, Krámu
arch, achi
arid, wisi wisi
arm, abau
army, edam

Arrived, du
arrow, egandua
art, eguin
ashes, insun
ask, to, bisa
asleep, da
ass, assu ponkor
ass, wild, kwaim ponkor
assault, tuiya
assistance, bua
asthma, intihí
astonish, to, wangwang
astray, hara
astride, apongkwanan
attack, tuatua
attempt, to, yewi
aunt, nánua
autumn, epi
awake, yan
away, nunghung
awl, fichi,
axe, ekuma
Baboon, akónson
back, ekil
backward, ekíri
bad, bon
bag, kutuku
bake, tung,
bald, pa
ball, musket, kurábu
ball, cannon, tubu
bamboo, adube
bank, insunua
bar of iron, daban
bar, bolt, krakra
barber, yifu
bargain, diarnu
bark, of tree, duyauabun
barrel, of a gun, etudua
bashful, nitun

Basket, kenten, birefi
bath, guari, jari
battle, ekung
bay, sea, epu-faka
beach, impo-anu
beads, ashiri, ahuni
beak, anumanu
bean, adua
beard, bagivisi
beast, abua
beat, bau
beauty, ahumfao
because, sainchi
beckon, sunsa
become, to, nyin
bed, impa
bedroom, ipiyem
bee, nua
beef, nanchinam
beer, beyel
before, inkan
beginning, stasié
behind, ekil
believe, gidi
bell, edon
bellow, to, sung
belly, yafun
belong, deya, edi
below, asi
belt, afon
bench, mangu
bend, to, pun
benefit, ye
besides, susu
best, oyepapa
betray, to, dada
better, oyaisin
big, kessi
bird, anuma
biscuit, panu

Bite, to, ka
bitter, uinin
black, tuntum
blame, asung
blanket, kuntu
bleed, to, esan
blessing, hira
blind, fura
blister, pupunga
blood, simoga
blow, bo
blue, bibil,
blunt, kum
board, tabiu
boat, batiade
body, unam
bog, tiké
boil, to, nuyang
bold, ko-kudu
bone, ibio
book, buku
bore, to, fichi
borrow, fem
bosom, abul
both, ebyenina
bottle, badamau
bough, sinemen
bow, egan
bow, cross, tegia
bowels, yefunim
bowstring, eganhuma
box, adaka
boy, afra
brag, to, tu
brain, ahoal
branch, senemen
brass, ebroan
brave, berima
bread, panu
break, to, bu

Breast, arku
breath, ahum
bribe, imuaba
bridle, menamfidi
bring, fabra
bristle, prakuin
broad, tetel
broil, tutung
broken, uabo, uabu
brook, asuchin
broom, emina
brother, inuana
bruise, bubu
bucket, bokchi
bud, su
bug, pulki
build, si
bull, nankwinin
bullet, kurábu
bullock, nenkwininba
burden, adisua
burn, hu
burst, pai
bush, haban, efu
busy, niadagil
but, na
butterfly, franfranta, petu
buy, tor
by, near, inkin
Cabbage, efan
cabin, ahenpeam
cable, sikehuma
cage, ibbu.
calabash, apeki
calamity, ehiyan
calf, nankwi ba
calf, of leg, anantu
calico, krada
callous, epi
call, fere
calm, fun

Calumny, ahuruba
cameleon, abusumanki
camp, inserem
can, be able, botum
cane, sugar, ahuil
cane, not sugar, awiri
cannon, epirem,
cap, ekaiu
capacious, tetel
cape, bipau
capsize, to, botu
captain, safohin
captive, insi
caravan, anantifu
carcass, ifún
care, wasam
care, take care, uie
careful, yansa
caress, eyen
carpet, insa
carrier, suafu
carry, fasuya
case, adakaba
cask, ankora
castle, aban
cat, eginamua
cataract, insogu
catch, ki
catch cold, awaugin
cattle, immua
cauldron, esen
caulk, to, sisu
cause, ajosenchil
causeway, ekuan
caution, inkai
cedar, tree, bako
cemetery, seman pom
censure, to, adona
centre, finfin
century, ingfiha
certain, umpa

Chaff, tosi
chain, inkonson
chair, abrogua
chalk, chaku
chamber, ipiyem
change, to, sisang
chapel, asolfi
character, ijin
charcoal, ibiru
charge, to take, wadu
charitable, edoum
chase, fan
chaste, papa
chatter, sung
cheap, ebumeno
cheat, to, sisi
cheek, afun
cheer, to, ahumka
cheerful, ahumka
cheese, chosu
cherish, to, yen
cherry, edor
chest, adaka
chew, ui
chief, paniñ
child, afrába
chill, awa
chin, abogui
chip, kua
chop, to, kua
clay, dechi
clean, fil
clear, chu
cliff, kukumiang
close, tum
cloth, etam
clothes, atam
cloud, esuisu
coach, uil
coast, bipo, emu

Coarse, kors
cockroach, kakráka
cold, auau
colic, ayeo
come, bra
command, ahum
common, oká
companion, yenkung
conceal, to, fasumang
conduct, to, abrobau
constant, daba
content, abugui
continue, to, kwen
conversation, asemkang
cool, gui
copper, korbri
coral, ninkinimá
cord, ahumang
cork, putisi
corn, ebru
corpse, ifun
correct, right, neniuádu
cost, price, ebu
cotton, asába
cover, to, katadu
cough, aiuo
count, to, kan
country, kro
countryman, kroni
couple, ebiyen
courage, imórjin
cow, nenkuíbri
coward, kwehútan
cowries, síriba
crack, pai
crafty, konkonsa
crawl, uiya
creek, taka
crime, ebon
crocodile, denkem

Cross, traverse to, tra, im-
bumu
crowd, asikerai, futu
cruel, chuadifu
cry, to, su
cunning, konkonsa
cup, korpu
cure, to, ahungsang
curse, impai
custom, amamra
cut, to, chua
Dam, to, ena
damp, aua
dance, sau
danger, ahíya
dare, to, sebotum
dark, isum
dash, ke
date, inkrisíya
date-tree, inkrisíya-dáya
daughter, ebaba
daunt, to, suro
dawn, adiking
day, eda
day, to-, adikingí
day-light, ahinamaking
dead, uau
deaf, ichu
dear, costly, daufu
death, iu
debt, ekau
debtor, kafuni
deceit, dada
decoy, dada
deep, dänkron
defeat, to, kangu
deficient, aunsung
descend, to, san
desert, akwi
despise, to, tum
destroy, to, sikau

Detain, to, kigina
devil, ayen
dew, ebau
die, to, wu
different, ausun
dig, tu
dine, to, didi
dinner, edidi
dip, bom
dirt, dechi
dirty, ifing
do, yé
doctor, dachil
dog, bodom
done, wi-ye
door, abu
double, ebiyen
dove, ebul
down, daji, asi
dream, adasung
dress, to, si-ya-si-ya
dress, *noun*, he
drink, to, num
drink, *noun*, num
drum, ekini
drunk, bu
dry, wisiwisi
duck, dabu-dabu
dumb, imum
dung, sumina
dusk, adisangi
dust, huntuma, fotro
duty, guma
dwarf, ipire
dysentery, ayemua
Each, bakung
eagle, ekodi
ear, asúa
early, intem
earnest, ampá
earth, soil, daji

Earth, globe, iwiáji
earthquake, weadi
east, bukang
easy, ang-yefúna
eat, to, didi
ebb, huam
eclipse, akora-waki-duani
eel, abriku
effeminate, imesiadi
egg, kirefua
eldest, penin
elephant, esun
empty, biribinum
end, awi-ye-í
enemy, edóm
enough, ausung
enter, kor, bra
equal, sefu
err, infum
escape, finsé, guam
even, sefu
evening, inwibil
every, yiná
ewe, igwánbiri, eguanba
exchange, to, sisang
eye, eni-wá
eyebrow, inton
Face, enim
fade, to, pa
faint, to, gu
fall, to, wi
falsehood, apaú
fan, ahú-te-i
far, ekil
fashion, ebau
fast, quick, intem
fasten, kikil
fat, *adj.*, angwá
father, egá
fatigue, efuna

Fear, suró
feast, epunto, afahe
feather, eta-u
feeble, gu
feel, to, chi.
feet, anan
female, basi-ya
ferment, kau
fever, awau
few, kumébi
fiddle, senkung
field, esal
fife, betu-yá
fight, to, kung
figure, idol, ikum
fill, to, hénuma
filth, ifing
fin, tátire
find, to, hung
fine, fefé-u
finger, inséchiaba, satiwa
finish, wi-e
fire, ojia
firestick, gen-chi-a
firewood, e-hin-a
firm, intúkanan
fish, enam
fisherman, feni
fish-hook, ekwába
fist, kutúku
fit, fitch
flag, franka
flame, igatekelma
flavour, ingkang
fledge, tiklebo
flesh, hunaym
flint, kwerabu
float, tau
flood, insupram
flour, esikirísam

Flower, inhíren
fly, to, tu
fly, a, wansíma
fog, ifúa
folly, inkwasiádi
food, ediban
fool, abúa
foolish, imu-adi
foot, anan
forbear, gai
forbid, maumen
force, hen
ford, kwa
forehead, emuadú
foremost, eken
forest, ekwai
forget, wirefil
forgive, fafiri
fork, faka
form, inyebia
fort, aban
foul, onchu
found, hung
fountain, esuchil
fowl, akukor
fox, esor
free, dihi
fresh, nipapa
friend, yenkyng
Friday, Efida
frog, akwel
from, fi
fruit, edwarba
fry, ku
full, ema
fun, fedi
funeral, siya
fur, awuma
further, enimnuhung
Gain, infasu
garden, ture

Gate of town, abukasi
gather, to, buanu
gay, ahumkang
gentleman, buronpu, berema
ghost, sunsum, saman
gift, akedi
girdle, asinimtan
girl, aketasia
give, ma
give him, ma nu
give me, ma emi
glad, ahumkang
glass, glasi
gloss, hem-hem
glutton, iful
gnat, kawili
gnaw, wi
go, kor
go down, san
go in, kor mu
go out, po ye
go up, kor esul
god, yankumpon
gold, sika
gold-dust, sika infutu
good, o-yia
goods, akwadi
grand, efeü papa
grandchild, nanah
grandfather, nanah
grandmother, nanah
grape, waninama, abrowi
grass, efu, ehun
grave, tomb, ada
gravel, imusabu
great, awsu, kessi
green, ebun
greet, to, ki-ye
grief, e-yau
grind, to, yam
groan, wum chin, kummi

Ground, earth, daji
ground nuts, akwing
guard, wen
guess, buchilmsi
guest, horhu
guilty, efor
gulf, epufakaba
gum, e-he
gun, itul
gunpowder, atudul
gut, ful
gutter, sukang
Hair, i-u-ing
half, efang
ham, hamnam
hammer, hamel
hamper, kenten
hand, insa
handsome, fa-u-papa
hang, sen
hard, e-jin
hare, asu asu
harp, senku
harpoon, kama
hat, e-ke-u
hatchet, ekuma
hate, to, etan
have, yang
hawk, sansau
he, awnu
head, chil
headband, abuchil
healthy, hunamjin
heap, iku
hear, chi
heart, akuma
heat, ahu
heaven, asul
heavy, idul
heel, ananchin
heir, wu-o-ji

Hell, hel
help, buwa
hen, akukorbini
herb, efu
here, harmu
herring, eban
hide, suma
high, esul
hill, kukwa
hip, gwenku
hippopotamus, baka ponkor
hit, bo
hoarse, afang
hoe, a saw-u
hog, prako
hoist, si
hold, to, som
holdfast, som-ejin
hole, tokura
hollow, ebon
home, ifi-ye
honest, nukwa
honey, e-wu
hope, to, enidal
horn, amel
horn, music, aben
horse, ponkor
horse-shoe, ponkor aspachil
hot, e-hu
house, edan
how, yendiné
hump, efu
hung, sen
hunger, ekom
hungry, ekom
hunt, aha-ya
hurt, mi yang
husband, ikuni
hyena, pataku
I, emi
idle, enihau

Ignorant, kwasia
ill, yari
in, mu
increase, dawsu
indigo, edul
infidel, yamintanfu, gimfo
ink, inki
inquire, bisa
inside, numu
insist, kechi
instant, sese
insult, kasam
interpret, yanu
iron, daji
island, supru
itch, hin-hin
ivory, asumel
Jar, pol
jealous, ningkun
joy, ahumkan
jump, huru
just, nukwa
Keep, si-e
key, safi
kick, won-chia
kill, kung
king, ehen
kiss, kis
kite, bird, akroma
knee, anangkruma
kneel, kuto –
knife, sikan
knit, win
knot, apau
know, hung
Labour, guma
ladder, akwiri
ladle, inkwanta
lady, bahíma
lake, sotai-i
lame, apaki

Lamp, kanía
lance, kama
land, imu
landing, egru-i
lane, insanba
language, kasa
lantern, lantel
lap, asiri
large, kessi
last, final, e-wi-é-i
last, endure, to, kel
laugh, siru
lay down, to, dadaji
lead, metal, sumwi
lead, to, kirekwan
leaf, atau
lean, thin, kwil
leap, huru
learn, to, sung-ya
learned, yang-safu
leather, ahuma
leather bag, ahuma-kutukú
leave, to, dang-ga
leg, anan
lend, to, fem
leopard, gahin
less, kumabá
let, to, ma
letter, awuma
lick, to, tafil
lid, abwadu
lie down, to, dahaw
lie, falsehood, apaukwa
life, inkwang
lift, to, madu
light, in weight, ahal
light, not dark, akan
lightning, sinaman
like, adj., pe
limb, hunam
lime, kadu

Line, cord, ahuma
linen, krada
lion, awindadi
lip, anu-fam-fa
little, kakraba
load, he-yeh
load, to, su-ya
loaf, drof
lock, daku
lock of gun, sabun
lock, to, tum
locust, imbebau
long, chin-chin
look, to, we
looking-glass, we-di
loosen, to, san
lose, to, san
loss, yu
love, to, daw
lover, dofu
louse, igu
low, ongwal
Mad, abodam
maid, aka-tes-i-a
make, to, yeh
male, inin
man, komel
mankind, adasa
many, pinada
market, igwum
married, war
marrow, angwa
master, wura
mat, impá
mattock, sóso
measure, sung-sung
meat, enám
medicine, edul
meet, hi-ya
melon, anumúna, anemura
melt, nan

Memory, inkui
merchant, baténi
middle, finfin
midnight, esuyem
milk, to, ki-milki
mine, my, midia
miss, to, fum
mist, if-wa
mistress, od-if-i
mix, fura
money, sika
month, busum
moon, busum
more, i-bi-su
morning, i-no-pá
morrow, ekina
morsel, tromá
mosquito, intuntun
mother, en-á
mountain, bipó
mourn, to, awira-hú
mouse, kura
mouth, enum
much, pi
mud, kurabá
mule, ponkor
murder, a-wi-ji
murderer, a-wi-ji-fu
musket, itul
Nail, of finger, ewiraú
naked, adagá
name, igin
narrow, kakai-hi-hing-a-bá
nation, eman
nature, inchibía
navel, funama
near, inkan
neck, ekwan
neck-band, abasu-kunmu
needle, dúruba
negro, donkor

Nest, ibú
net, ebua
never, debída
new, fuful
news, dewu
next, aukangdu
night, adafung
nimble, ha-hal
nipple, enúfú
no, debi
noise, ba
none, ibéra
noon, e-wi-a-bil
north, ekwaí-i-mu
nose, e-win
not, yenib
nothing, biri-bi-a-da
now, sia-sia
nurse, gi-gi
nut, akwi
nut-tree, akwi-duya
Oakum, itu
oar, tabun
obtain, to, yang
ocean, epu
offence, ebufu
offer, ke
oil, ingu
old, dadau
old-fashioned, inchichidí, odedada
old man, akwada
old woman, abiriwá
on, du
one, akwul
one-eyed, initol
onion, awíngu
only, arangkung
open, bo-i
ostrich, anamasung
other, ekuln

Our, yi-re
out, po-yi
out of, fim
outside, nekil,
oven, furunu
over, above, e-chi fing
owe, makua
own, *pron.*, da
owner, i-wu-ra
ox, nenkwi, nenchibri
oyster, adan-chi
Paddle, tabun
pain, eyau
paint, edul
pair, inta
palm-oil, ingumun
palm-tree, abi-dúya
paper, kratá
pardon, fafiri
pass, kwamú
passage, ekwan
passion, anger, ebufú
path, ekwan
patience, abutal
pay me, tu-ya
pea, pea
peace, asumgwi
pen, pen
people, nimpa-pi
pepper, red, amoko
perhaps, ang-kwa-i-ye-a
person, nunpa
physic, edul
piece, isin
pierce, woh
pig, prako
pin, punsangbá
pinch, ching
pipe, eb-ú a
pity, ahun-mo-ba
plain, etai

Plantain, brodi
plate, pretch
play, to, gul
pleasant, o-ye
please, to, pe
pleasure, anigi
plenty, pimára
pluck, to, bir
pocket, kutuku
pod, ahun
point, chin
poison, edul
pole, idu-ya
pond, ibura
poor, hing-ya
pot, sinabá
pound, to, sisu
pour, to, wu-e
powder, etudul
power, ahum
powerful, ahum-a-jin
pray, sol
prepare, sia-sia
present, here, wa-ha
present, gift, ke
press, wumdu
pretty, fe-u
prick, to, woh
price, ebu
pride, inten
priest, sau-fu
prison, fi-a-di
probe, wi-wa
profit, infasu
promise, to, si-sí-a
provisions, ediban
proud, inten
prudent, yansa
pull, kwing
punish, akatua
purchase, toh

Push, to, sunu
put, to, fatu
put down, fatu-daji
put in, fatum
putrefy, potau
Quarrel, ham
quick, intem
quiet, fung
quill, tekire
race, ampire
rage, ebufu
rain, yankum
rainbow, yankungton
rainy season, yankum-tobil
raise, madu
rare, aungka
rash, hurupu
rat, kwisi
raw, emun
ray, sansama
razor, ansiwe-yi
reach, to, kang
read, kinkan
ready, kiradu
recollect, to, kaie-i
red, mimim
reeds, indembil
reef, kikil
refresh, to, de-de
refuse, to, pu
release, to, yin
remain, to, ka
remove, to, yi, fi
repay, to, hianém
rest, to, ahumgi
restore, to, hianém, debá
return, to, san
rib, infing
rice, emung
rich, buronpon
ride, ku

Right, enuádu

right, dexter, abeninfa

ring, ankle, dechinan

ring, finger, impechi-ya

ring, nose, kaba

ripe, biri

rise, tausu

river, esu-chin

rivulet, esu-chin-ba

road, ekuan

roast, hu, tung

rob, wi-ya

robber, wi-fu

rock, ebuten-chim

rogue, ho-win

roll, pira-u

roof, edanechifing

root, ing-gu

rope, tampi

rotten, pota-ú

rough, saka-saka

round, apurau

row, to, kwan

rub, pusa

rum, insang

run, gwan

rust, inkanal

Sad, ayau

safe, fihiwum

sail, aton

salt, inkin

salute, to, inki-ya

sand, ang-wi-yang

sandals, impabówa

sap, iduamunsu, duansu

savage, bo-yá-fo

save, to, ghi

sauce, apehsí

saucepan, dadisei

say, to, si

scar, ituang

Scent, iwum

school, sesrau

scissors, apasu

scorpion, yankumkicha-bóa

scrape, kwirau-kwirau

scratch, kwirau-kwirau

scream, kem

sea, epu

sea-gull, ingwaunuma

seal, sel

sea-water, epu-insu

seat, egwa

second, aükangdu

secure, siyania

see, to, wi-ya

seed, ama

sell, to, ton

send, suma

sense, yansa

separate, pem

set, to, ku

sew, to, pam

shade, sumsum

shadow, sumsum

shake, to, wusu

shallow, seserau

shame, enitung

share, arfang

sharp, indam

sheep, igwan

shell, ebun

shield, ekem

ship, ahen

shirt, inkeminsang

shoal, seserau

shoe, asupachil

shore, insuanu

short, isu-i

shot, tubu

shoulder, abechil

shout, bom

Show, kire
shower, yankum
shun, to, pan
shut, tum
sick, yari
sickness, yariba
side, arfang
sigh, wunchin
silent, efung
silk, siriki
silly, kwasiye
silver, gweté
silversmith, gwete-gwinfu
singer, awintufu, nyontóni
sing, to, tu
single, akul
sink, to, daw
sip, saw
sister, akiribá
sit, to, ku
skin, awuma
skip, huru
skull, itchiguiriba, nepiti
sky, asúl
slack, gu
slate, seretel
slave, akúa
sleep, iná
slide, chiru
sling, samo
slit, pai
slope, chiru
sloth, enihau
slough, ahum-ahum
slow, yang
sly, howini
small, krakaba
smear, yankam
smell, to, hungwang
smile, sidu

Smith, gwinfu
smoke, wisu
smooth, nam namu
smother, to, hihu
snail, inwaba
snake, abuwatinu
snare, afidi
sneeze, to, honichi
snore, to, inkurom
snuff, asira
so, da
soak, to, dunon
soap, semina
sober, enikan
soft, emirau
softness, emirau
soil, ground, daji
soil, dirty, ifing
soldier, sudani
some, ibi
something, biribi
sometimes, awtaw-febi
son, eba
song, e-wim,
soon, intem
sorcerer, ai-yen
sore, ikul
sorry, e-yau
sort, sasu
soul, sun-sum
sound, noise, ekekum
soup, enkwan
sour, yire-yirau
south, epum
sow, pig, prakobiri
sow seed, ping
span, sechiyama
spare, to, ghe
sparrow, esurum
speak, kasa

Spear, kama
spider, anansi
spin, tu
spit, to, tu-intasu
spit, at, tu-intasu
spittle, intasu
split, to, pai
spoil, sikewu
spoon, achiri
sport, enigi
spot, bebi
spread, tire
spring, jump, huru
squabble, huhung-huhung
squeeze, king
squint, eniku
stagger, taünsisen
stain, kaikem
stairs, asinaji
stand, to, ghina
star, wuraba
stay, wait, kwen
steal, to, insuwise
steam, wiye
stem, stalk, duyaba
stench, bon
step, nanchew
stick, rod, du-yaba
stifle, to, su
still, quiet, tung
stir, kanghung
stocking, astagiri
stomach, yafun
stone, buba
stool, egua
stoop, to, kutu
stop, ghai
story, tale, tufusem
stout, kesi
straight, *adj.*, taw-ching
stranger, ha-hu

Straw, efu
street, eson
strength, ahumjin
stretch, to, chin
strew, to, pichi
stride, aponkornan
strike, to, bah
string, ahumang
striped, pah
strong, jin
struggle, intukwau
sugar, sikari
sugar-cane, a-wil
sultry, ahu
summer, epe
sun, a-wi-ya
sunrise, adiking
sure, tuangbi
surely, ampah
surly, bo-ya-fu
swamp, su
swarm, bibi-ibi
swear, intemka
sweat, fifil
sweep, to, prah
sweet, daukor
swell, to, hung
swift, haha
swim, bul
sword, afuna
Table, epun
tail, du-ya
tailor, tedel
take, fah
take away, fah-kor
take care, wa-i-ye
talk, kasa
tallow, abroaüngu
taste, saw
teach, to, kire
teacher, kirekirefu

Tears, inisuaba
tell, to, kangkira
tent, ibu
terrify, ákumelu
thank, darsi
thatch, awnu
theft, ahun
then, inkiri
there, her
they, won
thick, dudul
thief, wifu
thigh, asire
thin, fan
thing, aji
think, gwin
thirst, sukum
thirsty, sukum
thorn, esaw-yi
those, i-yi-num
thou, ewu
thousand, apim
thread, ahumang
throne, ahingwa
throw, to, tu
thumb, kokonin
thunder, pirem
tickle, to, nunu
tide, ebb, epuhuami
tide, flow, epumangi
tie, to, kikil
till, until, mang
timber, duya
time, emil
tin, chin
tinder, apega
tired, tu
tiresome, awyaefuna
toad, akwel
to-day, ine
to-morrow, ekina

Tobacco, etua
tongue, takirema
tooth, esing
toothache, esing-yau
torrent, insu-pram
torture, eku-yau
touch, kang
town, ikuro
trade, igwa
trap, efiri
tread, chi-ya-du
tree, idu-ya
tremble, to, wusu
true, ampa
trumpet, tutubentu
trust, furi
truth, inukwa
try, to, ye-we
tub, torpu
tune, hen
turkey, krekun
turn, to, dan
twine, tu, fira
twist, to, kim
Umbrella, ikim
uncle, worfa
under, asi
understand, chasi
unripe, ibun
until, kire
unwilling, impi
up, esul
Valley, bonsa
veil, akatanim
vein, inchin
very, papa
vex, to, ebufu
village, ekroba
villain, nimpabon
visitor, wafu
vomit, fi

Vow, intemkang
Waist, asin
wait, to, kwen
wake, yan
walk, to, nanchu
wall, eban
wall, of town, arban
wander, to, yu
want, to, wi-we
war, ekung
warm, ahu
wash, hul
waste, to, sikau
water, insu
waterpot, insu-kurubá
wave, suraki
way, ek'wan
we, eyen
weak, emirau
wear, he
weary, funa
weave, to, win
weaver, win-fu
week, dapen
weep, to, sung
weigh, keri
weight, ebu
well, *adv.*, i-ya
well, of water, ibura
well done, ayen-iya
west, ane
wet, faw-u
whale, bonso
what, ebin-adi
whatever, biribiadi
wheat, ebru
when, dabine

Where, hine
which, hineda
whip, abai
whiskers, abogwiputu
white, fufu
white man, broni
who, wana
whole, niyina
why, asiya
wide, tetel
wife, e-yil
wilderness, akwai-i
wind, inframa
window, tokura
wing, ataban
winter, esusau
wish, to, pe
with, aw
within, numung
woman, be-si-ya
wood, idu-yal
wool, igwanumang
word, asem
work, egwima
world, i-wi-adi
wound, pira
write, to, kireü
wrong, ebon
Yams, egu
year, afi
yes, inyau
yesterday, inida
you, awu
young, afra
yourself, wada
youth, abrama
Zealous, imojin

THE END.